The Lost Mills
A History of Papermaking
in County Durham

by
Jean V Stirk

**University of
Sunderland Press**

© Jean V Stirk

ISBN 1 873757 85 9

First published 2006

Cover Design by Murphy Creative Ltd

Published in Great Britain by
The University of Sunderland Press
in association with Durham County Local History Society
The Teleport
Doxford International
Sunderland
SR3 3XD

Tel: 0191 5252410
Fax: 0191 5201815

All rights reserved. No part of this publication may be reproduced, stored in a retrieval system, or transmitted, in any form or by any means, electronic, mechanical, photocopying, recording or otherwise, without the prior permission of the University of Sunderland Press.

British Cataloguing-in-Publications Data
A catalogue record for this book is available from the British Library

Printed in Great Britain by the Alden Group Oxford

Acknowledgements

No work of this kind can be completed without the help of many people, whether specialists in their fields or interested, keen amateurs. I am indebted to several members of the British Association of Paper Historians who helped with the glossary and the technical detail: Mr Peter Bower, Professor Alan Crocker, Mr Ian Hendry, Dr Richard Hills, Mr Barry Watson, Dr Derek Priest. Those who kindly shared their expertise included Dr Margaret Wills on Gibside Mill, Mrs Marjory Lodge on Tudhoe Mill and the Anderson family, and Miss Shirley Lister on several papermaking families. Dr Winifred Stokes generously shared her knowledge and understanding of the general historic industrial situation. Other local, industrial and family historians willingly delved in to their own research.

As always, the staff at the Birmingham Local Studies Library and at St Bride Printing Library were very helpful, but the staff at Durham County Record Office took the brunt of my questions and demands for documents with infinite patience, for which they deserve due acknowledgement.

Three people to whom I owe specific appreciation for being so generous of their time, material and expertise are Mr Robin Clarke, Dr Eric Clavering and Dr Stafford Linsley. The late Professor Peter Isaac, who originally was to have published this work as part of *The History of the Book Trade in the North* had it not been for his untimely death, was particularly encouraging and supportive.

Professor Gordon Batho and Dr Winifred Stokes of the Durham County Local History Society have made editorial suggestions and offered challenging questions that have opened this work to a wider audience; it will be much the better for it. I am indebted to them and to the Durham County Local History Society for their support and encouragement.

I would also like to offer my thanks to Mrs H. K. Bell for her work in compiling the index.

Durham County Local History Society

The publication of this book has been facilitated by support from a bequest made to the Durham County Local History Society by its first chairman, the late Dr David Reid. The Society was founded in 1964 to encourage and promote interest in the study of the history of County Durham. It is a registered charity, no. 235567. The Society's work focuses particularly on the period of modern history during which County Durham has played a major part in the economic and industrial growth of Britain.

Details of the Society's publications and other activities can be found on its website: www.durhamweb.org.uk/dclhs.

This book and other DCLHS publications can be purchased from: The Editor, DCLHS, c/o Miners' Hall, Red Hill, Durham DH1 4BB (0191 3709941).

Contents

List of Illustrations	vii
Map of Location of Paper Mills	vix
Abbreviations	xi
Glossary	xiii

Introduction
An Overview of the Development of Papermaking in County Durham — 1

Chapter 1
Paper Mills Established 1670 to 1728 — 17
Croxdale, Lintzford, Chopwell, Egglestone Abbey, Blackhall, Gibside

Chapter 2
Paper Mills Established 1750 to 1777 — 49
Fellingshore, Lamesley, Lendings, Relly, Shotley Grove, Langley

Chapter 3
Paper Mills Established 1779 to 1803 — 85
Hett, Tudhoe, Urpeth, Cornforth, Butterby, Ewhurst, Moorsley Banks, Stone Bridge, Snowden Hole, Thinford

Chapter 4
Paper Mills Established 1814 to 1838   121
Washington, Aycliffe, Blackwall, White Hill,
Tyne, Wearmouth, Egglescliffe, Ford

Chapter 5
Paper Mills Established 1841 to 1891   159
Springwell, Team Valley, Hendon, Swalwell, Marsden, Hartlepool

Chapter 6
Review of Trends and Changes in County Durham Papermaking   189

Appendices   197

I Duration of Mill Production 1670-1980

II Number of Mills Working Per Decade 1670-1980

III Number of Paper Makers (Craftsmen) Employed who were Members of a Trade Union

Bibliography   201

References   207

Index   227

List of Illustrations

Cover Images

Front
Croxdale Mill 2005
John Banham

Back
Making Paper by Hand Early Nineteenth Century
Source: *The Commercial History of a Penny Magazine* Part 1 in The Monthly Supplement of the Penny Magazine of the Society for the Diffusion of Useful Knowledge. Issue 96. August 31-September 30, 1833

Inserts

Excise Label Mill no.242 Shotley Grove
With kind permission of Mr H Dagnall, from his private collection

Shotley Grove Mill Nineteenth Century
With kind permission of John Buxton, artist and the North East Mills Group

Early Papermaking Machine
Source: *The Useful Arts and Manufacturers of Great Britain 1861*

Ord Family Watermark

Plan of Cornforth Mills
With kind permission of Dr D A Kirby, from his Ph.D. thesis 1968 Durham

Commemorative Sheet – Opening of Ford Mill 1838

Plan of Ford Mill 1896

Plan of Springwell Mill c1900

Map of Location of Paper Mills

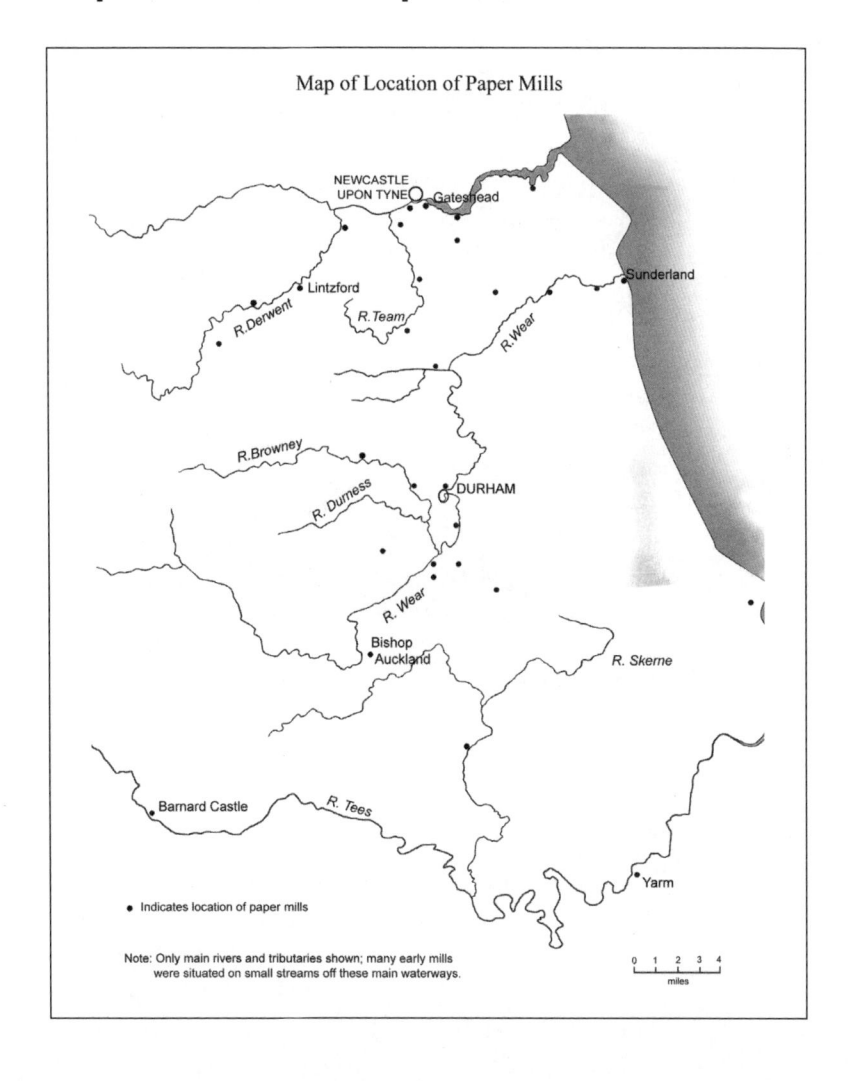

Abbreviations

AR/date	Notes from Original Society of Papermakers (OSP, trade union) papers and recollections of last Secretary of OSP, J. J. Highstead, recorded by Alex Robertson, member and ex-Secretary of OSP.
ASPM	Amalgamated Society of Paper Makers
BCA	Birmingham City Archives, Central Library, Birmingham
BL	British Library, London
BLPES	British Library of Political & Economic Science
CKS	Centre for Kentish Studies, Maidstone, Kent
DCRO	Durham County Record Office, Durham City
DUL	Durham University Library
EGL	Excise General Letters at TNA
HofC 1852	House of Commons Papers, Session of 1852, vol.51, no.128: *Return of the Number of Paper Mills at Present at Work in England, Wales, Scotland & Ireland on 13th June, 1851*
HLRO	House of Lords Record Office, Westminster
LG	*London Gazette*
NCRO	Northumberland County Record Office, Newcastle upon Tyne
NUPMW	National Union of Paper Mill Workers
NZ	Ordnance Survey Grid Reference

OSP	Original Society of Papermakers (Trade Union): Accounts & Reports 1850-1940
P/L	Private Letter
PMD	Paper Makers' Directory
REXFI	Royal Exchange Fire Insurance Policy
SFIP	Sun Fire Insurance Policy. Originals, and partial index, held at Guildhall Library, London
TNA	The National Archives (formerly Public Record Office) Kew, Surrey
TWAS	Tyne & Wear Archives Service, Newcastle upon Tyne
UBPM	United Brotherhood of Paper Makers
VCH	Victoria County History

Glossary

[No attempt has been made to define chemical or engineering terms unless those terms are used specifically in papermaking.]

Alfa	Esparto Grass q.v.
Antiques	1. Machine-made paper imitating hand-made printing paper. 2. Good bulking paper with rough surface.
Backing	Brown paper formed in a mould by compression (also called stereo backing)
Bagasse	Non-wood fibre derived from sugar cane; used particularly for fibreboard and printings.
Banks	Thin, tough writing paper no larger than 16½" x 21".
Beater	Tub with axle/spindle set horizontally within a wooden or metal roll around which are set long blades at angles that in rotation beat the fibrous material against the bedplate to break down the fibres (also called Beating Machine or Hollander).
Beating Engine	Beater q.v.
Blottings	Unsized and absorbent paper made from specially prepared cotton; cheaper qualities made from wood or esparto.
Board	Thick sheet of paper, homogeneous, or layers of paper pressed or glued together (also called cardboard).
Bond	Tough machine-made writing paper.
Browns Coarse	Dark wrapping paper made from commonest materials.

Calender	Set of cylinders or rollers on the machine through which paper is passed to glaze the surface.
Calendered	Smoothed on machine to produce surface of varying degrees of smoothness.
Caps	Thin wrapping paper.
Cardboard	Board q.v.
Carpet Felt	Imitation felt manufactured from waste fibre and used for underlaying carpets.
Cartridge	Hard, tough paper of varied quality for drawing, cartridge-making and wrapping.
Casings	Thin glazed paper, buff or drab colour, used lining cardboard cases and wrapping. Size of wrapping paper 36" x 46" (also known as white rope).
Chromo	Pigment-coated, usually on one side, used for better-class letterpress and offset lithography work.
Coated	Paper with material applied to surface after making.
Colourings	Paper that has had dye added at the beater stage to change finished sheet colour.
Common Writings	Waste paper grade covering white papers printed with script.
Copying	Strong unsized tissue used for letter copying books.
Couch Rolls	Couch is the action of transferring sheets of newly formed paper on to felt blanket so that water can be pressed out. Couch rolls on a Fourdrinier machine are situated at the end of the moving wire from which paper is transferred on to a felt blanket.
Cover	Extra strong paper for outer covering.
Dandy Roll	Metal roll (cylinder) covered with wire cloth that imprints on paper as it passes under the roll.

Deckle	1. Width of papermaking machine. 2. Feathery/deckle edge of paper resulting from the edge of the mould frame, the deckle, (handmade paper); artificial means, straps, on papermaking machine. Retains pulp while water drains through.
Drawings	Stout strong papers in a range of qualities, suitable for drawing.
Dry(ing) House	Building or loft where paper is hung on racks to dry, or laid on scrim (woven jute).
Duplex	Paper or board consisting of two layers of material differing in colour or quality brought together in the wet state and pressed in to one.
Duplicating Papers	Absorbent or semi-absorbent paper used for making copies on duplicating machines.
Enamellings	Pigment paper coated on one side to give higher finish than the other side. Medium quality used for box covers or lining boxes; better quality for litho work.
Engine-sized Writings	Machine-made paper hardened by addition of vegetable size (rosin) and alum to the paper pulp during beating, to be suitable for use as writing paper (also noted as ES Writings).
Envelope Papers	Highly glazed (by machine) on one side and possessing special qualities of folding strength, durability, opacity etc.; the smooth surface more suited to writing, the rough side taking the gum better than a burnished surface.
Esparto Grass	Material used in papermaking from c1860 as a major part of the furnish; mainly imported from North Africa and Spain.
ES Writings	Engine-sized Writings q.v.
Filler	(Also called loading) Mineral material, often china clay added to paper pulp to fill interstices in the matted fibres, imparting solidity and a good printing surface with improved opacity.
Fine (& Superfine) Printings	Best quality paper for printing.

Fourdrinier	Standard type of papermaking machine developed at the beginning of the nineteenth century, financed by the Fourdrinier brothers, stationers. Subsequently, all papermaking machines tend to be referred to as Fourdriniers.
Furnish	Materials from which paper is made.
Glazed Papers to	High gloss or polish imparted during manufacture or applied subsequently by various means such as passing paper through zinc rollers. Glazed Backings are formed in a mould by compression on to type.
Greaseproof	Thin wrapping paper made from chemical wood, beaten so that the pulp becomes hydrated.
Grocery Papers	Low grade wrapping paper for making in to bags for grocery products.
Gummings	Papers coated on one side with adhesive gum, such as labels or stamps.
Half Stuff	Partially broken or unbeaten source of fibres for papermaking (see Stuff).
Hollander	Generic name for beating machine.
Imitation Kraft	Quality of wrapping paper made from unbleached sulphite, mechanical pulp and waste papers, coloured brown.
Kraft	Strong flexible paper, light brown colour, made from chemical wood pulp prepared with a mixture of caustic soda and sodium sulphide. Used for wrapping; may be used as the body paper for some abrasive papers (also called Sulphate Board).
Laid	Ribbed effect of wires on mould or dandy roll being laid not woven.
Litho	Well sized, made short way of sheet across the papermaking machine, lie very flat; suitable for printing by lithography.
Long Elephants	Paper in rolls 22" x 12 yards, used in wallpapering trade.
Manil(l)as	Coloured paper, often buff, used mainly for strong envelopes, folders etc., not necessarily containing Manila fibre.

Map Papers	Paper of good folding quality and durability, with a good finish and high opacity for good register of printing needed for maps and plans.
Mechanical Wood Pulp	Mechanically ground wood, often spruce; lowest grade of wood pulp.
MF	Finish imparted on the machine.
MG Skips	M(achine) G(lazed) on one side of skips paper, thin brown used for lining crates and dress patterns.
Middles	Coarse board made from mechanical pulp and waste papers, used for tickets, tubes and centre layer in certain other boards.
Mill Wrappers	Coarse packing paper in which reams are wrapped and baled.
Music Demy	Paper suitable for printing musical notations; demy indicates the size and quality.
Newcastle Browns	Good quality brown wrapping paper.
News/ Newsprint	Paper suitable for printing a newspaper usually made from mechanical wood pulp or de-inked waste paper.
Off-set Papers	Hard, free from waviness and cockles, with grain in long direction of a sheet, suitable for off-set printing method.
Paper Machine	Fourdrinier q.v.
Parchment	Originally skin of animal, particularly sheep in England. A type of paper in varying qualities but with a high machine finish imitating the effect of parchment.
Pasteboard	Cardboard formed by pasting finer papers to either side of middles of inferior quality.
Pastings	Thin quality paper used for pasting purposes, usually with rough underside to improve pasting.
Plain Linear	Thin, lightweight paper for overseas correspondence.
Plate	Thick, soft-sized paper used for printing from engraved steel or copper plates, and for photogravure printing.

Potcher	One of a series of beaters or engines used in washing and preparing especially esparto in to a pulp.
Printings	Papers suitable for printing of a range of sizes and quality.
Pulp	Aqueous stuff (beaten) containing disintegrated fibrous material from which paper is made; stock is unbeaten.
Pulp Board	Board manufactured in one thickness by bringing two or more thicknesses in to a single structure; not pasted together.
Purples	Size of wrapping papers: 17" x 25" and 18½" x 28".
Rag Engine	Beater q.v.
Rolls or Rollers	Cylinders that may be used in pressing paper, for glazing, or covered in felt for drying.
Rope Browns	One of the better grades of brown wrapping paper made partly from old rope stock.
Samplings	High class wrapping paper, usually dark shades, used for wrapping samples of textiles.
SC Skips	SC (see Super Calendered) Skips are thin brown paper used for lining crates or for dress patterns.
Scotch Papers	Also called Tyne Casings. q.v.
Shops	White glazed or unglazed wrapping papers used in grocery trade.
Size	Water-resisting material, such as rosin or gelatine, added to paper during manufacture to render it impervious to ink.
Small Hands	Thin straw-coloured wrapping made from low-grade material.
Sorts	Types of paper.
Stuff half	Paper pulp beaten and ready for making in to paper (see stuff).
Sulphite Pulp	Raw wood pulp prepared with bisulphate of lime.
Super Calendered	An improved finish by passing paper through 8-12 rolls of various materials under pressure.

Surfacing	Paper coated in different colours.
Tea Lappings	Papers used for packing tea, often with a foil side; lapping refers to large sizes being folded in to three for packing.
Tips	Very thin Mill Boards used in bookbinding.
Tub	Circular or oval container in which raw material may be washed or pulp could be held.
Tub Sized	Formed paper dipped in to tubs of size to coat surface.
Twin Wire	Paper or board made as two separate sheets at the same time on a papermaking machine, joined with two under sides together at an early stage giving both surfaces without any wire imprint.
Tyne Casings	Casings q.v.
Typewriting Papers	Slightly more softly sized than ordinary writing papers, suitable for use in typewriters.
Vat	Oval or oblong tank containing stuff in which sheets of handmade paper are made; tank in which cylinder of a mould machine is partially immersed.
Wire Frame	Frame that supports the wire or continuous web of wire gauze on which paper is made.
Wove	Paper made on woven wire rather than laid to give a smoother finish.
Wrappings	Brown paper for wrapping various types of goods.
Writings	Paper suitable for writing use. General term for white papers.

Introduction

An Overview of the Development of Papermaking in County Durham[1]

Papermaking was an important industry in County Durham for at least a century and a half, yet its history and role in the life of that county have been sadly neglected. This is probably because historians have concentrated on other industries, particularly the extractive industries that dominated the North East's economy for much of the last three centuries. It may also have been because of the relative paucity of material relating directly to the history of papermaking in the county. Destruction of records in fires, flood, and explosion, by animals, and manufacturers not keeping their records, may also be reasons for the lack of historical material. This work is an attempt to rectify that situation by revealing something of County Durham's papermaking past, in the hope that more will be unveiled by other researchers.

After the introductory chapter this study moves chronologically from the first paper mill known to have been erected in the 1670s to c1900, moving past that date only to give an indication of subsequent continuance or closure of mills. In the review following the mill histories, trends and particular developments in the papermaking history of the county will be considered in relation to those of papermaking in England over the same period.

To appreciate the importance of papermaking in County Durham, how and why it developed and became, eventually, one of the lost industries of the county, it is necessary to understand the basic elements needed for making paper and to be aware of the evolution of the industry in England generally. The roles of geographic location, economic forces, technological changes and skilled manpower in the papermaking industry are highlighted to give a context to what happened to each paper mill in the county, and show the extent to which the detail of their individual histories reflects that of England's paper mills generally. Indications of the kind of information available from the main type of sources are noted as they may be useful for subsequent research.

Some Sources for Paper Mill History

Papermaking and paper mills are rarely mentioned in general histories of the county, then in passing. The only reference in the Durham Victoria County History's pages on manufacturing is minimal: 'Iron and steel forges and paper mills clustered round the [River] Derwent. Fordyce (1855: II, 276) refers to County Durham in general terms as the home of lost industries, some because of geographical position or their inability to compete, and others because industrial sites were exhausted or more lucrative for other uses; papermaking would qualify for such a list. In other histories, such as Lewis (1849: III, 303) reference to a specific paper mill under place name is rare and equally minimal: 'There is also here [Fellingshore] a paper mill', and 'At Cornforth are paper mills and tile kilns'. Lewis is a little more forthcoming when he comments that 'paper is extensively made at Shotley Grove, and in the neighbourhood of Durham'. Only one history (Chester 1976) and one article (Walker 1984) have been found of a particular paper mill, that of Ford Mill near Sunderland.

The paucity of material has meant that research has been a matter of painstakingly building the story of papermaking in the county from passing references, where paper is incidental to a study on another subject such as that on water resources, or in a record made for other purposes as that of a company supplying machinery to a paper mill. Excise correspondence, trade directory listings, insurance policies and notices of bankruptcy or dissolved partnerships are sometimes the only indications of a paper mill's existence. Wills of known paper manufacturers may yield information about a mill. Census returns sometimes indicate paper manufacturers and paper makers living at a paper mill site, and mills are usually noted on Tithe schedules. Where a paper mill was part of an estate then an estate archive may give a wider picture of a mill's history. Maps of almost any kind and date if compared should show when a mill was in existence in a particular place. Document and deed collections may include a relevant document.

Standard histories of the industry yield a certain amount of information as will some local histories of a relevant area. Research among records of the employers' association and those of the relevant trade unions add to the picture in terms of attitudes and the involvement of people concerned locally in the industry. A particular mill may be featured in any one of a wide range of trade and technical journals where changes in type of business, ownership or tenancy are likely to be recorded. Local newspapers report incidents such as fires and closures, but are not usually indexed so not easy to use.

Origins of Papermaking[2]

Papermaking was first known in China some 2000 years ago. Knowledge of the hand craft and expertise in its practice gradually filtered across the orient to reach the Middle East around 700 AD and Europe c1000 AD. Paper was not needed in England for nearly another 500 years as parchment could be produced cheaply from sheep and other animal skins, and sheep were abundant in England at that period, while paper from Europe was extremely expensive. During the fifteenth century the balance of price was reversed and paper became considerably cheaper to produce than parchment.

First Record of Papermaking and Early Development in England

The first record of paper being made in England occurred in 1495 when John Tate of Sele Mill, Hertfordshire made paper for a book translated by William Caxton and printed by Wynken de Worde. To be given this order he must have been working a mill for a few years before that. Confirmation of his activity here occurs in the 1498 accounts of King Henry VII for 23 May when the king visited John Tate's mill and 6s 8d was noted 'for a rewarde yven at the paper Milne'. In the following year another reward was recorded to 'Tate of the Mylne'. However, Tate could not compete with the price of paper made in Europe; he complained that 'foreigners bought up our broken linnen cloth and ragges' and sold them to the English in the form of paper 'both whit and browne'. Sele Mill ceased to produce paper sometime during the first few years of the sixteenth century.

On the little evidence that remains it is thought that paper was only made in England sporadically at perhaps three or four mills, and only for very short periods at each of them, during the mid and later 1500s. The most significant development occurred in 1588 when John Spilman, a German jeweller to Queen Elizabeth I, then to King James I, was granted the lease of two royal mills near Dartford, Kent and converted them for papermaking. The following year he was granted the monopoly for buying and dealing in rags, also for licensing others to make papers, a monopoly that was extended for another 14 years in 1597. It is said that his establishments became the main nursery for paper makers both in Kent and England generally. The growth of the industry in England was dependent on many factors, not least the availability of raw materials and the physical conditions conducive to paper manufacture.

Essential Elements for Making Paper[3]
Paper can be made from any vegetable matter, or material made from vegetable matter. Linen and cotton rags were used for good quality white paper, rope and canvas for making brown paper. In the simplest terms this material is cut up, and beaten in water to break down the fibres and form a pulp. The pulp is held in a vat, then formed by hand in to a sheet of paper within a mould with a removable deckle edge, then turned out of the mould and dried.

Once a papermaking machine had been invented the pulp was poured on to a continuous web, dried on the machine and reeled of in to a roll of paper.

Five main elements were essential for papermaking: a market, raw material, water, a skilled workforce, and finance. The significance of these elements, and the relative importance of a combination of those elements, underlies the success and failure of papermaking in certain mills.

A *market* for paper was essential, whether the demand was for good quality paper used in printing, writing and drawing, or for brown paper for wrapping and pressing purposes. These markets had to be within reach of the paper mills so that the paper produced could be delivered reasonably quickly, whether by horse-drawn cart or waterborne before railways were established from the 1830s or, a century later, by mechanised lorries.

The market for paper in County Durham was twofold: those institutions such as the cathedral, Egglestone Abbey and various seats of learning, businesses such as the coal, shipping and mustard industries required good quality paper for records and commercial use; a range of local industries, like the mustard industry, required cheaper but quality brown paper for wrapping and packing their products. Both these requirements could be supplied from within the county during the 1700s. As businesses generally expanded and literacy spread towards the end of the eighteenth century and in to the nineteenth century, demand increased rapidly from these sources, from the University once established in 1832, and from paper merchants and businesses in Newcastle and Gateshead, also from the textile areas of Lancashire and Yorkshire whose manufacturers sought glazed papers for pressing, also brown paper and board for wrapping and packing. With the introduction of papermaking machines coarser, tougher papers became a north-eastern speciality earning a good reputation throughout the country, the most famous, Newcastle Browns (from which the local beer took its name) also Tyne Casings, called Scotch papers in Manchester. (Coleman 1958: 226; Shorter 1971: 131)

Raw material, whether in the form of linen or cotton rags for making white paper, canvas or cord for brown papermaking and, later, other materials such as esparto grass and wood, had to be in regular and accessible supply at a reasonable price. The raw material also had to be available from a source that was relatively nearby in the earlier centuries. A sufficient supply of good quality rags was available from within the county for the smaller, white paper market, and there was canvas and cordage in abundance from the shipyards on the Rivers Tyne and Wear, and in smaller coastal ports, to support the brown paper trade.

During the first half of the nineteenth century changes in the economy of the country, the introduction of steam engines replacing sail, and the replacement of ropes with chains, had reduced the availability of material for making brown paper and, consequently, increased its price. The rag trade became concentrated in the hands of a few capitalists and the shortage was reflected in the price of cotton rags that doubled between 1848 and 1855. County Durham manufacturers were under considerable strain as the demand for paper increased at the same time. By mid-1800s when some Lancashire cotton mills ceased production there were no longer offcuts of material from that source. Various kinds of vegetable matter had been tried in papermaking but were either too difficult to process, too expensive or produced very poor quality paper.

An important development initiated in County Durham by Thomas Routledge in the 1860s was that of using esparto grass from North Africa and Spain as a furnish for making first brown then white paper, a development that was to benefit the English papermaking industry generally. It was cheaper than rags and available in quantity. During the latter part of the 1800s there was a further development as pulp made from wood chips gradually overtook the use of esparto grass as the main furnish, especially when a way had been found to neutralise the acidic effect that caused early deterioration of finished sheets of paper.

From the earliest days *water* was needed for cleaning the raw material before it could be processed, to provide power for the waterwheel that drove the machinery for beating the raw material, later to drive papermaking machines, and for adding to the raw material to make a pulp. The source of water needed to be reliable and of a sufficient quantity and flow to provide the necessary power. Once steam power had been introduced coal, readily available in the county, could be used as fuel replacing dependence for power on a river or stream. For making white paper the water needed to be pure and clear, but some discoloured water could be used for poorer quality brown paper.

Good clear water could be found on tributaries of the River Wear hence mills such as Tudhoe, Cornforth, Langley and Relly became established in those areas. Clean water could also be found by sinking wells in to the magnesium limestone, as at Hylton Mill, and reservoirs were built to conserve water, at Lintzford Mill for example. Clavering refers to the 'social discipline' of earlier times when rivers and streams would automatically have been separately used, or a stream partially diverted to ensure one branch was sufficiently clean for drinking water and uses such as papermaking; the other branch would be used to carry away polluted water.[4]

Streams that could be fouled by coal dust and water used for washing coal had to be avoided. (Shorter 1971: 82, 83n65) Frozen rivers and lack of a reliable river flow in dry summers was an irregular frustration for paper manufacturers as at Ford Mill. Such was the importance of reliable water that one manufacturer cited in his will detailed, shared arrangements with the corn mill on his paper mill site.[5] Coleman (1958: 230n1) comments on another County Durham paper manufacturer [not identified] who was noted by the Excise authorities as complaining that his mill 'from the frequent want of water is only calculated to make a small quantity of Paper and that he has frequently been obliged to purchase Paper from the Paper Mills in the Neighbourhood in order to supply his customers'.

A *skilled workforce* was also essential and had to comprise men who had completed a seven-year apprenticeship, initially in making paper by hand, later in making paper by machine. When paper mills were first established in County Durham the journeymen had to be brought there to work at the craft and train boys in the art of papermaking. Initially the paper makers were usually part of a clandestine combination that formalised as a British trade union in 1800, albeit illegally, as The Original Society of Papermakers (OSP). Discipline within the OSP and strict adherence to paper trade customs was such that the employers were not able to curtail its activities, even with the support of the law, partly because they were dependent on the members craft skills. The OSP operated a closed union and a closed shop, with which employers complied, so it was necessary to join the union if accepted as an apprentice and remain a member once qualified or be unemployed.

Neasham (1881,81) records that many paper makers came to County Durham at different times

> ... from the county of Kent, where the best white papers were made, and where the choice workmen were in demand; and though they were deemed interlopers by the old denizens, yet they brought with them a travelled intelligence, together with a peculiar accent and use of their mother tongue, by which they were distinguished.

The movement of paper makers in to and out of the county can be noted from local parish registers, especially between 1798 and 1812, and from the analysis by Dye (2001: 11) of the censuses 1841-1901 as that revealed birthplaces in Scotland, Ireland and several counties in England and Wales.

Unskilled men, women and children were also required for basic work to support the skilled men, but they were not unionised until towards the end of the nineteenth century. Among men who became skilled in making paper on a machine alternative trade unions were eventually established, but not until the mid nineteenth century.

Finance, too, was always an important consideration but became crucial with increasing mechanisation and the introduction of machines that could make paper. Many more manufacturers were tenants rather than proprietors of paper mills relying on borrowed money for funding and insurance policies against the inevitable hazards of this particular industry – fire, floods, and drought. Fire and flood damage would have required extensive repairs and, in some cases, rebuilding with a mill shutdown, inevitably causing a serious strain on finances.

Excise duty was imposed on paper from 1643 to 1861 adding to financial concerns. The charges were complex, frequently varied and were always considered excessive, forcing manufacturers to increase prices or evade duty. Some County Durham businesses were particularly affected by the imposition of duty on brown paper made from tarred rope in the early eighteenth century. Paper manufacturers petitioned Parliament in May 1826 to ask that the seizure of machinery and utensils against arrears be stopped as it 'was to the detriment and injury of petitioners'; without machinery and utensils they could not make and sell paper to help pay off arrears. The equipment belonged to the mill owners in many cases and could not therefore be sold. Overall the charges were so punitive that at one particular time in the 1820s only two paper manufacturers in the county were not in prison for non-payment of duty.

The period around 1800 was particularly fraught financially as the manufacturers had to contend with general inflation, rapidly rising prices for rags, and wage demands from their employees as well as high levels of excise duty. For those who invested in a papermaking machine early in the 1800s the pressure on finance was even greater, including several County Durham paper manufacturers who introduced machine papermaking at an earlier stage than many in the south of England. The relaxation of partnership laws brought a change to multiple partnerships in several mills, whether purely among paper makers or with other businessmen, their occupations not always noted, which reflected the need to introduce more capital in to the papermaking businesses.

Expansion of the Industry

It was during the last quarter of the seventeenth century that papermaking in England began to be extended from being concentrated within or near the home counties to areas more distant from the capital, and Shorter (1971: 23, 74) gives County Durham as an example of this 'noteworthy development'. Such expansion was partly stimulated by the repeal of printing press licensing in 1695, but also by the rising demand for paper. In the eighteenth century increasing use of news sheets, then the introduction of newspapers, the fashion for cards for social use, increasing trade generally requiring business stationery and records, also administration of all kinds of institutions, stimulated demand for writing and printing paper; growing literacy with an increasing print culture added to demand for paper.

This provoked papermaking enterprises along the River Derwent as well as on tributaries of the River Wear south west of Durham City and Shorter (1957: 74, 82n55, 83n61) notes that the growth of papermaking in England generally accelerated during the last quarter of the eighteenth century. Along the River Tyne and the River Wear, and their tributaries, the attraction of a range of industries developing there increased demand for writing paper for records and correspondence as well as for cheaper paper used for packing goods; this helped extend papermaking further in to those areas. (Shorter 1957: 74, 82n55, 83n62)

During the second half of the eighteenth century particularly there were a number of technical developments that were to prove advantageous for English papermaking. The most important was probably James Whatman's innovation of wove paper, a method that gave a very high quality smooth finish to the surface, as it helped England become self-sufficient in quality white paper and, Hills (1988: 22, 34, 55, 56) reports, to the extent of exporting to Europe, an impetus that benefited many paper manufacturers.

Originally dependent on a waterwheel to drive stampers for breaking down the fibres of raw material, then to drive a device for mixing the fibres with water to make the paper pulp, manufacturers welcomed the introduction of steam engines to provide the driving force. The invention of the Hollander beater, a vat with a central cylinder set with a series of knives at different angles, proved very efficient and provided better pulp with less effort; it could also be driven by a steam engine. Once the paper had been made excess water could be pumped away more easily.

Ways had been found to control bleaching agents more effectively and so reduce deterioration, and the introduction of heat in drying lofts ensured more reliable finishing times. For County Durham manufacturers where the local market had been relatively small, at least business, comments Clavering (1999: 1) 'had been parsimonious of paper', by the late eighteenth century there was 'a fast-growing culture of print that included newspapers and Thomas Bewick's works'.

A Pivotal Point in Papermaking History

The last quarter of the eighteenth century was a period of growing problems and anxiety for all paper manufacturers. While some industries benefited from supplying goods needed during the Napoleonic Wars, paper manufacturers did not. With business already curtailed by the French Revolution in 1789 and its aftermath, exporting English-made paper to Europe, and importing raw material from Europe, was extremely difficult. The difficulties were made infinitely worse during the Wars. Coleman (1958: 170, 179) explains that rag prices soared; canvas and cordage was a rapidly diminishing source of raw material, inflation generally rose rapidly and the journeymen paper makers demanded higher wages; in addition Excise charges became more complex and excessive. These concerns were exacerbated by the general atmosphere of serious alarm in the country at the possibility of a revolution in England or a French invasion and, at the turn of the century, the rumour of a machine that could make paper.

During the last decade of the eighteenth century the paper manufacturers met at *ad hoc* meetings in different areas of the country, alarmed at the financial difficulties, scarcity of raw material and the increasing pressure from the hitherto relatively quiescent employees. They considered ways to combat their problems, one of which was to petition Parliament to pass the Paper Makers' Combination Act of 1796, but the employers were not able to enforce it against the journeymen. In 1803 the employers formed the United Society of Master Paper Makers of Great Britain specifically to counteract the OSP members, but were diverted by discussions about pressing trade matters as cited above, and the constant debate as to the financial risk of installing a papermaking machine. Several manufacturers from County Durham, including some major employers, the Annandales, Ords, Smiths, and Cooke for example, attended these meetings.[6]

Despite these problems, Kirby (1968: 73) states that local demand for paper in County Durham increased and 'the quickening of the economic scene in England', that occurred once the post war depression was over, accelerated demand for paper of all qualities in to the early 1800s. In places like Sunderland and Gateshead where industry generally was expanding, Shorter (1971: 85-86, 88) considers that other industries were thus encouraged to expand thereby stimulating further work. The paper industry was one that benefited from a range of trades increasing output and requiring more paper for wrapping, packing and commercial intercourse. This expansion was demonstrated by the number of paper warehouses that appeared along the River Tyne.

Both Shorter (1971: 129, 167) and Coleman (1958: 220) are of the opinion that the problems of the war years and immediate aftermath changed the character of the industry nationwide. Many small mills closed, some amalgamated or formed conglomerates, while others were established, often to supply a particular type of market. The financial commitment required to install a papermaking machine in what were mainly one-vat mills, some in areas relatively distant from emerging markets, with competition from enlarging and amalgamating mills often in areas where new industries were developing, overwhelmed many manufacturers. Certain mill sites were sold for other commercial activities that would be more lucrative than papermaking. This trend was mirrored in County Durham. With some two thirds of mills here making lesser qualities of paper that could be produced more cheaply and more quickly on machines, mechanisation became attractive to manufacturers who could afford to risk that investment. Easy access to coal became vital to power steam engines and support growing mechanisation.

Excise Label, Mill no. 242 Shotley Grove

Excise Duty and Raw Material

Two problems that were of constant and major concern to all paper producers were eased in the mid-1800s. Coleman (1958: 330-332) cites paper manufacturers having had to battle with the authorities for two centuries to have Excise charges reduced or removed; apart from the cost to their businesses, there was the ignominy and inconvenience of having to have an Excise officer check every pack of paper and stamp it. They finally succeeded in 1860, with accompanying lifting of other restrictions, so local manufacturers could then use jute waste available in the form of bagging from the importation of sugar and cotton as part of a furnish. To the relief of everyone business could continue without the continued presence of an Excise officer. Neasham (1881,81) expressed that relief in his comment: 'along with the duty, the Exciseman, a daily visitor, made his exit, ... and trade, freed from such trammels, breathed more healthily'.

In the same decade experiments with esparto grass as a furnish at Ford Mill proved especially successful for producing newsprint initially, brown then quality white paper. This almost certainly saved Ford Mill from being among the earlier casualties of developments in the industry. (See Ford Mill history). Sunderland was a major port where more than 1500 tons of esparto grass arrived from Tripoli in 1898 for example, some of which was sent on to Edinburgh and parts of Lancashire by train.[7] Linsley (1994: 8) noted that ships brought lightweight esparto from Spain, sharing cargo space with heavyweight valuable mineral ores so at minimum cost, returning there with coal and coke. When the use of wood pulp as a furnish came to be favoured by the manufacturers from the 1880s most of this also had to be imported.[8]

A Matter of Scale, Competition and Specialisation

During the latter half of the nineteenth century papermaking became a question of scale throughout the country, and this was even more the case in the twentieth century, apart from a few mills that produced paper for specialist markets on a smaller scale, some still by hand. Paper was last made in England by hand on a commercial scale at Hayle Mill in Kent until 1987. There is insufficient evidence to say which mill in County Durham was the last to make paper by hand.

Marsden Mill that became the North Eastern Paper Mills Company is an example of increasing scale, modernisation and rapid expansion of business. In 1894 the mill was producing 60 tons of newsprint a week, 179 tons by 1905 and 200 tons a week by 1912; in one year, between 1911 and 1912, the speed of the papermaking machine had been increased from producing 260 feet of paper a minute to 500 feet per minute. Hendon Mill was on such a scale as to be considered the largest paper mill in northern England. Competition internally and from abroad became extremely strong and many paper mills closed down around the country; in County Durham mills such as Tyne, Swalwell and Shotley Grove are examples. The trends of increasing scale and more specialisation continued, creating more competition and forcing closures; by the end of the second world war there were only five paper mills working in the county. An analysis of the number of paper mills functioning at different period shows the rise and decline of papermaking in County Durham. (See Appendix I and Appendix II)

The Decline of Papermaking in County Durham

The decline of the County Durham papermaking industry during the quarter of a century after the first world war was, in the main, the result of escalating competition from other papermaking businesses, often those abroad, and the relative value of the land on which paper mills were situated. European manufacturers, particularly in the Scandinavian countries, had raw material in abundance and could produce paper more cheaply and efficiently than older concerns here, and their technology was more advanced. In County Durham, the financial investment needed to compete became prohibitive. As in the latter part of the nineteenth century and early twentieth century, paper mill sites could prove more valuable and lucrative because of underlying deposits of coal or minerals, or as waterfront sites for shipping and commercial trading. Even the largest and most modern companies eventually failed to survive.

County Durham Paper Mills

The individual history of each paper mill in the county follows, providing examples that illustrate the needs and problems of the industry across the centuries, how some of these were overcome while other attempts at successful manufacture failed. As far as possible the stories of the mills, the employers and the workforce have been set in the local context, but they do also reflect the more general trends that affected paper manufacturing throughout England.

Chapter 1

Paper Mills Established 1670 to 1728

During this early period from the 1670s, when the first paper mill was recorded, six paper mills were established. Three of these were converted from corn mills; one worked in parallel with a corn mill (this was sometimes a form of financial insurance for the manufacturer against demand decreasing in one of the products) and a further three shared their source of water with at least one other commercial activity.

Croxdale Mill[1]

Croxdale Mill has the distinction of being the first mill in County Durham known to have produced paper. The relative wealth of information found, considering the early period in question, is fortuitous in that the mill was built on an estate and the owners, the Salvins, kept detailed records many of which have survived. Because this estate was Recusant property it was registered at certain times by the authorities, thereby adding to the record of its history.

In 1650 Gerrard Salvin made an agreement with John Palmer of Flasse, a mason, for the building of a mill and mill house of local stone on the Croxdale Beck, River Wear near Croxdale, but whether for grinding corn, making paper or other purpose was not then specified.[2] By 1658 Croxdale Mill had been built and was being used as a fulling mill with a watercourse, according to a description of the Croxdale property of 4 January, 1658.[3] Details of an agreement between John Palmer and James Salvin, dated 4 February 1658, refer to the building of this mill at Croxdale.[4] It had become a paper mill by the 1670s, Salvin's, the first paper mill to be established in County Durham (Gooch 1989: 52) was listed by the Excise authorities as no. 79. The mill stood on a level terrace deep in Croxdale Glen at the point 'where the stream makes a marked crook'. A leat c400 yards long served the mill, with the wheel probably set inside the building (Kirby 1968).

The Salvin Family Proprietorship

References to paper makers in the parish registers of St Oswald, Durham might refer to paper makers here but could also relate to paper makers in neighbouring mills, so it is difficult to be certain exactly when the mill at Croxdale was converted to papermaking. For instance, John Benson is noted as a paper maker of Sunderland [Bridge] in 1678 when his wife was buried, but not of which paper mill.[5] The first direct reference to the paper mill was in 1682 in a reclaim lease to Robert Bell, 'and upon ye payment of the Rents and pforming all ye other Conds in a reclaime lease of ye paper mill at Croxdale'. Anthony Salvin was the proprietor at this period.[6] The Salvins were a well-established County Durham family that derived its wealth from agricultural rents and papermaking revenue, later exploring other commercial involvement, such as investing in railway companies (Gooch 1989: 52, 53).

Gerard Salvin, although only born in 1654, as fifth of the Salvin family line, inherited Croxdale Mill from his grandfather in 1663 (Gooch 1989: 50). The Salvin rent books show the tenant to have paid an annual rent of £10 in 1710 and £13 in 1717, until 1720.[7] Clearly the Salvins continued to be the proprietors for some years and, as a Catholic family, they were required to register their properties with the Clerk of the Peace, so the paper mill is mentioned in descriptions of their properties. In 1717 Jerrard Salvin, noted as of Croxdale, listed his lands including 'a paper mill with appurtenances in the possession of Edward Clarke as tenant ... to whom I have let the same for three years to begin from 1 May next ensuing under the yearly rent of £9'.[8] However, payments by Edward Clark (Clerk) listed in the rent book for 1716 show £10 for that year, £13 each year from 1717 until 1720, then £15 a year in 1721 and 1722.[9] Similarly, in 1723 Bryan Salvin registered property, land, rents and profits 'come to me by the death of my father Jerrad Salvin [including] a paper mill with the appurtenances in the possession of Edward Clarke as tennant thereof', at an annual rent of £15.[10] Later, in 1752, Bryan Salvin's son, William, was to register his property including the paper mill (See below).

The Tenants

Changes of tenancy can be deduced directly from the rental book and, incidentally, from other documents. Wallis (1981: 2) suggests a Richard Clarke was at Croxdale in 1714, possibly related to a subsequent tenant Edward Clarke. We know from the rental book that the paper mill was under lease to Edward Clarke for £10 per annum in 1716 (Gooch 1989: 52). A William Clerk, perhaps a relative, may have taken on the tenancy from Edward Clarke, as two years later he (William) was buried in St Oswald's parish churchyard, Durham City, and registered as 'of the paper miln near Croxdale' (Shorter 1957: 163). 'From May day 1720 he [Edward Clerk, the tenant] must pay for ye mill and a close £15'. A further comment in the rent book explains that £7 10s was to be paid in May and again at Martinmass; this rent was held at £15, at least until 1722.[11]

The paper produced was mainly brown and whitey brown, relying on a cheap supply of rope from Sunderland port to use as the raw material (Shorter 1971: 131). Such paper was produced by Joseph Eyre, the tenant for the next several years. He was a paper maker, probably the master paper maker at Croxdale by 1738 until 1756, his surname variously spelt as Eyre(s) and Ayre(s). By 1752 the owner was William Salvin (Shorter 1957: 163). From details in Recusant Estate papers, we note that William Salvin's Croxdale Paper mill was registered with the Clerk of the Peace in 1752 and described as 'a paper mill and a close therwith now lett to Joseph Ayres the Elder from year to year at the yearly rent of £35 out of which he has an allowance of all taxes, sesses and repairs'.[12]

A notice in the *Newcastle Courant* of 14 February 1756 advised that William Salvin was offering the mill for leasing, and the rent was specified as £33 per annum[13] and confirmed in the rent book showing Joseph Ayres, the tenant, paying this charge until 1758.[14] A similar advertisement appeared offering the paper mill for rent in 1768.[15] Thomas Cummins had been the tenant for a period, from 1759 until 1773, possibly the master paper maker there, but then there were major changes.[16]

Rebuilding and Improvements

In the normal way of maintaining, updating and enhancing property to make it more efficient, and more attractive to prospective tenants, William Salvin began to rebuild the mill in 1771 and installed new machinery; this included a 14' diameter oak waterwheel, a steam engine and 3,000 new laths[17] on which the paper could be dried. He added an additional drying house the following year and then the rebuilding was complete. There are numerous bills concerning this rebuilding among the Salvin papers.[18] Among these are mentioned a 45-yard walled-in millrace with an arched wall over it, and 'buildings of ashlar stone with pantiled roofing supported by deals and firs'. The waterwheel is described as having 'iron bolts and nails and deal buckets, oak axle trees and cast iron gear wheels, a large cistern and troughs 6 feet long, rollers, press frames, a new vat and stove and two chimneys'; also mentioned were an engine, tub, vat and stuff trough (Chapman 1977: 17). An undated bill or estimate for major items, such as wood for nine King posts, may well have referred to this rebuilding.[19]

Uncertainty of the Ords' Tenancy

Salvin leased Croxdale at a rent of £72 a year for 21years to Christopher and Jonathan Ord, paper makers, proprietors of Lamesley Mill. Several members of the Ord family were connected to other paper mills in County Durham at different periods. A note that Croxdale was currently in the occupation of Thomas Cuming (or Cummins), tenant, does not make it clear whether Cuming continued as a sub-tenant or was no longer connected with the mill. The Ords were required to keep the property in 'good Husbandman like manner'. It was agreed that 'if at any time during the said term hereby granted any of the Bank shall fall in to the Mill race', Salvin and the Ords were to share expenses equally towards cleaning it out.[20] Jonathan Ord paid rent to Salvin from 1773 until at least 1781 according to the rental.[21]

A document of 31 March 1783 refers to Salvin reclaiming the land (paper mill and thirteen acres) and discharging the Ords from £9 12s rent,[22] yet it is clear that of the Ords, Jonathan, at least, held the mill at Croxdale, if not the land, for another nine years. References to Jonathan Ord imply he may have continued alone, for it is his name that appears in a paper makers list in 1786,[23] in the *Newcastle Courant* on 27 October 1792, and again in 1793 (Shorter 1957: 163). However, it would seem that William Salvin became dissatisfied with Jonathan Ord for a letter of 23 October 1792 from Christopher Ord, on behalf of himself and Benjamin Ord, to Salvin, concerning a 21 year lease of Croxdale Mill states: I am 'given to understand that my Brother Jonathan Ord is not to have the Paper Mill and Farm at Sunderland Bridge'. He proposed rents of £94 a year for the mill and £44 a year for the farm. Christopher Ord added: 'N.B. The Farm house to be put in to proper repair at the expense of the Landlord and also an additional Dry house at Sunderland Bridge adjoining the present one - the Landlords to find Wood & Stone for the same ... the tenant to be at the expense of leading all Materials for the above'.[24] Clearly the lease was not renewed, whether because of dissatisfaction with the Ords as tenants, or because they did not wish to continue at Croxdale is uncertain.

The Lonsdale Period

There are references in the parish registers of St Oswald in 1718, 1756 and 1795 to paper makers called Lonsdale and Lumley, of whom William Lumley and John Lonsdale snr and John Lonsdale jnr became tenants in 1795, but that tenancy was to be short-lived as the partnership was dissolved in the same year.[25] It seems that William Lumley moved to establish Butterby Mill while John

Lonsdale snr continued the lease in partnership with John Lonsdale jnr (Shorter 1957: 163). When John Lonsdale, the elder, died the younger John Lonsdale continued to run the business alone. He was described as a paper manufacturer of Merrington, occupying Croxdale Mill as tenant holding a draft seven year lease from 13 May 1803 at a rent of £130 per annum, 'with all and singular Houses, Outhouses, Edifices, Buildings … Dams, Damheads … Together with Liberty, Licence and Authority to carry on the Business of a Paper Manufacturer within or upon the said premises'.[26] However, he was declared bankrupt in 1803 and described as the surviving partner of John Lonsdale the elder, deceased, of John Lonsdale & Co., so the lease was not executed.[27]

Further Rebuilding and the Teasdale Era

The mill's annual income in 1783 had been £130. By 1812 a balance sheet revealed the turnover of the business to have been £6,000 per annum yet no record of a tenant is extant for that year.[28] It is possible that the mill was idle for a year or two while it was being rebuilt by W.T.Salvin, as several bills, including one for rebuilding the mill in 1816, suggest.[29] It was then leased with two vats, a dwelling house and contained 'by estimation one Acre and sixteen perches more or less', as well as a Dry house and meadow land, from 13 May 1816 to Robert Teasdale at a rent of £154 per annum Salvin was to 'find all materials, maintain and keep all the machinery belonging to the said mill [and] renew the two vats when required'; Teasdale was required to pay all rates and taxes.[30] Teasdale was noted at this mill in an Excise listing of 1816,[31] but both Robert Teasdale snr. and Robert Teasdale jnr. were acknowledged as tenants of Croxdale still in 1824.[32]

From a Poor Law Settlement Examination document it can be confirmed that one of the Robert Teasdales was tenant at Croxdale until 1823, for he took William White as an apprentice there from 1818 until 1823. Robert Teesdale had moved to manufacturing paper at Stonebridge Mill, at least by 1823, and was listed at Low Street, Sunderland Bridge between 1831 and 1834.[33] Perhaps the Teasdales were too ambitious in trying to manufacture paper at several mills at the same time for they became insolvent debtors in 1826: Robert Teasdale, senior, late of Stonebridge, and Robert Teasdale junior late of Croxdale, trading as Robert Teasdale & Son, also of Butterby and Whitehill, were so recorded in the *London Gazette*.[34]

A Parsons & White directory of 1827 showed a change of tenancy to James Teasdale, and correspondence with the Excise authorities in 1827, 1828 and 1829 acknowledged James Teasdale as tenant at Croxdale Mill. From further Excise correspondence it was also elicited that business had been discontinued in 1829.[35] James Teasdale, paper manufacturer at Croxdale, and his wife, probably Jane, who had buried their two-year old daughter, Mary, on 17 January 1818 in St Oswald's parish, is probably the same James Teasdale noted above.[36]

Simmons (nd) puts James Teesdale at Langley Mills in 1834, probably at the second mill as Anwick Smith was well-established at Langley. Robert Teasdale was noted as a paper manufacturer of Sunderland Bridge, County Durham, but not of a particular mill, in a list of subscribers to a history of 1834, (MacKenzie & Ross, 1834: I, viii), although he was at Butterby Mill between 1832 and 1837 according to Excise correspondence.[37] A Tithe Map of 1839 defines the area of the Croxdale paper mill, but no mention is made of it in the accompanying Tithe Apportionment.[38]

Change of Function

Small mills such as this only survived while cheap raw material such as rope and canvas was available from the port of Sunderland (Shorter 1971: 131). Inevitably they were converted for an alternative use, as at Croxdale. Unfortunately no information has been found for the years after the papermaking ceased until 1869. On 23 January that year Mr G. Hauxwell, of a company in North Road, Durham called Engineering & Millwright Works, wrote to a Mr Fleming concerning Croxdale Mill, indicating that he proposed to make and fit a silk machine, 'taking the old Machinery which is now in the Mill'.[39] The latter comment suggests that the mill may have remained unused for some thirty years as the machinery was still in position, unless this referred to machinery of a subsequent use. By 1974 only the gutted ruins of the mill could still be traced (Atkinson 1974: II, 277).

Lintzford Mill[40]

Lintzford Mill at Lintz Green in Ryton parish 'lies next to the boundary between the Manor of Chopwell and Winlaton'.[41] The mill was situated on the south bank of the River Derwent, five miles down river from Shotley Grove Paper Mill, (Neasham 1881: 77, 81), two miles south of Rowlands Gill, and a quarter of a mile from Lintz Green station, (Linsley, 1989: 3), near the old ford that was replaced by an elegant, single arch bridge before papermaking began. (Ridley nd: 61) 'It has a fairly flat arch with four circular escape-holes in each spandrel': (Atkinson 1974: II, 294) This has been described as a 'one-span eighteenth-century bridge' (Pevsner 1953: 180).

The existence of a corn mill here by 1578 is noted in a history of Blaydon, but no source was given for this detail, (Maughan 1955),[42] however, an original deed of 1692 refers to a corn mill here. (Maidwell, 1987: 13) It was let by Christopher Hunter, a student of St John's College, Cambridge, to John Sandford in 1694, (Ridley nd: 61;Neasham 1881: 81), and it is thought that paper was being made here by 1695, (Maidwell 1987: 13), but there is no evidence to substantiate that. It can be confirmed that by 1703 John Sandford had converted the mill to papermaking, but there is no record that indicated whether or not he was a paper maker himself. (Shorter 1957: 161; Neasham 1881: 81) In 1703 the mill was rented by Thomas Weatherley of Leadgate and Thomas Bage of Armonside Farm (Ridley nd: 74; Neasham 1893: 301) for £7 a year and 'one sword blade, well made and tempered' (Neasham 1893: 301). By 1710 the rent had been increased to £10 a year but the requirement for a sword blade remained. (Ridley nd: 74)

A Double Paper Mill

The next reference found to Lintzford was from the *Newcastle Courant* of 22 September 1739 when the mill was offered for sale or let and advertised as a 'double mill'. From 1739 Isaac Gilder, paper maker, was in possession of a double mill here, that is two vats, (Shorter 1957: 70, 81n12) and continued in occupation at least until 1743. Good quality paper was made here from water that was considered clean for pulping as it contained only a little clay. (Neasham 1881: 81) However, Reinhold Angerstein, a Swedish ironworks director visiting in 1754, who was interested in the metallurgical industries of the Derwent Valley, referred to the 'trouble with rusty water … at Lintz Green', due to iron that would stain the finished paper. (Linsley 1989: 3) Despite that problem, this mill is thought to have been the only one making paper in County Durham with more than one vat before 1800. (Shorter 1957: 407)

A Sun Fire Insurance Company certificate no. 263906, dated 19 November 1768, shows the proprietor of Lintzford to have been James Bell, a merchant of Newcastle upon Tyne, who insured the mill that was in the tenure of Alexander MacKey, a paper maker. Whitehead's trade directory of 1775 and of 1790 mentions a paper warehouse belonging to Gilder in Newcastle upon Tyne. Wallis (1981: 1) also places James Bell here until 1790. It has been suggested that 'sometime around 1780 this mill came in to the possession of the Annandale family,'[43] but other records indicate that the Annandales acquired the mill in 1840. (Neasham 1881: 81)

Paper found with the watermark *1797 AM* was probably made by Archibald McKinlay who appears to have occupied both Lintzford and Urpeth Mills. (Shorter 1957: 161) A paper maker, Mr Scaife, carried on a paper manufactory here, at least from 1811.[44] He had leased part of Lintzford Mill to two cordwainers, Ralph Shevill and Jonathan Stephenson in 1797. (Maidwell 1987: 13) Archibald McKinlay was probably Master Paper Maker at Lintzford and at Urpeth from 1771 according to Shorter (1957: 161). He noted that a number of paper makers appear in the parish registers of Tanfield who may have been connected with Lintzford Mill:

Archibald McKinlay and David McLeod in 1798, Simon Garling from 1798 to 1800, Thomas Bennet 1798-1802 and the Grays, Robert from 1799 to 1811, Thomas 1799 to 1806, both probably more connected with Urpeth Mill yet recorded at Lintzford; from 1800-1807 also William Cruddas (Cruddace) of Urpeth Mill, 1802-1805 Robert Lawes, 1803 Thomas Heel and, in 1804, Ralph Reid.

In 1799 the Chopwell Estate was for sale, including the paper mill at Lintzford. The mill site with land comprised five acres that yielded a rent of £35 a year.[45] Mr Scaife appears to have continued here, possibly from 1797, for he was recorded as having 'built reservoirs on the edge of Chopwell Woods to ensure an adequate water supply during the summer months' about 1800. (Turnbull 1978: 5) Yet Archibald MacKinlay representing Lintzford Mill was recorded at a meeting of Master Paper Makers at the George & Vulture Tavern in London in 1803.[46] A paper maker named Thomas Heel was noted here in 1803, but whether or not as an employee is not clear. (Wallis 1981: 4)

Although Excise authorities listed Lintzford Mill under different mill numbers, 239 in 1816 then 234 by 1853, they do not appear to have been used concurrently, so it was probably the result of an administrative adjustment rather than an indication of two paper mills here. The Excise listing of 8 October 1816 showed George Pearson & Co to be occupying the mill, and Parsons & White directory located him with premises at 2 Side, Newcastle in 1827, but in partnership with Thomas Pearson. Bailey (1990:11, 19) searched the records of a Newcastle engineering firm, R. Stephenson & Co: they show that the company supplied Messrs G. & T. Pearson of Lintzford paper mill in June 1829 with five small paper rollers valued at 29/- each and other paper machine components that together cost £53. That, with other sightings of the Pearsons there, indicates their continued occupation until 1837.

A Francis Pearson, paper maker, was cited in Excise correspondence of 28 November 1832 but was, presumably, not the main occupier. By 1835 there was a bankruptcy case against George Pearson and Thomas Pearson, paper merchants and manufacturers of Newcastle on Tyne, of Lintzford Mill, Durham and of Haughton Mill, Northumberland. It was agreed by the authorities that a certificate could be issued from 8 December 1835; the case was confirmed as finalised in November that year by listings in the *London Gazette* of 15 September and 17 November 1835, also on 23 February 1836. The Pearsons were still in correspondence with the Excise authorities over this matter during 1837.

The Annandale Papermaking Business

The business did not prosper, but whether from poor management or from lack of adequate finance cannot be ascertained. In 1840 Peter and James Annandale of Shotley Grove Mill acquired Lintzford paper mill by purchase from James Thompson, currier of Morpeth; Thomas Hunter, farmer of Kettlesworth; Nathaniel Grace, paper maker of Scotswood; John Scaife snr, Gentleman and John Scaife jnr, Gentleman, and this is confirmed in a document of 10 September 1842.[47] This was probably to expand their business from Shotley Grove Mills. By this date (1842) there were three beating engines here, 'driven by a metal waterwheel 20½ feet in diameter and 12½ feet wide, and three new drying cylinders'. (Chapman 1977: 18) They installed new machinery to make fine writing, printing and envelope papers. (Turnbull 1978: 5)

It is possible that the Annandales came to live in Lintzford House well before they had papermaking businesses here. It is said, but has not been substantiated, that John Annandale built this house in 1790, but probably incorporating an older house as dragon wing roofing was discovered during renovations in mid 1900s. (Ridley nd:61) While viewing County Durham, Pevsner, (1953: 180) came upon Lintzford House and described it as a 'handsome five-bay, two storey, Georgian stone front, [with some] buildings of a former paper mill'.

Maidwell (1987: 14) considers that the Annandales took over Lintzford Mill in 1842, possibly from Nathanial Grace, whom the Excise authorities recorded as the occupier on 1 December 1842, or with Nathanial Grace working the mill initially. Also in 1842, the Annandales (Peter and James) leased of Sir Thomas John Clavering some adjoining land measuring ten yards by eight yards, to provide access from the River Derwent to Lintzford Paper Mill. This was for a term of twenty one years, back-dated from 2 August 1842 at a rent of 10/- a year, as the lease was dated 10 September, 1842. Perhaps this was to formalise an understanding or complete the transaction.[48] According to Excise authorities, George Pearson and his fellows had 'left off' working 'Mill 240' (Lintzford) by 1842, but George Lightfoot and John Lightfoot were also noted here in 1841 and as having 'left off' working the mill in 1842.[49] This apparent contradiction may be the result of different tenants working the mill for short periods between which it was idle, or that the Excise authorities comment referred to the paper makers themselves having ceased working at the mill.

Other than that the Excise authorities noted on 1 February 1844 that Peter and James Annandale were still running the mill in 1844, we cannot always be sure which members of the Annandale family were in charge of this company at particular periods. It is clear that the papermaking business of John Annandale & Sons continued here until 1897, and became a limited company in 1898, a status maintained until the firm's demise in 1907, as paper makers and other trade directories show.[50]

Housing had been provided for at least some of the workforce from an earlier period, as we learn from Bourn (1896: 164) in his parish history: 'the houses occupied by the workmen at Lintzford Paper Mill' in 1800'. The Annandales continued this provision; there were some 20 houses opposite the works each comprising two or three storeys and built of stone and brick, houses that were eventually demolished in 1966.[51]

In addition to the paper mill at Lintzford and their mills at Shotley Bridge, the Annandales owned extensive farms connected with both mill sites, including a large stud of horses for carrying out farm work and also work related to the paper mills. They were also well-known sheep breeders, particularly famous for their prize-winning Border Leicesters.[52]

Initially producing about five to six tons of paper per week,[53] the Annandales increased this output by installing a 62 inch machine; the mill was then making fine writings, printings and envelope papers. (Maidwell 1987: 14) Seven beating engines were recorded working in 1851 during a national survey.[54] A tithe assessment of the Chopwell estate in 1852 noted James Annandale, paper manufacturer, as the owner and occupier of Linty Ford (sic) Mill; he was assessed for a tithe of £5 8s 0d on a property of eighteen acres.[55] A William Palliser, paper maker of Linty Ford (sic), formerly of Shotley Bridge, publican, was declared and discharged a bankrupt and listed in the *London Gazette* on 23 August and 29 October 1867. His relationship with the Annandales is not clear, nor whether he had ever been apprenticed to a paper maker.

By 1871 both rag and esparto were being used as furnish for quality papers, and writings were being advertised in Kent's Trade Directory as engine sized; five years later Craig's Trade Directory indicates that cartridges were also being offered.

Lintzford Mill Saved from a Fire

On 20 September 1873,

> An alarming fire, which we believed to be the work of an incendiary, took place at Lintz Ford paper mill, the property of Messrs Annandale. This was the second fire that had occurred at this place within four days.
>
> Annandale was also the proprietor of an extensive farm and a 70 ton haystack also caught fire. The attention of the fire brigade was diverted [to] the paper mill itself. [Soon] … by pouring a continuous stream of water [from the River Derwent] the fire was prevented from spreading, and the following morning had burnt itself out. (Fordyce 1876: II, 256)

The Annandales firm's business was being conducted from Shotley Grove by 1872, although paper was also being made at Lintzford according to Kent's Trade Directory, but the company was also listed in Kelly's Trade Directory at Winlaton 1873. Simmons (nd) papers give details of the paper products being made at

Lintzford. The motive power was derived from both steam and water by 1880 and, as an experiment, blottings were added and remained in the range of papers produced until 1893 when they were withdrawn. Enamelling papers were tried in the latter years. Engine sized cartridges and hosiery papers were advertised in 1895, and fine printing offered in ream or web by 1905, and noted in paper trade, and noted directories. In summation, large quantities of all kinds of superior paper were manufactured here, and, by 1895, output had reached about 120 tons per week from five machines.[56]

Changing Fortunes

Although the mill ceased to function in 1907 and was then advertised for sale by private treaty, Lintzford continued to be advertised in paper makers directories in subsequent years until sold in 1913; the sale of machinery had been mentioned specifically in 1911 directories. A change in 1913 when the Lintzford Paper Mill Co was formed by Vincent Jackson of Darwen, Lancashire, who may have been an Annandale heir, and a Mr Musgrove, cotton spinner of Bolton, was an attempt to make Lintzford Mill profitable. (Maidwell 1987: 14)

The new company installed a considerable amount of additional machinery: a new boiler and economisers by Messrs E. Green & Son, Wakefield, Yorkshire; super heaters and a new unaflow steam engine by Messrs J. Musgrave & Sons, Bolton, Lancashire; a water turbine from Messrs James Gordon & Co, Knightrider Street, London; a bleaching plant produced by Messrs Masson, Scott & Co, Fulham, London; a new wet end to the papermakng machine with other additions from Mr A. Robertson of Darwen, Lancashire; a duplex cutting machine produced by Messrs C. Walmsley & Co, Bury, Lancashire; two 57 kw British Westinghouse generators and a first class reeling machine. Thus, Lintzford Mill became fully electrically equipped for power and lighting, with a 60 inch web machine capable of producing 30 tons of paper a week.[57]

Paper Makers directories of 1914 and 1915 noted agents in London, and in Birmingham, Bristol and Edinburgh suggesting an expanding concern, and that another papermaking machine of a 70 inch web width was installed in 1915 to enhance the business. Despite all this the concern was short-lived, for a paper merchant of Gloucester and a chocolate firm acquired Lintzford Mill mainly for making greaseproof paper, (Maidwell 1987: 14) and the company was registered on the Stock Exchange Register as Gloucester Paper Mills Ltd in the same year.

Within two years this company went in to voluntary liquidation and this appeared on the Stock Exchange Register of 1917; the mill again changed hands, to be taken over by Charles Marsden & Co Ltd paper makers and merchants of Sheffield. (Maidwell 1987: 14) This firm introduced a 72 inch width machine and, by 1922, paper trade directories listed the company as Charles Marsden & Sons Ltd. This venture lasted longer than some others of recent years and the mill did not cease production until sometime between 1922 and 1924; authorities such as Maidwell (1987) and Turnbull (1978) differ about the year. Shorter (1971: 175) commented on the tendency for several mills to have been in a group for economies of scale but still having failed if the management was poor; he cited Marsden & Co as an example, in which group Lintzford was one of six mills.

The premises was taken over by Richardson's Printing Ink Co Ltd of Team Valley in 1923. (Atkinson 1974,: II, 181) Lintzford Mill was still operating in 1966 as Dufay Paints,[58] but closed in the 1980s. (Linsley 1989: 22) Considering the site, Atkinson, (1974: II, 294) wrote: 'Some nineteenth-century buildings from the earlier paper mill have been incorporated in to a later (1923) printing ink factory'. By the 1990s the mill site had finally been converted in to a picturesque collection of Georgian style houses.

Chopwell Mill[59]

As with Blackhall paper mills nearby, it is sometimes difficult to distinguish references to paper makers there from those at Chopwell Mill. Both were described as on the north bank of the River Derwent, with Chopwell Mill one and a half miles south of St John's Church in Chopwell, and just east of Blackhall Mills.[60] Both were in Ryton parish but an Excise number (241) distinguished Chopwell Mill. Situated on the River Pont, a tributary of the Derwent, 'coarse grey paper was made from old rags and sails [at the mill]. This was the only kind that could be made there because the water, which was said to have come from a coal mine, was heavily charged with iron, and would discolour finer paper'. (Flinn 1955: XXIX, 261) Water in the tail race of Blackhall Mills was used to provide power for the paper mill situated at the end of the mill race, presumably Chopwell, but it could refer to the tail race from Blackhall iron mill forge providing power for Blackhall paper mill, or both mills. (Turnbull 1978: 5)[61] It could also be construed that the dam and mill race, that produced power for Blackhall forge and Blackhall paper mill, also served Chopwell paper mill. (Maughan 1955) This appears to have been a relatively small mill that eventually could not compete financially or perhaps in quantity or quality of paper, with larger or modernised paper mills.

The Paper Makers

Parish registers of Ryton and Ebchester referred to paper makers who may have been associated with Chopwell Mill or, equally, with Blackhall Mills. Not until 1697 do we find a precise reference to Chopwell Mill. (Shorter 1960: 103) The first mention of a paper maker of Chopwell occurred in Ryton parish registers in c1697, that of Jonathan Ord of the paper mills, (Shorter 1957: 162) then a record including Thomas Sage of the paper mill, Ryton in 1706. (Wallis 1981: 6) Christopher Bowman, paper maker of the paper mill, appeared from 1713 until 1719 in both Ryton and Ebchester registers at different times. Others were also noted at the same period, so it is difficult to know which were proprietors, tenants or employees. Paper makers so noted were Richard Clarke 1714, Nicholas Hurst of Ebchester 1714-1716, and John Vintin of Ryton in 1716. (Shorter 1957: 162) William Bonsor of the paper mill, Ryton, appeared in Ebchester parish registers in 1722, as did John Jackson of Ryton in 1726 and in 1734. When Mr Angerstein, a Swedish business man, visited Chopwell Mill in 1754 he noted that a Richard Clark owned the mill. (Linsley 1994: 20) By 1768 the mill was being rented by a Newcastle merchant, James Bell. (Turnbull 1978: 5)

The burial register of Ebchester parish for 1788 shows William Harvey to have been of Chopwell Paper Mill, and it is possible that the Joseph Harvey, paper maker of Ebchester noted in 1800, may have been related and also associated with Chopwell Mill. (Wallis 1981: 4) Soon after William Harvey's death, Chopwell Estate was advertised for sale by auction on 30 August 1799. Particulars of the property included 'Paper Mill, with Five Acres and Three Quarters of Land, is let on lease for an unexpired Term of about Nineteen Years' at a rent of £35 per annum to Joseph Whitfield.[62] In that year a William Whitfield was also noted at the mill. (Shorter 1957: 162) Reservoirs built in Chopwell Wood in 1800 may well have served both Chopwell and Blackhall paper mills. (Ridley nd: 62)

It appears that Messrs Harker (Joseph), Pearson (Richard) & Gladston (Thomas), paper makers, took over the tenure of Chopwell Mill for, by 1803, they are known to have insured their fixed machinery and utensils in Chopwell paper mill.[63] A Lease & Release of property between the Earl Cowper and Isaac Cookson Esq of Whitehill on 18 and 19 October 1809, included Chopwell Paper Mill and appurtenances, but there is no evidence to determine whether or not Isaac Cookson was a paper maker.[64] Joseph Harker, Richard Pearson and, until he died in 1828, Thomas Gledstone, were subsequently mentioned at various dates in the parish registers between 1807 and 1814. (Wallis 1981: 3)

It was Henry Jefferson & Co. that was named in an Excise listing of 8 October 1816 as making paper at Chopwell Mill, and specifically John Jefferson Harrison, as the occupier on an 11 July 1822 listing. He continued there until at least 1828 because his name was still listed as paper manufacturer and occupier at Chopwell Mill in Parsons & White trade directory in 1827, also in a directory of paper makers in 1828. A subsequent Excise list of 28 November 1832 noted that mill no. 241 was not in use. A Tithe revision of

1852 for the Chopwell Estate referred to the owner and occupier of the mill but there was no indication of paper being made there at that time.[65]

Egglestone Abbey Mill[66]

Egglestone Abbey Mill, variously called Abbey, Egglestone or Eccleston, even Athelstone, was situated on the River Tees one mile south east of Barnard Castle. It was first mentioned in 1717 as part of the Manor of Dalton as *'unum molendium papir'* in a Recovery Roll of the parish; it remained a manorial mill until 1807.[67] Chapman (1977: 18) commented that it was 'sited just where the Tees dissolved in to the rapids of Abbey gorge', and implied that a dam or weir directing water towards the mill race, and controlled by a sluice gate, might act to some extent for storage. The mill was said to have been formed from domestic buildings of a convent there.[68] Egglestone Abbey was a one-vat mill where paper was made by hand throughout the paper mill's history, but it proved to be too small to survive the technical changes that pervaded the industry in the early 1800s.

Messrs Henry Cooke & Co.

The occupiers are not known before 1773, although the mill was to let in 1756.[69] James Cooke of Messrs Henry Cooke & Co had leased the mill from the Morritt family by 1773 (Bower 1994: 15), and the firm continued there until 1830. The accounts books of 1778 show that the company paid £20 per annum in rent for the mill, £47 18s 10d for four fields near the mill, and £2 per annum. for a house and stables. (Cornett 1908: IX,161) Robert Hutton, who ran Ford Mill from 1838 until he moved to Deptford Mill, served his apprenticeship here with Henry Cooke. (Chester 1976: 2)

> A Robert Crampton was noted as a paper maker here in 1793, perhaps the occupier, as he was named as the person to whom to apply when the mill was to let in 1799. When the famous painter Turner visited the mill in 1797 James Cooke was the proprietor, but he died three years later in 1800 aged 55. James Cooke left seven young children, to each of whom he bequeathed

£50, except to his daughter, Elizabeth, who received £100. James widow, Elizabeth, as legatee, received the major part of his estate and the remaining years of the lease on the mill. She continued working the mill while bringing up seven well-educated children, until her own tragic death in 1809. (Bower 1993: 3; 1994: 5)

Tragedy of a Major Fire

A major fire at the mill caused tragic deaths to members of the Cooke family that were reported in detail in several newspapers:

> On the night of Friday, 16th June, 1809 the drying house of Mrs Cook of Athelstone(sic) Abbey paper mill near Barnard Castle, Co. Durham was discovered to be on fire. Mrs Cook and her two daus. in endeavouring to remove what paper could be saved, were soon enveloped in flames. Mrs Cook and one of the daughters died afterwards.[70]

It was also recorded that:

> The neighbours were obliged to break in the shutters and with much difficulty got them out of the place from the top windows. Mrs Cook was carried down apparently lifeless, and expired the next day; the eldest daughter leaped out of one of the windows, but was so much burnt that her life was despaired of; the other one was carried down in the same manner as her mother, nearly suffocated.[71]

The second son, Henry Cooke, took over the mill in 1809 after the fire and the death of his mother, Elizabeth Cooke, paying rent of £190 a year for the mill, a house and 42 acres around the mill for growing and grazing. Henry Cooke, with his sister Catherine, described as son and daughter of the late Elizabeth Cooke of Egglestone Abbey, near Barnard Castle, paper maker, petitioned on 9 September that year for repayment of the duty already paid on paper destroyed in fire.[72]

Conversion to Corn Milling

Henry Cooke married Hannah Wilkinson in 1811 and continued to produce hand-made paper. (Bower 1993:4) He was listed by the Excise authorities as a paper maker at the mill under Excise no. 74, as on 8 October 1816. Cooke also held 42 acres around the mill at an annual rent of £190 and used that land partly for grazing cattle, partly for growing grain. (Bower 1993:4) His name was recorded in trade directories with the Egglestone Abbey Mill address until 1830 when the family moved to Richmond in Yorkshire, and operated Whitcliffe Mill there. Egglestone Abbey Mill was then converted to grind corn. (Bower 1993:16) One can only speculate that there was no opportunity at Egglestone Abbey to extend the mill to accommodate papermaking machinery, so the Cookes moved on. There is no evidence to suggest that the mill was ever again used for papermaking. A great flood in 1881 severely damaged the mill and it was never repaired.

Some small part of it remained, but in ruins. Atkinson (1974: II, 315) noted that only the shell of the mill was then intact; the roof and floor had been removed and the rest gutted. 'The stone race remains for an internal undershot wheel measuring approximately 17 inch x 7 inch x 9inch'.

Note: Turner's painting of this mill is said to depict sheets of paper laid out to dry on the grass, but these sheets are too large for paper made by hand, and paper was not usually dried outside by this period. It was more often dried in drying lofts within the mill. More likely is it these were felts that were to be used, layered between the sheets of paper to soak up surplus moisture, laid out while being cut to size for couching. (Bower 1993: 3-4) The so-called sheets of paper may just have been artistic licence.

Blackhall Mills[73]

There were two paper mills called Blackhall in Ryton parish, two miles upstream from Lintzford Paper Mill on the River Derwent. They were situated about one hundred yards off the main road, on the right hand side if travelling south. Maidwell considers that one of these mills may be on the site of the Lintz Old Paper Mill, shown on a 1 inch to the mile Ordnance Survey map NZ 151556 on the River Pont, but Lintz Old mill is shown one mile south of Lintzford therefore not Blackhall; it came to be called Ewhurst [Paper] Mill. (Maidwell 1987: 12, 14) Surprisingly no Excise number has been located for a mill or mills called Blackhall. The development of these mills demonstrates the advantage of sharing an existing dam and millrace to fulfil water requirements, even though they eventually failed to compete with larger mills.

Origins of the Paper Mills

A fulling mill and a corn mill were worked here originally and a steel mill with a forge was established at Blackhall in the eighteenth century. The paper mill was operated by the same dam and millrace as the forge, producing coarse grey paper from old rags and sails. It was said that the water, being charged with iron, discoloured finer paper and the bridge on the River Derwent was frequently swept away by floods. (Maughan 1955)

According to Maidwell, (1987: 15) a reference in Ryton parish registers to Jonathan Ord 'of the paper mils' in 1697 could apply to Blackhall Mills, but Shorter (1957: 162) considers this reference to concern Chopwell Mill. Between 1706 and 1800 many people connected with the paper mills were noted in Ryton parish registers and in Ebchester parish registers, but it is not often clear whether they were connected with Blackhall or with Chopwell. A Mr Henrik Kalmeter, an engineer from Sweden visited Blackhall Paper Mill in 1719 so confirming that the mill was working then. (Flinn 1955: 259) It is known that the Surtees family owned Blackhall Estate from sometime in the seventeenth century. (Surtees 1820: II, 282)

Working the Paper Mills

A journal advertisement on 18 January in 1732 announced that the two paper mills were available for letting. Unusually perhaps, the rent was to be paid in kind, as sheets of paper. (Shorter 1957:

162) No further references to Blackhall Mills occur until 1768; an insurance policy of that year indicated that James Bell, a merchant of Newcastle upon Tyne (perhaps a paper merchant) insured the stock of paper in the paper mill. As the policy noted that the mill was in the tenure of a paper maker, Alexander MacKey, either James Bell was the proprietor, or the two men were in partnership with James Bell having a financial interest rather than providing papermaking expertise.[74] At this time the mill was producing inferior, coarse grey paper made from old, poor quality rags. It is also noted by Turnbull (1978: 5) that 'The tail waters from Blackhall Mill were used to provide power for a paper mill situated at the end of the mill race'; this refers to Chopwell Mill. Ridley (nd: 62) mentions reservoirs built in Chopwell Wood 'by the Paper Mill people', reservoirs that may have served Blackhall Mills as well as Chopwell Mill.

Mention in records of people who worked the mills at Blackhall is only occasional, as is comment on any activity at the mill; it is rarely clear whether or not a paper maker worked at either Chopwell Mill or Blackhall, or even if he was the proprietor, tenant, a paper maker craftsman or a paper mill worker. However, there is no doubt from the parish register of Ebchester that the paper maker called Archibald Donkinson, buried there in 1794, was at one of the Blackhall Paper Mills as it was so stated.

Maidwell (1987: 14) comments that John Jefferson Harrison worked Blackhall Mill in 1820, and is recorded as having paid annual rates of £32 10s for his mill in 1826. This is confirmed by Parsons & White trade directory of 1827, in which it was also noted that Harrison occupied an office at 63 Side in Newcastle upon Tyne. At this date Harrison was paying £32 10s 0d in rates, calculated at 2s 6d in the pound, for the paper mill; this compared with the payment by other local businessmen of £2 5s for a public house, £9 for a slate quarry and £50 for a forge. Harrison continued there until about 1834.

Demise of Papermaking

Either one, or both, of Blackhall mills was laid still in 1829, (Maidwell 1987:14) but may have started production again as comment on the mill in 1834 refers to it having been lately carried on by John Jefferson Harrison but being now unoccupied. (MacKenzie & Ross 1834: I, 205) A Tithe revision of 1852 for the Chopwell Estate included Blackhall Mill and noted that the owner, John Cookson, had let the mill. There was no mention of papermaking so perhaps it had reverted to being used for grinding corn or converted for some other use.[75] Fordyce writing in 1855 commented: 'a paper mill, formerly carried on here, has long been discontinued'. (Fordyce 1855: II, 679)

No further evidence of these mills has been found, perhaps partly because of the occasional confusion with Chopwell Mill, and partly that few records appear to have survived. It was recorded that the mill furnace stood as a ruin until 1916 when it was demolished to allow a house to be built for the headmaster of a nearby school. A postcard sent in 1900 is illustrated with a drawing by Angerstein that depicts the mill as it was in 1754.[76]

Gibside Mill[77]

As with Croxdale Mill on the Salvin estate, we are fortunate that the Strathmore estate records are full and survive, as the story of Gibside Mill has been compiled mainly from that source.[78]

As far back as 1325 there were two water mills at 'Gipsete' [Gibside], one a fulling mill, the other a corn mill, three miles downstream of Lintz Green on the River Derwent. As part of the Strathmore Estate the mills became the property of George Bowes in 1722. Five years later, in 1727, he began to establish plantations in the grounds where it was too steep for crops, and put up small buildings to interest visitors. Among other changes, Bowes converted the corn mill to papermaking in 1728 in the hope of making it more profitable. Initially he took visitors on 'Paper Mill Walks' but later preferred walks to other new buildings.[79]

An Earlier Paper Mill

There are three references that may indicate an earlier paper mill here. Articles of Agreement drawn up on 5 August 1719 between 'Jonathan Ord & Sons Paper Millers of the first part and George Hunter Corn Miller both of Gibside of ye other part' detailed how the water was to be used for their respective mills; it was mutually agreed to share by weekly alternating use. If there was sufficient water both were entitled to use it concurrently but, should there have been a dispute it was stated, and accepted, that Mr William Boulfield, millwright, would be the arbiter. No specific indication was given of the function of each mill; it may be that each party held a corn mill, but the Ord men were described only as 'Paper Millers'.[80]

In the accounts for 1728, the year it is said that George Bowes converted the corn mill to papermaking, Joseph Palliser was paid £5 for work 'at the new paper mill made from the old'. Probably the 'old' referred to the corn mill, but it is not entirely clear in view of the contents of the 1719 document mentioned above. More direct is the comment in a memorandum of a lease in 1731: Benjamin and Robert Ord were 'to have to Farme All That Paper Mill called Gibside Old Paper Mill'. These references are ambiguous so it is impossible to be certain about the existence of an earlier paper mill, but they leave open the question as to whether or not paper had been made previously at Gibside.

The Paper Mill Site

The paper mill marked on T. Jeffry's map of Durham for 1767 is almost certainly that of Gibside, (Shorter 1957: 161), and a plan of the mill site appears on a Gibside estate map dated 1767. This indicates the leat cutting across a broad peninsula, itself formed by the meandering route of the river. A building is indicated at the downstream end of the leat that may have housed a rag engine driven by an undershot wheel. In a deposition of 16 June 1789 John Maugham, who 'wrought at said mill as a Wright', declared that he had heard Mr Ord say 'that before the Race was cut, that there was no island in that part of the Darwent (sic) ... untill a great flood which made it overflow that part of the Tenter Garth 'tween the Island and the Race, which has been ever since tearing more and more away'.

The mill was situated at the bottom of a gill west of Snipe's Dene, as shown on the first Ordnance Survey six inch map.[81] Being in the tidal area of the River Wear the mill possibly benefited from higher water catchment areas and reservoirs (originally the investments of coal mill builders) that escaped pollution. (Clavering 1999: 3) Dr Wills confirmed that the river water was considered to be clean, that is without much clay, so good for pulping.[82] Although Reinhold Angerstein, Swedish steelworks Director visiting in 1754, wrote of Gibside: 'In addition to everything else, there is also a paper mill to be seen, that has the same trouble with rusty water as the mill [Lintzford] at Lintz Green',[83] but clean water must have been available here as the mill was known to have produced good quality paper. (Shorter 1957: 161)

Structure and Equipment

There are some clues to the mill's structure from notes of repairs in the accounts. We can reasonably assume that the roof was thatched as there was an entry for 'Thatching ye mill' £1 16s 6d, and 'straw for Ord's mill' costing 18s paid to John Hopper, on 20 and 27 May 1760 respectively. Similarly, Thomas Coltman was paid 11s 0d for drawing straw and thatching at the paper mill on 31 August 1764. The mill house, presumably Widow Ord's house, was also thatched as she had been charged £1 12s 6d for thatching of the mill house roof on 11 May 1751.

How the mill was equipped and kept in good order is reflected further in the accounts. A new press was being built, or an existing one being extensively repaired in 1755, as Mr William Wouldhave was paid £3 6s for '36ft of Elm and two nutts for the paper mill' on 25 October. Similarly, a note of payment on 23 December, 1771 to Cuthbert Palliser of £2 11s 4d, measuring wood for the paper mill hanging [drying] house, suggests new or major work. Six months later (26 June 1772) John Maugham & Partners had been 'putting in the Cogge wheels, making new arms for (?), putting in and making a gang of rodds, making 2 pairs of trindle heads and making a fall for the waterwheel at the paper mill' at a cost of £4 15s 8d.

It is not clear why an inventory was taken of the fixtures at the paper mill on 11 April 1780, but the listing gives a minimal view of the contents of the mill and in what is referred to as the 'Workman's House':

> Two Wood Presses in the Dry House
> In the Mill an Iron Press
> A Water Wheel a Cog Wheel ... and an Ingine
> 1 Vatt Stuff Chest with (?) Wood Presses

Problems of Flooding

The variable behaviour of the River Derwent is well-known locally and this, combined with the nature of the paper mill's location, made the site vulnerable to flooding. This is reflected in the frequent need to repair the sluices and the dam. An undated document refers to a dam, possibly a rice dam, being built to regulate the flow of water, but neither the proprietor nor tenant nor the tradesman concerned is named:

> An Estimate of Wood and Workmanship for Making a
> Dam at Gibside Paper Mill from the fludgates to the
> Sand Bed 95 foot.

To 292 Foot of Fir Wood at 10s ft	£12 3s 4d
To 60 Deals	£ 3 5s 0d
To 28 Square of frame at 7s ft	£ 9 16s 0d
	£25 4s 4d

Attempts to control excessive water seem to have failed as the estate accounts show frequent entries of payments for repairs to, or rebuilding of, the sluices and the dam. One example is the entry for 30 May 1752 when Joseph Palliser was paid £3 0s 1d for 'pulling down the old paper mill', followed by 3s 0d paid to Richard Elliot on 7 November 1752 for 'walling up ye sluices at Ord's Mill carried away by ye flood'. The implication is that the flood damage was so great that the mill had to be rebuilt. Later problems resulting from flooding are indicated by entries such as: 17 November 1764 James Barras 'for woodsmen for mending the paper mill sluices for three days at 3s 9d', and Joseph Palliser 6s 3d on 31 December for 'repairing the flood gates and nailing on laths at the paper mill'. Another indication of possible flood damage is the entry of 19 June 1772 that notes a payment of 4s 6d to Henry Bedson far walling in the paper mill race 4s 6d.

Continuing problems with the dam from earlier years are evident in notes of repeated repair work. For example, an £8 bill [no name] 'for his half of £16 for repairing the Mill Dam, 16 years ending May Day 1744' and, for repairing mill dam 17 January and 5 October 1749, respectively 2s 6d and 14s 7d. Then on 17 May 1766, a note of 'cash disbursed by James Barras for building a shade and repairing the Dam at Gibside paper mill'.

The Tenants

An advertisement in the *Newcastle Courant* of 9 January 1731 announced that Gibside paper mill was to let. It is unclear when Robert and Benjamin Ord became tenants at the paper mill, but they were named as such in the advertisement, and as the people to be contacted by interested parties. Although their trade is not stated, from the connection with the Ord papermaking family and their connection with paper mills, Shorter (1957: 161) feels there is little doubt that they were Master Paper Makers. Despite a suggested change of tenancy by the insertion of the advertisement, the Ords continued to occupy the mill. A Memorandum of a Lease of Gibside Old Paper Mill for 31 years, dated 2 March 1731 was agreed between Thomas Hall, gentleman on behalf of George Bowes, and Robert and Benjamin Ord, 'to have to Farme All That Paper Mill called Gibside Old Paper Mill together with the Drying house and other houses thereunto' at a rent of £20. This included appurtenances and a new engine to be built at the landlord's expense, but the Ords were to pay interest at 1s 6d in the pound for the money expended; the Landlord would find the wood for any repair but it was the Ord's responsibility to ensure necessary repairs were carried out. The tenants were also required to pay all cesses and taxes, 'save the Land Tax'.

By August 1731 a new engine had been installed at a cost of £52 1s 4d, detailed in 'an account [11 August 1731] of the charges of Making a paper Engine for Robert & Benjamin Ord'. These charges add up to £1 8s 2d less than the given total; either the total is incorrect or the amounts have been mis-read. It was arranged that payments were to begin on 11 November 1734; the rent was noted as £18 per annum for a lease of 31 years for the mill and ground.

	To: Cash paid them at several times	
	Which they laid out as of [unclear]	£38 0s 0d
10	Hundred single tack nails	9s 6d
3	Hundred sixpenny tack nails	1s 6d
1	Hundred fourpenny tack nails	4d
30	Thraves of straw	1s 10d
101	foot Oakwood at 20	£8 9s 2d
60	Deals	£2 15s 0d
2	Small firr baulks	2s .6d
2	Gung 16 coggs at 6d	13s 4d

Continuing Repairs and Improvements

Excerpts from the accounts depict continuing repairs and necessary alterations to the paper mill during Robert Ord's tenure, usually under a heading of Repairs and Improvements.

24th January, 1736 Robert Ord on account altering his mill	£5 0s 0d
9th February, 1736 Robert Ord on account repairs for paper mill	£7 4s 0d
4th June, 1736 Leading wood to Benjamin Ord's house at paper mill	9s 0d

The paper mill wheel needed close attention. It was repaired in 1759 at both ends of the year by John Maugham, including the mill axle tree in December, and charged at £1 12s on 22 February, and again at £1 12s on 22 December, this time for 23 days work.

Another instance of repairs to the paper mill wheel was noted on 23 April 1763 when Joseph Cockram was paid £6 8s 6d for 55ft Oak Wood delivered and used for that repair in the preceding year. Unspecified repairs were listed through the Gibside Mill's history: 16 February 1760, Joseph Palliser paid for 'repairing ye mill' £2 15s 9d; 26 October 1764 John Barras paid for 'a Fother of lime and leading for repairs at ye paper mill' 8s, and James Barras £1 2s 10d for 'repairing the paper mill roof'. A Cash Accounts entry of 9 February 1735 shows 'By repairs: Paid Robt. Ord on account of altering his Mill £7 4s.'

Changing Tenancy

It appears that sometime after 1736 the partnership may have been dissolved or Benjamin Ord had died, for he is not noted in any documents later than 4 June 1736. However, paper purchased by the Estate from the mill on 7 March 1735 refers to buying paper from D. Orde's wife 'for [the] Gardiner to raise melons'.[84] Presumably other members of the Ord family were working in the business, but continuing references in the accounts confirm Robert Ord's tenure, at least until 1742 when a newspaper advertisement offering Gibside Mill to let, described it as late in the possession of Robert Ord, now deceased.[85]

Further evidence of the Ord's supplying paper for use by the incumbents of Gibside appears in estate accounts, suggesting that David Ord may now be the tenant.

Contingency Expenses:

12th June, 1746 Paid David Ord, Miller, for paper bought of him for covering little books	1s 6d
14th January, 1847 Paid Anne Ord for 2 reams of paper	8s 4d
16th July, 1748 Paid Ann Ord for 6 sheets of strong paper bought for book backs and for blue paper.	1s 6d

Here David Ord is noted as a miller, yet he is supplying paper. This could indicate that he held a corn mill as well as the paper mill, unless the word miller was meant to refer to him as a paper miller.

Change of Proprietor and Tenant

George Bowes died in 1760 and his widow became the proprietor; the mill was still leased by members of the Ord family. On 17 November that year John and Thomas Ord had the temerity to put this proposal to Mrs Bowes:

> Madam, as the Term of my Deceased Father's Lease is Expired, and as we have been of a long Continuance [as tenants] to the family; and the mill which we now have in possession, the walls are become Quite Ruieness and the working movements in General are failing, so that the same must be rebuilt, and as my Brother and me chuses to Continue in partnership, our proposals upon new Conditions for a term of thirty one years are as such that if you will be pleased to Build us Two mill, with Each a Drying house above them, with sufficient from'd (?) Dams, with the Dwelling houses in the place put in to sufficient Repairs; with stabling convenient for our horses and cows, we will give the Annual Rent of 6s a year, to have the whole Housing in place in to them; and to find us wood and lime we will be bound to keep the whole in Repairs; Exclusive of the Dams and Stabling for the [?] in which I hope you will be pleased to rebuild, as promised by the Happy deceased Geo: Bow's Esq; the last time we had the opportunity to speak to him on this occasion, and hopes you will continue your most Obedient and Humble Servants. Messieurs Ords.

Mrs Mary Bowes decided to grant a further lease of only eight years from 7 February 1761, and at a rent of £36 per annum. Articles of Agreement on 10 September 1761 with John and Thomas Ord confirmed the lease for eight years from May Day 1762 and detailed certain arrangements; 'Tenant to have £10 allowed towards Repairing the Water Wheel, making the Engine Tub and Repairing the Water Course, Tenant to have Wood allowed for repairs, and Coggs and Rounds during the Term …'.

The Paper Mill Demolished

The final part of the Gibside Paper Mill story was determined by the second marriage of George Bowes daughter to Robinson Stoney Bowes, who nearly ruined the estate. She had made provision that her husband had no rights over her property, but she eventually allowed him rights to her property because of his cruel treatment of her. Bowes then argued with a Mrs Garton (occupier?) and 'turned her off the same day' and destroyed the mill.[86] This is confirmed by entries in the accounts less than a month later: 23 December 1780: 'Paid Labourers taking the old Iron of the Ruins of Paper Mill'. A week later (31 December) there is a further reference to 'the Ruins of Paper Mill' and William Dixon being paid £3 18s 10d 'taking of old iron at the paper mill'. Beamish (2001: 10) comments that in December 1794 the remaining old walls at the paper mill were pulled down and used to build a wall round the old site. Beamish (2001: 5) describes what can still be seen of the mill site today:

> The visible remains of the infrastructure of the former paper mill at Gibside are limited to a stone cutwater on a now silted former channel of the River Derwent (the present channel now lying further to the north); a drystone walled leat and a small building foundation.

Chapter 2
Paper Mills Established 1750 to 1777

No mills had been converted to papermaking, nor built as paper mills, for twenty-two years since 1728, perhaps reflecting a lack of local demand or the state of trade generally. In this quarter century the beginning of an increasing demand for paper is mirrored in the development of another six paper mills. In five instances men of families that came to be well-known as paper manufacturers were the proprietors at some period of the mills development. Only one mill had a relatively short life of forty years; the other five were in production for eighty years or more.

Fellingshore Mill[1]

Fellingshore Mill was situated on the bank of the River Tyne east of Gateshead. The Excise authorities listed the mill by the name Heworthshore in 1816 under the Excise number 240,[2] but it was subsequently referred to as Fellingshore Mill with Excise number 297, perhaps to distinguish it from Snowden Hole Mill, also in Heworth parish. No other paper mill in County Durham appears to have been given the Excise number 240. Fellingshore was described as 'a brown paper mill', that is, making paper for wrapping and packing. (Surtees 1820: II, 85) It is possible that there were two paper mills in Heworthshore originally, but there is no evidence to justify that assertion.

Paper Mill Established c1750

Around 1750 Sir Robert Hawks established a mill here that was probably partly used to grind corn, and partly for making paper.[3] This is confirmed by a notice in a Tyneside newspaper in 1795 announcing that a half part of a paper mill was being offered for sale, with five vats, a drying house and four cottages; this was the part that had originally been used as a corn mill.[4] This also suggests that the papermaking business was prospering sufficiently for Sir Robert to forgo corn grinding and concentrate on making paper. Hawks was among the first in the region to recognise the value of steam power, employing this form of power at his ironworks, and then establishing the first steam-driven paper mill on Tyneside at Fellingshore in the late 1700s. (Manders 1973: 67; Shorter 1971: 110) William Reed, a paper maker, had joined Sir Robert Hawks in partnership by 1797, and R. Shafto Hawks became a partner of theirs subsequently. (Shorter 1957: 160)

Mill Destroyed by Fire

Unfortunately, the mill belonging to Hawkes & Co, referred to as the Tyne Steam Engine Paper Mill, was destroyed in a fire in 1803.[5] 'About five o'clock on the morning [of 20 December 1803], a fire broke out in the Tyne steam-engine paper mill at Fellingshore, near Gateshead, belonging to Messrs. Hawks & Co, which, in a short time, entirely consumed the stock, machinery and buildings'.[6] The fire was caused by 'the carelessness of a servant leaving a lighted candle in one of the drying rooms'.[7] There may have been another fire two years later, or that mentioned in *Tyne Industries* as occurring in 1805 is the same fire, but was so dated in error as no other reference to a subsequent fire has been found.[8]

Manufacturing Continues after Rebuilding

The mill must have been rebuilt because manufacture resumed and the partnership continued. However, when William Reed died in 1807 his widow, Eleanor, was named in his stead, but that partnership of Robert Shafto Hawks, John Grace and Eleanor Reed widow, described as paper manufacturers of Fellingshore Mill, was dissolved in 1808.[9]

It is difficult to be sure exactly who the tenants at Fellingshore were at some dates. Several men who were paper makers appear in the parish registers of Heworth, or are known to have been involved in papermaking but, either without specifying their status or without specific reference to Fellingshore Mill. Richard Blenkinsop, for instance, appears in Heworth parish registers between 1798 and 1809; (Shorter 1957: 160) David McLeod is noted by Wallis (1981: 3-5) in 1798, and in Heworth parish registers in 1800. Wallis also lists John Grace at Fellingshore between 1807 and 1809, and Robert Shafto Hawks, paper maker and draper from 1798 until 1830. This may suggest that the paper mill remained divided in to two or was sub-let at this date. It may also be that Robert Shafto Hawks, a draper, held a financial interest in the mill rather than an executive position.

It was recorded that a tremendous fire in a steam corn and paper mill in Gateshead broke out on 22 February 1810 at the premises of a Mr Harrison, a baker. 'A few minutes after the first discovery of the calamity the whole of the mill was completely in flames', resulting in extensive damage to the corn mill and dwelling, but the fate of the paper mill was not mentioned. It is uncertain but Sykes indicates this could be Fellingshore.[10]

Maidwell (1957: 14) refers to an advertisement that offers the mill for sale in 1810, comprising '4 cottages, Drying House, Paper Mill of 5 vats' etc. Elsewhere it is suggested that a Mr Salter held the mill from 1805 until 1826,[11] and a William Salter was listed in Parsons & White trade directory in 1827 as a paper manufacturer at Fellingshore during this period. He was cited as a bankrupt in 1832, a paper manufacturer, late of Fellingshore Mill.[12] However, Geo. Pearson & Co, paper makers, were on the 8 October 1816 Excise list for Heworthshore, mill no. 240 that seems to refer to Fellingshore Mill, so this may be a further indication of a split mill or a sub-let.

Messrs Thomas Gallon & Co, Tenant and Proprietor

From 1826, Fellingshore Mill no.297 producing brown paper was occupied by Messrs Thomas Gallon & Co as tenants of Sir Robert Hawks, from whom Thomas Gallon eventually bought it in 1860.[13] Maidwell (1987: 10) disagreed about the date on which Messrs Thomas Gallon & Co leased Fellingshore; he suggested 1834 but did not cite a source for this date.[14] As William Charlton Forster, a papermaker was noted in occupation at the mill in 1832, it seems likely that Gallon & Co either held a divided mill or further sublet. Salter became bankrupt in 1834.[15] Gallon & Co took over Salter's machinery, the power 'wrought by steam engine, for making brown and other wrapping papers' that Gallon continued to produce.[16]

One of the hazards of using papermaking machinery was the propensity to accidents resulting from an employee being caught up in the moving parts. Unfortunately, a boy named Kirkup, only about five years old, was so tragically injured:

> On 9th December, 1837 he had slipped, unperceived, in to Mr Gallon's paper manufactory, at Fellingshore, and climbed upon one of the wheels there. The weight of the boy, it is supposed, set the machinery in motion, and he unfortunately had both his legs wrenched off. He was found by one of the workmen, and conveyed to the Infirmary, where, we understand, he is likely to recover.[17]

Thomas Gallon, papermaker, is cited as the occupier of Fellingshore Mill in Excise correspondence in 1848,[18] and the firm is listed as Thomas Gallon & Co in various trade directories between 1850 and 1896.[19] In 1851 Mr Edward Smith of Gateshead exhibited the fine, strong brown wrapping paper produced by this company at the Great Exhibition in London. He was to become the mill manager by 1859.[20] Thomas Gallon & Co was then producing paper from one vat and one 80" machine with four beating engines working to produce the stuff.[21] Rope browns were then a speciality of the northeast. (Maidwell 1987: 10) In 1860 Thomas Gallon & Co acquired the business and the premises, so became the proprietor.[22] The firm continued to make rope brown, glazed browns and brown sorts of paper, adding a 74" machine in 1869.[23] Then disaster struck.

Boiler Explosion and an Inquest

On Tuesday, 9 May 1876 about 2.30 am a boiler exploded causing widespread damage; half the building was destroyed and a serious fire broke out leaving five people dead.[24] 'The effect of the explosion was deplorable in the extreme. The boiler was lifted from its bed and the greater part of it carried a distance of several yards'. Of those who died, three were crushed by debris: Patrick Abbott and his sons Patrick aged 20 and John aged 14; the two others were Alfred Smith, the 17 year old son of the Works Manager, and Robert Smart, 'an old man' aged 67.[25] The Foreman said there had been no warning: 'If the boiler had been working at an extreme pressure I would have known, because the pulping engine would have gone quicker'.[26]

At the Coroner's Inquest it was explained that boilers 'nos. 1,2,3 and 5 were fired all that day ... the [steam] pressure was about 25 or 26lbs ... and all had been well'. Fireman, Edward Burns, stated that the flues and tubes had been cleaned thoroughly only three weeks earlier and there had been no indication of 'wet or leakage in the boiler' nor any problem with gauge cocks that would have caused the pressure to have become excessive. A year previously an Inspector of steam boilers had checked no.1 boiler, pointed out some required repair work and it was understood that such repairs had been carried out.[27]

Edward Burns and William Pinkney had been relieved by Patrick Abbott and his son Patrick about 5.30 pm on May 8. Patrick Abbott, the Elder, took advice from a chemical company next door and used a little muriatic acid to help keep the pipes clean. This was not the cause of the accident. It was decided that the explosion was probably caused by a leaking sprung seam or sprung rivet, the result of corrosion and that the boiler had been 'worked beyond the age of safety'. The explosion had been set off by the sudden pumping of cold water in to the boiler. The Coroner declared the explosion to have been accidental but recommended 'more rigid supervision of repairs'.[28]

Expansion and Change

Another serious fire in the following year demolished the rest of the building, but work on rebuilding the mill began immediately and it was functioning again later in 1877.[29] An 80" papermaking machine had replaced the 74", but one vat continued to be used to make paper by hand[30] and, by 1880, steam was the only motive power employed at Fellingshore. Expansion is indicated by the addition of backing papers in 1882 to the browns and glazed browns produced previously, also output had increased to 24 tons a week, (Simmons nd) a level that was later further increased by the introduction of an 82" machine in 1896.[31] By 1890 the works site occupied three acres and covered a wide river frontage; the business prospered under the management of Edward Smith with the support of competent staff. Thomas Gallon had become the sole proprietor of a 'concern of recognised importance in [this] special industry'.[32]

Despite the apparent success of the business change was coming. Thomas Gallon died in 1897 and the mill was taken over by E. Richardson & Sons Ltd in that year; vat work was discontinued and all communication with the company was through the Team Valley Paper Mill.[33] The mill was converted to use electric power throughout and noted as an example of an electrically-driven paper mill in trade journals.[34] Only five years after taking over the mill E. Richardson & Son went in to liquidation and Fellingshore Paper Mills Ltd was formed in 1903 with J. E. Smith as Managing Director, making the same range of papers, with the addition of mill wrappers using rope and bagging; only the 80" machine was listed.[35] Fellingshore eventually became a casualty of the development of the high speed Kraft machine and was closed down finally in 1910. (Shorter 1971: 174)

Lamesley Mills[36]

Lamesley Mill carried the Excise no. 237 but consisted of two mills: Moor Paper Mill that adjoined a corn mill, and Turn Paper Mill. (Shorter 1957: 161) These mills were situated on the River Team near Chester-le-Street.[37]

The Ord Family: Proprietors at Lamesley

It seems probable, from somewhat patchy evidence of their involvement in these mills, that the Ord family provided the master paper makers at Lamesley for the second half of the eighteenth century. Several members of the family were cited in Durham Marriage Bonds: Benjamin Ord, a widower and paper maker who remarried in 1753, possibly the Benjamin Ord born c1694 who died in 1771, Christopher Ord, a papermaker who married in 1767, and another paper maker called Christopher Ord who married in 1787.[38] The marriage at Lamesley of a paper maker called Thomas Bage in 1781, (and another Benjamin Ord, a paper manufacturer, who married in 1790), may have referred to a tenant or an employee at one of the mills as the Ords continued as proprietors at the mill. (Shorter 1957: 161)

Trade directories indicate that a Christopher Ord had a paper warehouse in Newcastle upon Tyne and, by 1778, another warehouse in Gateshead.[39] A Christopher Ord continued to hold the mill, at least until 1795, making brown papers and insuring the utensils and stock in his paper mill in 1795, but noted as a miller and paper manufacturer.[40] He had also appeared as Bondsman for Benjamin Ord the second, paper manufacturer, who married in 1790. (Shorter 1957: 161)

By 1803 the Lamesley business had become a family company entitled Christopher Ord & Sons, and Christopher Ord was noted as a Master Paper Maker attending a national meeting of Master Paper Makers in London in 1803.[41] This makes it more difficult to distinguish between individual Christopher Ords, and to be sure whether any mention of Christopher Ord refers to a person or to the company. Certainly in 1803 a Christopher Ord of Moor Mills, described as miller and paper maker, 'insured the waterwheel in his corn mill, the fixed machinery and utensils in a paper mill communicating, and the fixed machinery and utensils in a paper mill at Turn Mill near'.[42]

Floods and a Hurricane

A Mr Ord was still at the mill when the elements overtook his business, on a Saturday, the day before New Year's Eve in 1815:

> In consequence of a rapid thaw, considerably heightened by a tempestuous gale from the west, the rivers in this neighbourhood were, on Saturday last, swoln to an alarming degree; and, we regret to say, considerable damage has been done by the watery element, and by the tremendous hurricane which lent its aid in the work of destruction. Mr Ord, paper maker, of Moorsley Banks, sustained considerable loss, by the water carrying away part of the dam, which he had erected at considerable expence.[43]

No record of rebuilding has been found but repairs must have been carried out as papermaking continued at Lamesley. However, it was Ann Ord who was listed as paper maker there in an Excise listing of 1816, although correspondence between Excise authorities and the Ords in 1817 was with Christopher Ord, and by 1823 with Benjamin Ord and John Ord.[44] Reference to an Edward Bowmaker, a flour miller, who relinquished the tenancy of Hendon Lonnin, a corn grinding windmill near Sunderland in 1823, and migrated to the conjoined paper and corn mill called Moor Mill near Lamesley in 1824, but returned to Sunderland in 1831, indicates that this mill was being used for corn milling as well as paper making. (Hyslop 1909: 163) A Thomas Graham at Lamesley Mill was mentioned by name in correspondence with Excise authorities in 1825, but his occupation was not mentioned.[45]

New Arrangements

The Ord family appear to have been unsuccessful at Lamesley Mill as Benjamin Ord became an insolvent debtor and was declared bankrupt in 1826. The official notice of bankruptcy in the *London Gazette* that year, described him as a paper manufacturer, formerly of Gateshead, afterwards of Newcastle upon Tyne, and lately of Lamesley Paper Mill.[46] The proprietor or tenant in 1827 and 1828 was a paper manufacturer called John Calvert,[47] who was also listed in directories (Parsons & White 1827; PMD 1828) at 185 High

Street, Gateshead, probably a sales office, with Christopher Ord as manager. No further mention of members of the Ord family has been found in connection with this mill.

The Ord family was involved in papermaking in several mills in County Durham so their resources may have been insufficient to sustain business at them all. One can only speculate that Lamesley Mills were the least profitable, or unable to compete in the brown paper trade as an increasing number of mills introduced machinery, or were more conveniently situated for transporting finished paper. There is uncertainty as to the fate of Lamesley Mill, and it is not known exactly when papermaking ceased. The most likely date is indicated by a statement in Excise correspondence that work (presumably papermaking) at mill no. 237 had been discontinued by 1830.[48]

Lendings Mill[49]

Lendings Mill could be found in the same parish as Egglestone Abbey Mill on the River Tees, half a mile from Barnard Castle. (Shorter 1957: 248) The mill was advertised to let in 1756 and 1757,[50] but no further information about Lendings Mill has been found until John Cooke, a paper maker of Lendings Mill, was listed in 1789 as a declared bankrupt.[51] He was probably of the well-known papermaking family that was working neighbouring Egglestone Abbey Mill, but may have been working the mill as a corn mill as subsequent occupiers were described as millers.

By 1793 a Mr Crampton of Barnard Castle had appeared in a list of paper makers in an address book. (Shorter 1957: 248) Could he be the same Mr Crampton, Robert, to whom enquiries concerning the sale of Lendings Mill were to be addressed in 1797?[52] The mill was still for sale two years later and the occupier noted as Robert Crampton.[53]

John Jefferson, a paper maker, was also at Lendings but, in 1815 when he was declared bankrupt, he was described only as a miller of Barnard Castle.[54] Matthew Jefferson worked Lendings between

1827 and 1834, possibly for longer, but whether as paper maker or corn miller is uncertain; his son (not named) is thought to have been with him for part of that period. A Robert Harrison was at Startforth, Barnard Castle in 1856 (Simmons nd) but, without further evidence, it is impossible to know whether or not he was at Lendings Mill and or even to know if Harrison was a paper maker or flour miller.

Relly Mill[55]

A mill at Relly was in existence before 1326, working as a fulling mill for the Convent of Durham. This mill, or a mill rebuilt on the same site, was converted to papermaking by the mid 1700s. (Surtees 1840: IV, 73) Relly, or Releigh, Mill stood on a level terrace five feet above the 1968 level of the River Browney, fed by a 400 yard leat that conducted water from a dam on the river 600 yards upstream; it would have been powered by an undershot wheel. (Kirby, 1968) Situated at Elvet, near Neville's Cross in the parish of St Oswald, Durham, this mill worked under Excise no.76.[56]

Financial Commitments and Paper Production

The paper mill was part of an estate being sold by a Mr Allen at public auction in 1762. A letter from Mr W. Fleming of February 1762 concerning this sale refers to a rent of £200 per annum being payable for the paper mill and land. The tenant, John Smith, was also required to pay the paper mill fire insurance of £7 17s 8d a year and would have expected to spend an average of £25 per annum on repairs to the buildings and the water dam. The letter also refers to an estimated sum of £50 needed against renewal of the lease every seven years.[57] Some years later, in 1795, Relly fulling and bleaching mills were being offered for letting and conversion. Whether these were separate mills from the paper mill, or the paper mill had reverted to a previous use, is uncertain.[58]

Shorter (1957: 162) noted several paper makers from St Margaret's, Durham parish registers that could have been at Relly or at Moorsley Bank or Stone Bridge Mill. He listed Thomas

Wennington in 1798, then Henry Lacey, Robert Smith, and John Graham in 1799; Joseph Douglas occurs in 1800 and there are numerous paper makers mentioned in these respective parish registers after that year. The type of papers produced at Relly was of a coarse brown sort, including paper bags (Kirby 1968), particularly rope browns produced on a 50" machine. (Shorter 1971: 155)

Deeds, Leases and Letters

John Ord, Master Paper Maker, is listed at Relly mill by the Excise authorities in 1816.[59] He, with Benjamin Ord, William Stoker and Henry Smales, took a one year lease of Relly smallholding from the Dean & Chapter, Durham Cathedral in 1817, and this may have been repeated for the following year, as a subsequent deed was recorded with the same details in 1819, with the addition of the names of Francis Smales and John Taylor.[60] During that year John Ord died so the records show the late John Ord to John Taylor, a debt to a mortgage on Relly Mill and land: the principal sum being £1600 from 13 May 1819, but the half yearly interest £40, and the annual rent of 10s 8d to the Dean & Chapter, Durham Cathedral; Excise Duty payable amounted to £200 and interest on that duty to £6 13s 4d; insurance to cover the value of £700 was to be £2 12s 6d per annum.[61]

The occupiers from 1822 until 1824 were a Mr Addison and Benjamin Ord. Whether or not Addison was a paper maker is not known, but he paid a quarterly rent of £42 10s 0d in cash.[62] Correspondence with the Excise authorities shows him to have been at Relly Mill in partnership with Benjamin Ord from 1822.[63] However, this partnership between John William Addison and Benjamin Ord of Relly Mill and Moorsley Banks Mill, trading as Ord & Addison, had ceased in 1824 and the mill appears to have been unoccupied during 1825 and 1826.[64] Addison and Ord were eventually recorded as insolvent debtors at Durham in 1826.[65]

Repairs and a Sale

Some repairs had been made to the mill while it was unoccupied as amounts paid to each tradesman have been entered in to the accounts: '13th Sep 1826 pd Danl Gleddle for attending Rilly Miles [sic, Relly Mill]; 21st Apr 1827 pd to Mr Humble Dbts Ad of Relly Mill', [debts for attending]. Presumably these repairs were ordered or sanctioned by Mr F. B. Taylor of Aldin Grange who, later records such as tithe assessments and an agreement inform us, was then the owner.[66] Subsequently, a 'For Sale' notice appeared in the local newspaper offering 'The Paper Mill, Dwelling House and Cottage situated at Relley [sic] 1½ miles from Durham and 9 acres of good grassland, lately occupied by Mr J. W. Addison'. Further details describe the situation: 'The mill is supplied by a powerful stream of the River Browney and the house is nearly new and is in capital repair'.[67]

Messrs Hand & Simmons, presumably the new occupiers, began to pay a quarterly rent of £35 from 6 June 1827, but only £25 from 11 September until 22 December because an allowance of £10 had been made for a mill engine; in December the purchase of machinery cost £89 5s 3d.[68] John Hand with John Simonds [sic] appeared in Excise correspondence as paper manufacturers at Relly Mill, but John Hand seems to have been carrying on the business alone later in that year, following the dissolution of his partnership with Simmonds in 1827.[69] To confuse the situation, we again find Benjamin Ord listed at Relly, but alone, during the following year, although the owner's papers suggest the mill was unoccupied between 1825 and 1829.[70]

Improvements to the Mill

The next tenant, Mr William Granger (sometimes Grainger), was at Relly from 1830 and, on 13 November that year, he was recompensed for the £194 19s 1d spent partly to pay tradesmen for repair work on the mill and items bought for the mill, and partly for several small payments he had made on Mr Taylor's behalf. These included a charge of £163 18s 10d for repairs to the machinery and £18 15s 9d for repairs to the mill and to the mill dam.[71] Granger remained at Relly for fourteen years with Mr Temple Fleming as the Foreman from 1833, and was noted there in several records including Poor Law Correspondence regarding an employee.[72] An agreement was signed on 12 September 1833 between Mr F. B. Taylor of Aldin Grange and Mr William Granger of Relly paper mill, paper manufacturer, tenant by yearly agreement.[73]

Four years later, in 1837 we learn of changes at the mill from a letter written by Granger to Taylor:

> Having occasion for certain new & improved machinery on the sd mill for the better carrying on of trade...' he asks if Mr Taylor 'will permit and suffer' Granger to install or erect at his expense, and move or dispose of in due course, if necessary, at the expiration of the tenancy, steam cylinders and necessary boilers and pipes attached with a cold-water pump and pipes for conveying the steam to the cylinders. Granger wished to establish that Taylor would pay for any machinery he might wish to keep at the end of the tenancy.[74]

The wording of several years of accounts suggests that the owner, Mr Taylor, paid bills for work carried out in relation to the paper mill, however, another letter between Mr Granger and Mr Taylor in 1837 indicated that Mr Granger would pay the bills. Some examples illustrate:

18th August, 1832 paid to P. Forster for 1000 Dry Lathes on rods from Stone Bridge Mill	£8 6s 8d
9th April, 1834 pd. Black & Gainsford for metal for Relly Mill for Mr Granger	£1 1s 8d
12th April, 1834 pd. T (J?) osh & Co. for Buckets & Water Wheel for Relly Mill	£19 11s 8d
24th March, 1835 pd. Mark Jopling for Relly Mill Finishing House for W. G.	£4 17s 1d
24th July, 1841 pd. John Snowball Timber for Mill Dam	£52 16s 5d
10th October, 1842 pd. John Forster mason repairing and rebuilding Relly Mill Dam	£72 3s 10d[75]

The Tithe Apportionment of Elvet, Durham City, in 1838 shows areas 87, 88, and 89 to include a paper mill, garden, garth and millrace covering three rods and thirty two perches. There was no mention of paper mill workers houses although the 1851 Census Returns listed twenty nine people living at 47 to 51 Relly Mill, presumably in mill houses. The tithe chargeable on this property was calculated at 12s 0d, the responsibility of the owner Mr Francis B. Taylor; his tenant, William Granger, was noted as occupying the mill.[76] Mr Granger was not mentioned specifically in accounts after 1837, but his tenancy continued until 1844.[77] A year later the *London Gazette* recorded the issue of a feat in bankruptcy for William Granger in 1845 and gave notice of a final dividend of 1s 3¾d in the pound 'for creditors who have proved their debts under the above estate'.[78]

Relly in the Smith's 'Empire'

The mill was not let again until August 1845 when the firm of A. Smith & Son became the occupier, but that company did not appear in Mr Taylor's accounts until 1 November 1845. A rent of £65 was paid half-yearly by A. Smith & Son from then until 1850.[79] As further rent and other record books are not extant, the continued occupation by this company can be assumed from other types of record, such as that describing three beating engines at work in 1851 and reference to Anwick Smith and John Smith in Excise correspondence.[80] From 1855 Relly Mill, with Langley Mill, was part of the Anwick Smith family business and the two mills were organised in conjunction with each other. (Kirby 1968) Wallis noted two paper makers living very near Relly Mill in 1847, Robert Best at Crossgate and Thomas Coward at Allergate, both in Durham City, but they were probably employees rather than tenants. (Wallis 1981: 2)

By a conveyance in 1862, John Ord and others assigned the Relly Mill smallholding to the Dean & Chapter, Durham Cathedral.[81] This does not appear to have affected the Anwick Smith & Son tenancy as the company appeared in various trade directories until 1874 under that name, then as Smith Bros until 1885.[82] The firm became known as Willan & Smith in 1894 and produced paper bags.[83]

The company produced grocery papers and middles and by 1879, as noted in a Post Office directory, rope browns generally; using one 50" machine. By 1899 the mill was too small and not sufficiently specialised to compete with larger mills so had to close. (Shorter 1971:155) The Dean & Chapter, Durham Cathedral, the owners, signed a deed conveying the mill site to a railway company.[84]

From the evidence of maps it would seem that the mill buildings were unchanged, except for small additions, from 1838 until they were abandoned. A map of St Edmund Bearpark of 1879 depicts Relly Paper Mill.[85] By 1968 nothing remained of the mill except a house of brick and stone construction with a pantile roof of eighteenth century style. (Kirby, 1968) Six years later Atkinson recorded that there were only a few remains of Relly paper mill to be seen, part of the foundations and one outbuilding. (Atkinson 1974: II, 279)

Shotley Grove Mills[86]

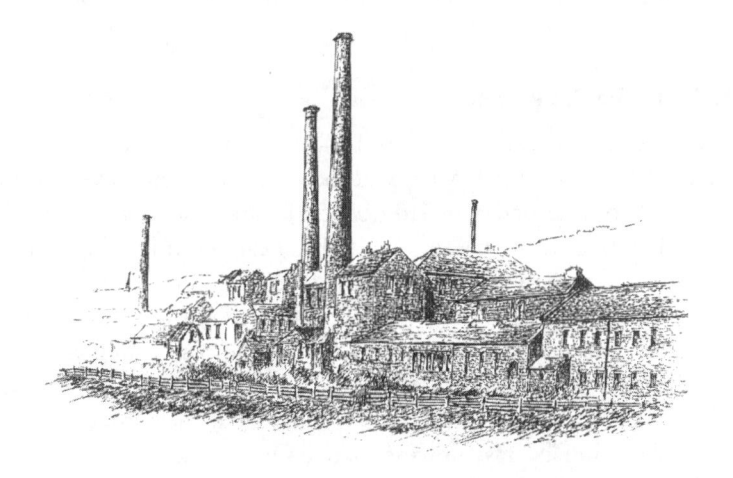

Shotley Grove Mill Nineteenth Century

Shotley Grove Mill at Shotley Bridge, also called High Mill or Grove Mill, was on a site above the higher bridge on the south bank of River Derwent. (Neasham 1881: 77) The mill's situation was described by Surtees (1820:II, 293) as:

> The surrounding scenery is wild and romantic; and the Derwent fringed with native wood, wanders through rich haugh grounds, finely contrasted with the heathy hills, which hem in the vale on the north and south.

More detail appeared in Benfieldside, St Cuthbert's parish magazine of July 1988:

> The river water was peaty and sometimes polluted and this affected the quality of the paper. So springs were diverted from a wide area in to pipes leading to a large reservoir above Forge Cottage. Another storage pond was in the wood above Sandy Path Cottages. Spring water followed the contours in to the pond.
>
> Four impressive chimneys dominated the mill and another ingeniously used the sloping ground as a flue from the boiler near the Mill Race, up through Chimney Wood to Bridgehill. Sticky white waste from the mill was led across the weir to be accumulated in to what were known as the putty heaps ... In flood times the horses could not cross the river and tipping took place on the south side.

Building the Paper Mill

The land on which the paper mill was built was first mentioned in a Deed of 20 July 1761 when Cuthbert Smith of Snaws Green was admitted to 'one parcel of land called Ealands, with a sword mill and a barley mill upon the same, lying near the mills there called Bishop's Mills, with a malting and corn mill'. Stone (millstone grit and sandstone) quarried from nearby Blackstone Burn, Middle and Low common quarries, was used to build the paper mill, the dam and the sides of the water race, with sluices fitted for efficient control of the water. The river below this was dredged, then stone-lined to prevent erosion by fast flowing water. On the fields opposite the mill water catchment drains were dug, and three reservoirs were installed on the south side, initially at the high mill, later at the low mill, and in Sodfine Wood. A further reservoir was constructed adjoining the dam on the north side of the river; roughly wedge-shaped, the dam measured some 230 yards by 70 yards, 20 feet deep and was stone-lined throughout. (Moore, 1988: 2, 6)

Ridley (nd: 62) commented that there had been two mills here, one a paper mill and the other a corn mill, conducted by the Slater family, but no particular period is suggested. It may have been prior to 1771, but no evidence has been found to confirm or refute this statement. By 1771 the paper mill had been erected and bequeathed by a Thomas Johnson in his will to his nephew John Johnson, with corn, sword and barley mills all previously called Ealands. This family of Johnson is said to have been descended from the German sword makers who worked one of the mills at Ealands. (Moore: 1988, 2) Various references to John Johnson suggest he owned the mill until 1812. For instance, in the 6 April 1776 issue of the *Newcastle Chronicle* he advertised for journeymen paper makers capable of brown work.

Simmons (nd) noted that John Johnson of Shotley Bridge owned two mills in 1781; Johnson occupied one valued at £40 a year; Thos. Sharp held the tenancy at the other, valued at £11.10s a year. We do not know if Sharp was a paper maker. John Johnson is noted at Shotley Grove Paper Mill in a manuscript of 1786,[87] and in 1793 listed in Richard Johnson's Address Book. (Shorter 1957: 162) The baptism of a son of Archibald McKinlay, born at Shotley Grove in 1811, was recorded in St Cuthbert's parish register. The wording specified McKinlay's occupation as paper manufacturer, formerly of Lintz; presumably he was a tenant of the Johnson family.

The Early Annandale Proprietorship

John and Hannah Johnson finally sold Ealands, with all the mills on that land, to the Annandales in 1812. (Neasham 1881: 80) John Annandale and his brother Alexander came originally from Scotland, and founded the firm of Messrs. John Annandale & Sons, paper manufacturers, on 1 May 1799 at Haughton Mill in Northumberland. When they purchased Shotley Grove Mill in

1812, High Mill as it became known locally, (Ridley nd: 73) housed two vats, a beater, a washer, and a small drying loft or stove house.[88] Originally a brown mill (Shorter 1971: 145), it had produced not more than four tons of paper a week at first;[89] by the end of 1812 output of hand-made paper had increased to five or six tons a week. (Neasham 1881: 80)

Conditions at the earlier period have been described by one of the managers of Annandales:

> As a lad I had to empty chests by myself with a grape or hand hook, my fingers would often bleed and my lungs often felt as though they were bursting with the fumes [bleach and vitriol] and the effort. [Some] rag boilers were just open pans, all of the rags and rope was manhandled ... When a beater was emptied in to the chest, a large hand bell was vigorously rung to warn the machine men to put more water on. My first machine ... ran at between ten and thirty feet a minute, it had wooden couch rolls, one set of press rolls, with three drying cylinders ... and five little calenders less than 4" in diameter. (Moore 1988: 4)

The Annandales mechanised rapidly, introducing a Fourdrinier papermaking machine 'and other novel mechanical appliances' such as sizing equipment, and drying machines to replace the old drying room; 'powerful, scientific motors' displaced ponderous or 'lumbering waterwheels'. All these changes were designed to cheapen the cost of production and increase output.[90] In 1812 paper cost 8d per quire to produce; by 1899 only 2d per quire.[91]

John Annandale was listed on 8 October 1816 at High Mill by the Excise authorities with no. 242 as the mill number, but from 1826 until 1859 John Annandale jnr was also noted as a paper manufacturer in connection with Shotley Grove. (Wallis 1981: 1) The list of partners at both High Mill and at Low Mill in 1830 and 1832, apart from John Annandale jnr, included Peter, Alexander and William Annandale, but only Peter and James Annandale in 1861.[92] This was because William had left the partnership on 1 May 1839, a partnership that was then recorded in the *London*

Gazette of 31 May 1839 as having been dissolved between Peter, William and James Annandale trading as John Annandale & Sons.

The firm of John Annandale & Sons at Shotley Grove Mill, and at 26 Old Butcher Market, Newcastle upon Tyne, continued to be listed in trade directories in 1827, 1828 (Kelly's), 1850 (Ward's, PMD), 1853 (Bradshaw's), 1855 (Slater's); 1862, 1864, 1866, 1869, 1875 (PMD), and 1876 (Craig's); then in paper makers directories from 1879 until 1911.

Flooding, Rebuilding and Refurbishment

Very severe flooding in northern counties on 13 and 14 July in 1828, the result of heavy rainfall, caused the River Tyne and others to overflow, the strong current and exceptional volume of water undermining river banks. It was reported:

> The Derwent rose higher by several feet than the oldest people in the vicinity can remember. The damage at the Paper Manufactory at Shotley Grove is very great.[93] The whole of the dam-head and apron is gone, and great part of a new quay for the erection of another mill is swept away. We are happy to say, however, that that part of the quay on which the new buildings are being erected, has received no injury from the floods; although, from the rain penetrating the new walls which were not covered in, some have fallen, and others will have to be taken down.[94]

Inevitably paper production was disrupted for a time, however, later in 1828 a second mill was added nearby, called Low Mill, and a map of 1829 shows both sites well developed with a 'mansion house and garden between them'. (Linsley 1994: 23) Evidence of the mill being re-equipped can be found in the records of Robert Stephenson & Co. That company's 'No.5 Paper Machine was completed in March 1829 for a mill being fitted out by John Annandale & Son at Shotley Grove near Consett in County Durham. The Annandales became the company's most important customer for paper machinery from this time. Additionally the first major order for Shotley Grove included two boilers, a steam engine, a press with a 4.5" ram and several other components including leather presses, all being delivered in the first half of 1829'. (Bailey 1990: 10)

In August of that year the same company installed two large hydraulic presses at Shotley Grove, each with a 12" ram, an order worth £350. The Stephenson ledger indicates a problem with installation, whether breakage or faulty installation is not clear, for they honoured their mistake by deducting the expense of repairing the hydraulic presses. John Annandale & Son took delivery of another drying machine in July 1830 that cost £352 13s 5d and some small items in November 1835. (Bailey 1990: 10)

There was a later reference in a local history by MacKenzie & Ross (1834: I, 240) to the 'extensive paper mills' belonging to Mr John Annandale of Newcastle having been repaired and expanded, with damaged machinery repaired or replaced; 'machinery lately much improved and enlarged'. In his history of Shotley paper mills Moore (1988: 8) refers to a new chimney, square-built of some 600-700 tons of stone, 120 feet high, with the inscription date 1834. The two mills were on the same general site with the newer mill at a lower level, hence the reference to Low Mill.(Shorter 1971: 129) Between December 1828 and November 1835 Annandales bought a range of machinery from Robert Stephenson & Co. of Newcastle, to be installed at Shotley Grove at a total cost of £2036. These items were listed among Stephenson's records: paper machine components, no.5 paper machine, steam engine components, two hydraulic presses, paper rollers and components, four drying cylinders, two press rollers, and two other paper papermaking machines. (Bailey 1990: 10, 11, 19) By 1840 the mill was working with twelve beating engines and two machines, all water impelled. (Shorter 1971: 111/112)

An Effluent Problem

Following a complaint from a Mr Wilson, Messrs Annandale & Sons were in dispute with the local authorities over the problems of effluent at Shotley Grove. In the initial order of 16 August 1848, it was decided that to abate the nuisance instructions for the necessary arrangements for the disposal of waste 'must be particularly defined and mentioned'. Mr Annandale was to be asked 'to abate the smoke of his Manufactories as much as he conveniently can'. A note of instructions, dated 30 August 1848, detailed how each kind of waste was to be conveyed to its specified disposal point. For example: 'The Refuse from the Chlorine Gas Still, be conveyed in a Leaden pipe to a barrel capable of holding 18 Gallons, which shall be placed inside of a Tank lined with Mastic & Gypsum'. The only discharge allowed from drains in to the river was that from the machine engine house sand boilers.[95]

John Annandale, who had set up the business in 1799, a man of great energy and perseverance, knew the value of good water supplies and 'well understood all the departments of the business … He was admitted by his most experienced workmen to be a thorough paper maker, an upright man and good Master, though a strict disciplinarian'. (Neasham 1881: 80) In 1834 he died, leaving the management of the mill to his widow, six sons and two daughters. (Moore 1988: 2)

Conditions at the Mills

An inspection for the Royal Commission in to the Employment of Children in 1843 noted 8 male and 19 female young persons, also 5 male and 10 female children, employed at Shotley Grove Mill. Of these some 40 children who were under the age of 18 years, 14 could write their own names but one 14 year old, John Leadbitter, could not write at all. Young girls, working in the rag house cutting rags from 6.30 am until 6 pm, six days a week, were paid 6d a day at nine years of age, increasing to piecework at 1s 2d a stone of rags at 16 years. They ate their meals there, the dust in the air so thick as to cover their food. Coughs and extreme shortness of breath, also torn or cut hands, were commonplace. Despite this, the mill was noted to have the best-ventilated rag cutting room in the district.[96]

Extending Range of Paper Types

We know from Excise records that mill no. 242 was Shotley Grove Mill, sometimes listed as High Mill or, in 1830, as Hall (sic) Mill. The firm was then in the hands of John Annandale junior, and of Peter, Alexander and William Annandale.[97] Nine years later the partnership was dissolved between Peter Annandale, William Annandale and James Annandale, paper manufacturers at Shotley Grove. At the same time a partnership of William Annandale, Andrew Annandale, James Annandale & Peter Annandale as paper stainers and hangers was also dissolved.[98] James Annandale continued to be listed in trade directories at Shotley Grove Mill, also at Lintzford, another Annandale mill, and at 37 Westgate Street, Newcastle until 1857. Excise records of Shotley Grove Mill, probably the newer Low Mill, showed it listed in 1832 as mill no.683.[99]

After the early days of making ordinary brown paper, John Annandale & Sons developed a wide range of papers: cartridge paper largely used by Her Majesty's Stationery Office, by artists and packers of hosiery; blue paper in which druggists put up Seidlitz powders and for sugar bags; paper for collars and cuffs, shirt fronts and artistic cards. Telford's family Bible was one of the first to be printed on Annandale paper. Even before white paper production Shotley Grove Mill had a high status in the estimation of paper maker journeymen who sought to move there. The level of skill was considerable and the craftsmen were paid high wages accordingly. They were described as 'conversant with the great commercial centres'. (Neasham 1881: 81)

The introduction of steam power reduced production vulnerability, output no longer dependent on the vagaries of water power. (Fordyce 1855: II, 700) By 1851 expansion can be gauged by the listing of twenty beating engines working with two more silent.[100] About this period the mill was extended downstream. (Moore 1988: 5)

The removal of excise duty from paper in 1861 came as a considerable relief to paper manufacturers from a commercial viewpoint.(Neasham 1881: 80) Abolition of Excise duty gave 'a great impetus to the trade and large additions were made to the mills'.[101] This cost relief is partly reflected in the widening range of papers offered. The making of paper sorts such as machine writings and printings was first mentioned in trade directories in 1862, but more detail appeared in advertisements in later directories. For example, in 1872 tub-sized writings and cartridges, self blue paper, engine-sized writing, envelope papers and fine printings were being offered for sale. Blottings, news, collar paper and hosiery cartridges had been added by 1882, and long elephants by 1890; manilla cartridges and envelope papers both engine-sized and tub-sized by 1894. A year later John Annandale & Sons were also offering gummings, surfacing, chromo and enamelling papers; by 1898 enamelling papers in web, label cartridges, also super calendered and plate papers had been added. Customers could buy news in ream and web by 1900, and packing paper suitable for export by 1904.[102]

Annandale's specialities included '242' cartridges, tub-sized and air-dried. One such paper provoked advice to authors; 'A pure rag printing [paper] deserves special notice in these days of "shoddy papers" and we recommend it to authors who fear that wood pulp will not preserve their works from oblivion'.[103] Thomas Bewick, the famous Newcastle engraver who died in 1828, regularly bought paper and card from the Annandales, initially from their Haughton Mill in Northumberland but probably latterly also from Shotley Grove Mill. (Thomas 1997: III, 4, 5)

Expansion with Commercial Difficulties

Despite this continued expansion, updating machinery, and widening the range of furnish, thereby the range of papers offered, there were commercial difficulties. One particular problem was demonstrated at a meeting of the Papermakers Association of Northern Manufacturers in 1870 that concerned price-fixing, a proposed increase of 10% in the price of paper. Some manufacturers withdrew support. This followed concern that the high price of rags was depressing profits, combined with a decrease in the average price of paper by 15%-20% between 1860 and 1863. Negotiations with the London and Edinburgh Associations of paper manufacturers had followed. Thomas Wrigley of Bridge Hall Mills near Bury, leading the Lancashire & Yorkshire Paper Makers Association, commented: 'I understand that the respectable, well-established House of Annandale, finding some little deficiency of orders, have withdrawn from the resolution of the trade'. Wrigley considered that Annandale's actions might have been different if printings had been discussed separately. He therefore advocated sectional action. (Tillmans 1978: 55-56)

Another factor in the increasing range of paper was the introduction of esparto grass as a cheaper furnish and, perhaps, one more easily obtained in quantity than rags. (Maidwell 1987: 13) Esparto became 'the principal raw material used in the manufacture of printings and news ... by its means the cost of paper was largely reduced'.[104] Certainly by 1881, using esparto grass and rag furnish, Shotley Grove Mills were working shifts to run the mills for twenty-four hours, producing 40-50 tons a week, employing some 300 hands, more than half women and girls picking esparto, sorting rags and overlooking final finishing. (Shorter 1971: 141) Whereas in 1869 the mill had boasted four 60" machines, by 1894 Annandales could claim in trade directory advertisements four machines up to 74" wide, producing 95 tons of paper a week.[105] Described at this period as one of largest manufacturers in the United Kingdom, Annandales had recently installed a Chapman multiple-effect evaporator, a rotary incinerator [for esparto waste?] and a gasometer; steam and water power were both used in conjunction with two Hercules turbines, the arrangement of the High and Low mills such that water power could be used twice. (Maidwell 1987: 13) An uncorroborated story circulated locally that Annandales had boasted on one occasion that the bulk of their business derived from only three customers. (Moore 1988: 7)

With the development of the iron and steel industry in the vicinity of the paper mill in the 1860s, the Derwent waters became polluted. The company had cast iron, fresh water pipes laid to safeguard the papermaking process and provide drinkable water for the local residents. Laid below ground, one pipe ran from above the ironworks pump house about 600 yards upstream, to the dam downstream, and across the river in to the mill. Another, laid immediately below and across the weir, followed a covered watercourse to its source further upstream, part of a much older water race. 'The water race extended to the low mill, there being a series of tunnels for the useful transport and utilisation of water either between the mills or, for disposal from a tailrace three hundred yards downstream, and in to the River Derwent'. (Moore 1988: 6)

Centenary Celebrations and Management Change

At the centenary celebrations of the firm in 1899 it was reported that 60 tons of esparto grass from Spain, Algeria and Tripoli was being used as the main raw material for making printings and newsprint. Rags used as a furnish for other sorts were being imported from India, Egypt, France and Russia; material for sizing came from North and South America. One statement that is not explained and appears contradictory is that 'Operations having been carried out at the low mills, it was found necessary to erect the high mills'.[106] Perhaps this is a misprint or misunderstanding. Almost in contrast to this sophistication, Simmons (nd) noted that in the early 1900s the waterwheel had increased its speed to 50 mph. Crocker comments that 50mph would have been an impossible speed for a waterwheel to achieve, and by 1900 would have been replaced by a water turbine.[107] Perhaps the date and the speed were incorrectly cited. Reference was also made in 1899 to a small drying loft or stove house, 'the latter name still clinging to one of the outbuildings. The disused chimney standing in the wood bears the date of 1834'.[108]

Despite the success of Annandale's business that firm was just as susceptible to fire as any other papermaking concern. In 1868 Shotley Grove Mill had nearly been destroyed by fire, damage amounting to several thousands of pounds.[109] On another occasion, in October 1892, a large stock of esparto grass was found to be on fire and appliances at the mill were put to work. Fire fighting apparatus from Lintzford Mill arrived quickly, but about 3000 tons of esparto grass was destroyed. The financial loss was covered by insurance but the inconvenience of delay in making paper must have been costly in itself.[110]

The Annandale family appear to have been proprietors of Shotley Grove Mill from 1812 until it closed, but in 1896 they appointed Mr J.Mitchell from Leeds to take over management of the mill, (Simmons nd) and the concern was converted to a private limited company the following year. Mr James Annandale, JP, of The Briary, Shotley Bridge, and Mr William M. Annandale of Lintzford, grandsons of John Annandale, became directors, their sons managers and son-in-law Mr W. R.Town, the Company Secretary.[111] In preparation for this, in 1895 James Annandale's two sons were being trained at Shotley Grove with Mr Town, son of the late Mr Annandale Town, former partner. William Annandale's son had been studying the papermaking business at St Cuthbert's Works, then in London, but was shortly to return to the mills in County Durham.[112]

Decline of the Business

In 1897 there had been a hint of some financial difficulty as an entry in a trade journal of that year referred to debts: 'Annandale, John & Sons, (James Annandale, William Mitchell Annandale, William Town, executor of Annandale Town, deceased, and Alexander Annandale), Shotley Bridge and Lintzford, Durham, and 28 Budge Row, London, paper makers. 22nd January as concerns A. Annandale. Debts by J. Annandale, W. M. Annandale, and W. Town'.[113] Centenary celebrations three years later suggest continued success.

In May 1906 it was recorded that, without prior warning, Messrs. Annandale 'have given the whole of their employees 14 days notice to terminate their engagements on 4th June. It is stated that about 500 men, youths and young women will be affected. The tenants of the firm's houses have also received similar notices. A good deal of consternation has arisen in the village, but it is hoped that the firm's action is in view of some re-arrangement of the business'. It had come as a considerable shock to everyone concerned that such a successful company could be in difficulties, to the point of rationalising that the problem would only be temporary.[114]

The mill closure affected the local community badly, subsequent unemployment forcing other closures, such as that of the Shotley Bridge Co-operative Society, originally formed in 1862. The irony is that the Annandale family had sold their flour mill to that Society in 1872. (Lister 1946: 30) Various members of the family had helped the community develop over the years. Parson & White's directory for 1827 listed John Annandale as Treasurer of the Friendless Poor Society. In 1851 Mr Annandale had provided a site on which to build the Baptist Chapel for two hundred people, a site that would also accommodate a house for the Minister. (Fordyce 1855: II, 701) The firm of John Annandale & Sons also presented a site for a Presbyterian Church in 1879 on which 'a building of stone in the early English style, seating 400 persons' was erected. (Neasham 1881: 76) The families of both Peter and James Annandale supported Highgate Baptist Church at Blackhill.

Mrs Annandale had established a school in 1855, with a residence for the Master, to provide for 120 children whose parents would pay pennies for their education. (Fordyce 1855: II, 700) The school was a little lower down river from the paper mill. MacKenzie & Ross, (1825: II, 357a) and Moore (1988: 9, 18) suggested that the school had been built by the Annandale family in 1841 at the junction of Shotley Grove Road and Cutler's Hall Road; whether a previous building or another school is not clear. A comment in a local newspaper suggested that a school had been erected as early as 1834.[115] The Bank at Shotley Bridge in 1872 was also owned by the Annandale family. (Lister 1946: 30) James Annandale was a County Councillor for Durham, a Justice of the Peace and Chairman of Consett & Lanchester Benches; he and William Annandale were both parish councillors.[116]

By July 1906 the mills were being advertised for sale by private treaty, 'for sale as going concerns, together or separately', with a detailed description given to entice prospective buyers: 'steam and water power, extensive reservoirs for Spring Water and Valuable Water Rights; T.S. & E.S. papers in great variety made from rags, esparto & wood pulp'.[117] Similar advertisements appeared in subsequent years specifying items of machinery, buildings and land adjoining according to Simmons. (nd) Shotley Grove Mills ceased working between 1908 and 1911 but some machinery was still being advertised in 1917.[118] The horses and timber were sold, machinery was eventually dismantled and used in other mills in this country and in India; once in that country crates were sent 300 miles inland by rail, then loaded on to the backs of elephants to be transported another 90 miles.[119] Moore (1988,8) records that when all this had been cleared only the two separate parts of the mill and four chimneys were left standing; the 120 foot chimney erected in 1834 was finally felled in 1951.

In 1950 Mr Maidwell (1987: 13) studied the site and 'found sole plates at the lower mill, what seems to have been the office and some farm buildings which could have housed raw material. In 1970 most traces of the High Mill had gone; a drying house for finished paper still stood on the power mill site, and several nice little cottages and houses plus the main Shotley Grove house'. Moore (1988: 8) commented that the reservoir adjoining the dam had been filled in with the waste and refuse from the paper mill in the early 1960s but that Sodfine reservoir remained.

Langley Mills[120]

Langley Paper Mill was built of local stone with a pantile roof and powered by water brought 300 yards from a dam below the confluence of the Rivers Browney and Deerness; it stood upon the level plain of the Browney, some six feet above the 1968 level of that river. (Kirby: 1 1968; Surtees 1840: IV, 25) Situated on a small feeder stream to the River Browney and reached by a lane from the south side of the Witton Gilbert road, Langley Mill was at Brandon joint township with Byshottles in Brancepeth parish, two miles south east of Lanchester. (Lewis 1840: II, 299) It was given the Excise number 84 and can be located on the 1902 edition of the 1inch to a mile Ordnance Survey map, downstream of Relly Paper Mill.

Corn Mill Origins

The first mention found of Langley Mill occurs in a Deed of Covenant dated 20 February 1777 relating specifically to the occupant of Langley Mill being charged 'a further sum of £200'; Mr James Eggleston to Mr Nicholas Chilton. It refers only to a corn mill.[121] An insurance policy taken out by James Eggleston, a miller and paper maker, in 1777 reveals Langley Mill to have been a corn mill; no mention was made of a paper mill.[122] References to Langley Park are differentiated from Langley Mill as the former seems to have been an estate or property within which the mill was situated.

Papers of 1780 that relate to the corn mill only mention George Skelton as formerly the occupier, and John Smith, a rope maker of South Shields, County Durham. (This clearly reads 'rope maker' but may have been an error as a John Smith of South Shields was a well-known paper manufacturer associated with this mill.) It may be that John Smith was a businessman who was turning his attention from rope making to papermaking, relying on his business acumen to succeed in this venture. (See below REXFI 15 Sep 1788)

A Release of Langley Mill, dated 21 November 1780 cited Mr Nicholas Chilton of Fishburn Esq and Mr James Egglestone of Langley Mill to Mr John Lowther of New Elvet, Durham City, Yeoman, for securing £900 0s 0d interest, redeemable by Mr John Smith, the purchaser. A further document of 21 December that year details a gift received by John Lowther Esq from James Egglestone, a Yeoman and his wife Mary, of Langley property including two paper mills, a coal mine, a stone quarry, twenty acres of land, pasture etc., also tenements, corn mills, three messuages, and three cottages. Despite its being a gift, John Lowther was required to pay one hundred marks of silver.[123] Clearly this is an extensive property with commercial income, of which Langley Mill is just one small part, hence the large sum of money mentioned.

The reference to two paper mills may be explained by a phrase in an indenture of 1781: a 'paper mill now erected'. This implies that a second paper mill had been erected to complement an existing paper mill already converted from grinding corn. Two paper mills were specified in a document of 1780 so, presumably, the second mill had been built by that date.[124]

The Smith Family in Occupation

It is surprising, however, to find that the cost to Mr John Smith of South Shields, paper maker, of insuring the paper mill and warehouse adjoining in 1788 was £250 per annum, a seemingly very large sum for a paper mill at that period, especially as he paid another £500 per annum for utensils and trade.[125] The paper mill house was similarly insured two years later for £600, the fixed machinery and utensils for £200.[126] Again, in 1807, Smith paid insurance 'On a paper millhouse with loft over situate at Langley nr. Durham in the occupation of his son Anwick Smith £500; on fixed machinery and utensils therein £300; on the Sizing house, Bleaching house, Packhouse and storeroom £150; on the Ragloft £200.' Despite the detailed description of the items covered, there is no separate reference to the waterwheels.[127]

It would appear that John Smith continued as tenant of Langley Mill until his death, probably in 1827. He also owned a paper warehouse in Newcastle upon Tyne.[128] John Smith attended a meeting of Master Paper Makers in London in 1803, listed as of John Smith & Sons, Langley Mill,[129] and was also noted among Excise correspondence on 13 June that year. In 1812 Messrs. Woodifield & Dobson, that is Matthew Woodifield, Gent. of the College, Durham and William Dobson, Gent of Bp Auckland, leased Langley Mill previously in the tenure of Matthew Charlton for a year, for one year to John Smith the elder, Gent, late of South Shields, now of Langley Mill (and to his wife Elizabeth): corn mill with closes, 'paper mill lately erected', part in the parish of Brancepeth, part in the parish of St Oswalds; in trust for Elizabeth his wife, heirs and assigns, and in trust for his younger son, Anwick Smith, heirs and assigns forever.[130] The implication here is that something had happened to destroy the paper mill, burnt down perhaps or beyond repair, so that a new mill had to be erected, or an additional mill had been built.

Anwick Smith at Langley

The younger son of John and Elizabeth Smith, Anwick Smith, took over the running of Langley Mill and he was noted there as paper maker by Excise authorities in their listing of 8 October 1816. Two years later, on 14 August, Anwick Smith received a licence to install a Fourdrinier papermaking machine, an addition to two existing vats. He was recorded in 1837 at a Fourdrinier Committee hearing as Abr Smith but, presumably, this was a misunderstanding for Anwick; no Abr or Abraham Smith was noted elsewhere in relation to papermaking or Langley Mill, and Anwick would probably have been a name unfamiliar to the recording Clerk.[131]

A further one year lease on 25 July in 1827 from Matthew Woodifield Esq to Mr Anwick Smith of Sadler Street in Durham and of Langley Mill, paper manufacturer, noted that the previous occupiers had been formerly George Skelton, late Ralph Lambert, now John Smith, he and Elizabeth Smith both now deceased. With the lease was a Conveyance of Langley Mill in the parish of Brancepeth, subject to Mortgage dated 26 July 1827.[132] No dates are known for occupation of the mill by George Skelton or Ralph Lambert, but the implication may be that they consecutively rented the mill from James Eggleston. A directory of 1827, Parsons & White, confirmed Anwick Smith's occupancy of Langley Mill as a paper maker at that date.

Devastation and Reconstruction

The Smith family was to suffer a major setback on 23 April 1828 when the paper mill was partially burnt down. (Richardson 1843: III, 160)

> About six o'clock on the morning, a fire of a most terrific
> appearance broke out in the extensive paper manufactory of Mr.
> Smith, at Langley, near the city of Durham. When first

discovered, the flames were ascending through the ventilators on the roof of the new part of the building, and very near to Mr. Smith's dwelling-house. The alarm was instantly given, and in a few minutes Mr. Smith's workmen and neighbours were on the spot. Intelligence having been speedily conveyed to Durham, the fire engines soon afterwards arrived at Langley, where also a great number of persons had assembled, who made the most praiseworthy exertions to subdue the destructive element. The room in which the fire broke out was used as a drying loft, and a great quantity of paper, in an unfinished state, was hanging upon lines within it. This burnt with amazing rapidity; and the timbers of the roof becoming ignited, very soon gave way under the weight of the slates, and the whole fell in with a tremendous crash. Masses of burning paper now rose in to the air, and were scattered to a considerable distance. The fall of the roof, by checking the flames, gave an opportunity to those who worked the engines to play upon the building with effect, and the opportunity was not lost. From the great efforts now made, the fire was entirely subdued before nine o'clock. The damage was estimated at about £1,000. The property was insured.[133]

Kirby (1968) writes that extensive reconstruction was needed, including an extension to the old mill to provide a drying loft roofed with slate rather than local tiles. Between September 1830 and April 1831 an engineering company, Robert Stephenson & Co, fulfilled an order from Mr Anwick Smith for Langley Mill, of paper machine components totalling £48 and a hydraulic press at a cost of £50. (Bailey 1990: 11, 19)

The mill had obviously been repaired and rebuilt where necessary as Anwick Smith is listed again, but with John Smith, (perhaps his son) as the paper makers at Langley Mill in an Excise list of 1832.[134] Simmons (nd) also noted that Anwick Smith was listed at Langley Mills in Pigot's Trade Directory of 1834, but Simmons (nd) suggests a James Teesdale, paper maker of Croxdale was also at Langley; that might confirm a second mill at Langley, or that Teesdale was manager or occupant of this mill at this date.

We hear again of Anwick Smith when a previous apprentice of his, Thomas Cockburn, (son of Mary and Thomas who had legal settlement in Brancepeth, and whose wife was pregnant and the couple in need of a house), made a declaration at his Poor Law Settlement Examination by the Overseers of St Oswald's parish on 5 December 1835. He stated that he had been apprenticed to Anwick Smith in Brancepeth parish for seven years from November 1827 until November 1834, confirming this period already found in other sources.[135]

Extensive Paper Manufactory

The survey for the Tithe Map and Tithe Apportionment in 1838 for Brandon and Byshottles parishes, that included Langley Mill, described Anwick Smith alone as the owner and occupier. The extent of his holding, including land such as arable, orchard and garden as well as the mill, was 16 acres 3 roods and 26 perches, and the tithe payable was calculated to be £5 15s 0d. Items connected with the paper mill were the Dam Head & Road (558), Langley paper mill with Mansion and paper mill yards (561), and the mill field (564). Elsewhere, Smith rented from William Russell, another field called Paper Mill Field (757), Ragpeth (223) and two other Ragg Peths (224, 239)[136]

Surtees history published in 1840, (IV, 25) in which he reviewed the City of Durham, refers to 'an extensive manufacture of paper is carried on by Mr Anwick Smith at Langley Mill on the Browney, about a mile and a half from Durham' [City]. A lease for one year dated 1 February 1839 and a reconveyance on 2 February 1839 from Miss Eliz Eleanor Fielding to Mr Anwick Smith in 1839 is the last document found before his death and recorded by Probate of his Will on 16 November 1842; a codicil was proved nine years later on 8 August 1851.[137] Thereafter his name remained in the title of the firm as Anwick Smith & Son, or Sons. The firm expanded, taking over Relly Mill in 1845 and Moorsley Mill by 1853 suggesting that the sons proved to be good managers. (Simmons: nd)

At Langley Mill business must have been brisk, with a substantial number of orders for paper, as eleven beating engines were recorded as working in a survey of 1851,[138] and a manager, James Hollingworth, had been appointed by 1855. Langley Mill was described as extensive at this period, 'the property of John Smith Esq. ... [that] gives employment to a considerable number of workmen'. (Fordyce 1857: I 435) In the 1861 census return he is shown employing 46 men, 60 women and 12 boys.[139]

The 6 March 1855 issue of the *London Gazette* published the intention of John Smith, paper manufacturer (presumably Anwick Smith's son), with James Hollingworth his manager, to apply for a patent in respect of an invention concerning 'Improvements in treating certain fibrous materials for manufacturing paper'. We do not know if the intention to apply for a patent was ever followed through, but the quality of paper being produced at this period included better class paper. Paper makers trade directories through the 1850s and 1860s advertised Anwick Smith & Son offering cartridges, writing and music papers as well as blottings, copying and pasteboards. An entry in a directory of 1874 emphasised the use of a 50 inch wide papermaking machine.[140] At that period it was noted in the *London Gazette* that a dividend of 1s 6d in the pound would be paid on investments.[141]

End of the Smith Era and Langley Paper Mill

Unfortunately, this apparently successful concern was in financial difficulties as John Smith was declared bankrupt and the mill ceased working for some months in 1875.[142] A copy of an Abstract of Particulars of Langley Mill c1875 indicates that the mill had been put up for sale with a colliery that was part of a nineteen acre freehold property; mention is made that 'a siding could be had' to connect the mill with the new railway 300 yards away. The description gives so much detail of the mill at that time that it is virtually an inventory.

The buildings and machinery consist of one large Rag House (to hold 1,000 tons and stalls for 20 cutters); One Dusting House, with chopper, willows, etc. driven by 8 horse power low pressure steam engine; Three Rag Boilers, viz. 1 – Rotary (25 cwt.); 2 – Tank (20 cwt.); there is a complete steam and water side, separate, steam side, consisting of two washers, (1¼ cwt.), and one (2cwt. Capacity), the latter supplied with hot water. Four beating engines (1½ cwt.) and one beating 3 cwt; the last-named beater driven by a 16 horse power engine, the remainder of the steam side by a condensing engine of 45 horse power. The water side consists of two washers (1¼ cwt.) and two beaters (1½ cwt.) the whole driven by a waterwheel of 18 horse power; one soaking house with hydraulic press, and one draining house with two presses, – the pumps for presses being driven by water or steam, – bleach and stuff chests, etc..

The Machine is a 54" Fourdrinier, fitted with five steam-heated drying cylinders, driven by waterwheel or 8 horse power engine; size rolls and tanks; large and well-fitting drying house, with steam-heated drying cylinder at end; one calender machine, with five rollers, – the sizing and drying house and cutter driven by 8 horse power engine, – one large finishing house, with 5 presses; an overlooking house; a plentiful supply of water from well; filtering and settling ponds, etc.. The Mill is supplied with water from these sources by two 8" and two 12" pumps (two on steam and two on water side.) The steam is supplied by three boilers, two high and one low pressure, fed by powerful donkey engines. Water power is derived from junction of two rivers by an artificial race – there is generally enough water to drive at least six months in the year.

There are extensive Blacksmiths' and Joiners' shops, fitted with lathes and machinery, capable of doing all necessary repairs. Two good store rooms. Extensive paper lofts over the finishing house and a greater part of Mill.

The papers made have been Blottings, Cartridges, Writings, Foolscap, etc..

> A handsome residence of 16 rooms is on the freehold, separate from the Mill, with Pleasure Grounds, Orchard, Kitchen Gardens, Vinery, etc. forming one of the most picturesque seats in the neighbourhood. There is also a Cottage confining [sic] 6 rooms and counting-house, etc..[143]

Business restarted during 1876 the mill producing News and Caps on 60 inch, 72 inch and 84 inch width machines under the title Langley Paper Co Ltd.[144] This was to be short-lived. A conveyance of 1877 completes the history of Langley mill in the papermaking trade.

> On 19th January, 1877 National Provincial Bank & others to Mr Benjamin Wilkinson Conveyance of Dwelling houses, paper mills, Land and Premises, situate in the parish of Brancepeth, County Durham. Release and quit claim of freehold messuage or Dwelling House called Langley Grove with Pleasure Grounds and gardens & outbuildings, formerly in the occupation of Anwick Smith, lately in the occupation of John Smith (now of Heaton, Northumberland, bankrupt) and now in the occupation of Benjamin Wilkinson and his undertenants, also those freehold mills, lands, tenements and hereditaments situate in the parish of Brancepeth: ie. a water corn mill on the River Browney and parcels of land called closes adjoining the corn mill and a paper mill and buildings and freehold land ... Peter Lowe of Chapel Town, Lancashire, paper manufacturer, John Short Hagan of Bolton, Lancashire rag and waste dealer (5th part) and Benjamin Wilkinson of Oswaldwhistle, manufacturing chemist (6th part).[145]

On the same day Mr Benjamin Wilkinson with Marmaduke Charles Salvin Esquire signed a Deed of Covenant for this property and the mill was closed. The closure is confirmed in paper makers trade directories of 1878 and 1879. What occurred in the intervening period is uncertain, but a reconveyance of hereditaments situated at Langley, on discharge of a mortgage on 5 May 1883 from Messrs Henry Haworth, Hargreaves Haworth and James Haworth to Benjamin Wilkinson Esquire, refers to coal and mineral rights, presumably far more lucrative than making paper. There is no mention of a paper mill. The site on which the paper mill stood was sold finally on 1 November 1889 to The North Brancepeth Coal Co Ltd.[146]

Chapter 3
Paper Mills Established 1779 to 1803

Demand for paper increased rapidly during the years 1779-1803, but the ten mills set up during this period were quite small, mainly in more rural, remote areas and not easily accessible, so were not able to compete in the market. Five mills worked for 40 years, three reverted to corn mills, and three installed papermaking machines in an attempt to succeed, but failed, although they continued for longer than the mills making only by hand, except for one mill.

Hett Mill[1]

Hett Paper Mill was situated about a mile east of the village of Hett on Thinford Beck in Tursdale not far from Sunderland Bridge. (Lewis 1849: II, 497)[2] Parsons & White trade directory of 1827 notes that Hett was a dual mill making paper and grinding corn. The mill was at the head of Croxdale Glen, where the Tursdale Beck begins to flow off the 300 foot surface to cut its way down to the River Wear. An 800 yards leat brought water from Tursdale Beck to the mill; the leat could be replenished by another sluice from the Beck within 150 yards of the mill. An undershot wheel powered the mill. (Kirby: 1968) An Ordnance Survey map of 1857 shows the mill race just south of Tursdale on the south side of the Tursdale Beck.[3]

Probable Origins

Two other mills and the site of Hett Mill are apparent on a rough plan of the Manor of Trillesden or Tursdale in 1430.[4] It was probably a corn mill originally that was eventually converted, at least in part, to papermaking, as a 'mostly newly built' paper mill was advertised for sale or rent by the owner, Thomas Eyre, in 1779, in conjunction with a corn mill.[5] However, Thomas Ayre was still in possession of a corn mill and a paper mill the following year as noted in the *Newcastle Courant* of 13 May 1780 and, according to Shorter, (1957: 163) probably Master Paper Maker, given that the Ayre family were well-known as paper makers.

Amoras and Joseph Ayre were noted as paper makers at Hett in 1798 and probably continued until 1800, with Joseph Ayre continuing there until 1802. (Wallis: 1981, 81) Several paper makers appear in the Kirk Merrington Parish Registers who could be at this mill, but their status is not specified: 1798 to 1802 Joseph Ayre; 1798 and 1799 Amoras Ayre; 1798 Anthony Oates; 1800 John Murray and William Moore. After 1800 there are numerous paper makers mentioned in these registers, but it is difficult to determine which were owners, tenants or employees. (Shorter 1957: 163)

The Cooke Family at Hett Mill

James Cooke, Master Paper Maker, was the proprietor at Hett Mill by 1799 until his death in 1807 at the age of 88. With other paper manufacturers from County Durham he attended a meeting in London in June 1803 of Master Paper Makers from counties in England.[6] In his Will, drawn up in 1805 and proved in 1807, James Cooke left the mill and other property in trust for his wife and children; he also cited arrangements for water usage:

The Water which Supply or serves the said Water Corn Mill and the said Paper Mill shall be held and enjoyed as follows, to wit, the said Water Corn Mill shall have the exclusive Use and Supply of the same Water between the Hours of Seven of the Clock in the afternoon and two of the Clock in the Morning And the said Paper Mill shall have the exclusive Use and supply of the same Water after that time.[7]

Cooke's Will also refers to the sale of the mill as well as terms of the lease; he may well have been noting details that concerned the corn mill rather than the paper mill.

The firm continued to use the title of James Cooke after his death. That the Cooke family remained to work Hett Mill after 1834, and until at least 1855, is recorded below.[8] One of his sons, John, had been working at the mill from 1805. Other sons, James and Robert Cooke, as proprietor and occupier respectively, paid Land Tax of 15s 6d in 1814 for property in the Township of Hett, but whether for the paper mill is not specified.[9] James Cooke is listed as paper maker here in Pigot's 1834 trade directory.

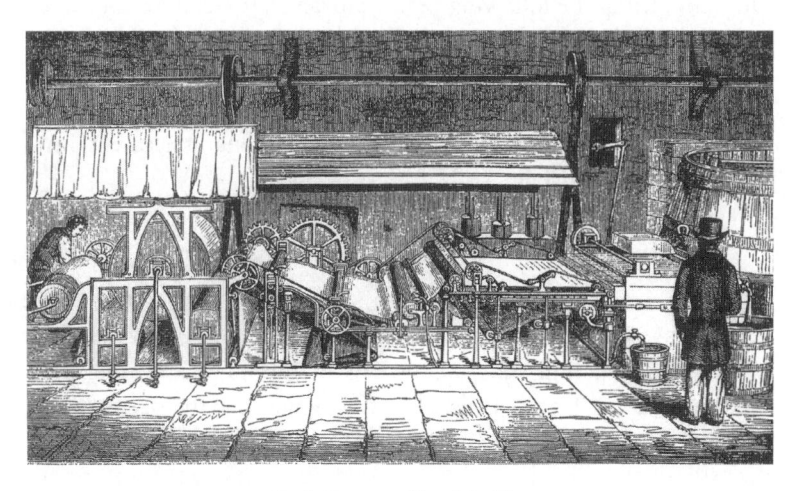

Early Papermaking Machine

The situation of ownership and occupancy is not entirely clear as Thomas Thwaites, paper maker, dealer and chapman, is mentioned in bankruptcy proceedings as the proprietor of the mill. The *London Gazette* reported the progress of those proceedings; first the Commission of Bankrupt on 6 May 1815; then the dividend at the Queen's Head Inn, North Bailey, Durham on 29 May 1815. Further stages were reported until the final certificate had been agreed, to be given on or before 16 August 1817.[10] A Matthew Jefferson was listed at Hett Mill by the Excise authorities in 1816, possibly a subsequent proprietor or tenant there.[11] Thwaite of Hett Mill, Excise no.75, was also mentioned in Excise correspondence, but no further evidence of his proprietorship has emerged.[12]

A son of James Cooke, Robert, paper manufacturer and Corn Miller, was also at Hett, seemingly as tenant, until his death in 1819.[13] Robert Cooke's son, another Robert, then took over the tenancy but was declared an insolvent debtor in 1825,[14] and petitioned for relief as an Insolvent Debtor at the Court House Durham during the following year.[15] However, it seems he continued at Hett Mill for he is listed in Parsons & White's trade directory of 1827, and in Excise correspondence in 1832 then, in 1833, with James Cooke who himself was noted here in 1825.[16] This James Cooke was possibly a grandson of the paper manufacturer James Cooke who had died in 1807.

The Latter Years

Hett is described by the Excise authorities as a new mill in 1835 with Robert Cooke, senior, in occupation.[17] It is shown on the Tithe Map of 1839 comprising two groups of buildings and one other building. Robert Cooke is listed as the owner, but the occupancy is shared between him and others not named. Cooke's property is described as a dwelling house, two cottages, gardens, paper manufactory, bath [barn?] and lane.[18]

That there may have been a son Robert also involved in running the mill is suggested by the mention of Robert Cooke, neither senior nor junior specified, but described as late of Hett Mill, paper manufacturer, an insolvent debtor, a prisoner for debt in Durham Gaol in 1842.[19] Robert Cooke jnr is specifically mentioned in correspondence with Excise authorities in 1844. [20] Robert Cooke, senior, is noted in Excise correspondence in 1847, again at Hett Mill.[21] In the 1851 census Robert Cooke is shown at Hett mill employing six men and four women.[22] A Robert Cooke occupied Hett until at least 1855 when he died, listed in Paper Makers directories in 1850 and 1853.[23] He had two beating engines at work in 1851,[24] and is noted there in 1855 by Fordyce (1855: I, 393). The mill is not noted in the 1861 census of Hett and is no longer listed in a directory of 1864 so, presumably, it had ceased working by that date. Kirby (1968) suggests that the mill reverted to corn milling until it became disused, certainly by 1914.

Tudhoe Mill[25]

Tudhoe Mill, in the parish of Brancepeth, can be 'reached by turning left about a quarter of a mile along the lane which goes from the village to Spring Wood and the River Wear'. (Simmons: nd) The mill buildings were in the area that is now part of Durham Wildlife Trust (Lodge 2004: 2) Constructed in a little dell formed by the Valley Burn as it descends from the 250-300 feet surface to the River Wear below, Tudhoe Mill relied on water fed to its 18 feet diameter undershot wheel on the outside of the mill. (Kirby 1968) This paper mill produced mainly brown and whitey brown paper manufactured from rope brought by packhorses from Sunderland. Employees at the mill earned considerably more than those in alternative work as wage rates for paper maker craftsmen were, on average, 33% - 50% higher than for other work in 1899. (Dodd 1899: 96)

Ord Family Watermark

A conveyance of 20 March 1795 cites the placing in trust for Jonathan Ord, a purchaser, a water corn mill and premises; whether or not these referred to a paper mill is uncertain for 'premises' was not specified.[26]

An earlier indenture of 1793 refers to the corn mill being converted to papermaking, but whether in part or as a whole is unclear.[27] Two years later a Proclamation According to Statute of 7 April 1795 refers to a lease to Ingelby Miller Gent, John Farrow, and John Clarke, of land, property, a water corn mill and a paper mill at Tudhoe.[28] A parish history noted that the mill was converted 'about 1865' (sic 1795) to papermaking, the finished paper being transported to Sunderland by cart, and that a saw mill was placed adjacent to the paper mill and worked by the same waterwheel. The mill later reverted to flour milling until, as a result of colliery subsidence, the wheel was thrown out of gear and the mill was dismantled. (Surtees 1925: 9)

Anderson Family Lease Tudhoe

The Anderson family were in occupation at Tudhoe for about 55 years from 1780. John Anderson was noted as the paper maker here until 1821 (Wallis 1981: 1) but, as Jonathan Ord attended a national meeting of Master Paper Makers in London in 1803 representing Tudhoe Mill, it is probable that he was the proprietor or main lessee.[29] Jonathan Ord died in 1805 and his will, proved on 8 December 1805 confirms that he was the proprietor of Tudhoe Mill. Apart from legacies to his son Benjamin, and his daughter, Elizabeth Pickering, Ord left his estate, including the paper mill, to his son, also named Jonathan Ord.[30]

Ord's name is also attached to Tudhoe, mill no.85, in an Excise listing of 8 October 1816. There was a general reference in a mill lease of 21 July 1816 for one year from Mr John Ord to Mr Peter Richardson, to the water mill having been converted to papermaking, but no date of conversion was mentioned.[31] That Ord was the proprietor is confirmed by a document that concerns the title and purchase of freehold of a messuage, mill and land at Tudhoe; it states, 'purchased of Mr. John Ord by Bryan John Salvin Esq.' on 2 November 1816.[32] The citing of John Anderson and Thomas Anderson in Excise correspondence of 4 August 1817 confirms the names of the occupants.

In the 27 July 1826 issue of the *London Gazette* there appeared a note of the appeal as insolvent debtors by John Anderson, the Elder, and Thomas Anderson, senior, late partners at Tudhoe paper mill, also of Thinford Mill, paper manufacturers in 1826. Later that year James Anderson was described as the occupier of Tudhoe Mill in Excise correspondence of 13 September. In 1827 Tudhoe Mill was listed in Parsons & White trade directory under the title Anderson & Sons, paper manufacturers. The Andersons were confirmed to be of Tudhoe Mill in the burial records of their respective wives: John Anderson senior's wife, Isabella Anderson, was buried at Tudhoe on 30 October, 1828, three years before her husband's death; she was 73 years old. John Anderson Junior's wife, also Isabella, had died seven years earlier than her mother-in-law;

each of them was described as wife of John Anderson, paper maker at Tudhoe Mill. (Lodge 2004: 2)

When the business was beset by commercial and financial problems, the mill was advertised to be let in 1831.[33] It appears that the Andersons managed to retrieve the situation for, despite being imprisoned in Durham Gaol for non-payment of a penalty relating to evasion of paper duty in 1831,[34] Thomas Anderson, a son of John Anderson snr was being mentioned in an Excise letter of 1832 as occupier at Tudhoe Mill.[35] Whether or not John Anderson had superseded Thomas Anderson before or after the mill had again been advertised to be let in 1834 we cannot be sure, but Simmons considers a John Anderson to have been the tenant there in that year. (Simmons: nd) This is confirmed by an entry in Pigot's Trade Directory of 1834. The public was advised:

> Tudhoe Water Paper Mill, with a Farm, containing about 37 Acres; a considerable part of which is good Old Grass Land, situated near the Turnpike Road leading from the City of Durham to Bishop Auckland ... To be let and entered upon at May-day next. Mr Fenwick of Tudhoe will show the premises.

Further particulars were available from F.B.Taylor, Aldin Grange.[36]

Changing Tenancies and Considerable Refurbishment

A William Wells, paper maker, was in occupation at Tudhoe Mill by 1836,[37] and remained there at least until 1842. (Wallis 1981: 8) [38] In that year he was mentioned in a survey of Salvin's Tudhoe Estate. Reference to Tudhoe Paper Mill Farm stated that William Wells was tenant of four of six fields that included the name of the paper mill.[39]

The tenancy had changed by 1845 when the Tithe Map and the Apportionment were drawn up. James Cooke was noted here as tenant of the paper mill and that he also held part of South farm on Salvin's Tudhoe estate. The old rent charge for the paper mill had been £6 8s 2d but an additional charge of £2 8s 7d was agreed, based on the rate of 5/- in the pound.[40] James Cooke had been the tenant since early in 1844 according to Excise records of 1 February 1844.[41] He was also noted in Salvin's Rent Book paying a half year's rent of £54 5s 11d at Martimas 1844, but was subsequently noted as paying £108 11s 10d rent for 71 acres 2 rods and 11 perches, including the paper mill, later in 1844; correspondingly Salvin repaid James Cooke £3 4s 5d for his outlay of one year's Income Tax. These amounts were noted for rent in 1845 and 1846; Salvin repaid James Cooke £2 10s 2d for Property and Income Tax on 6 March 1846.[42]

An estimate for extensive repairs to the mill in 1846, and to the office houses, dwelling house, dairy, stable, and store house for the paper mill, suggests that the paper maker was experiencing serious problems. The estimate for the paper mill is as follows:

> Water Course about 50 yards long – A New Top & Bottom.
> 22" wide each of 1 1/2" boards – say about 70 or 80 feet of Larch.
> <u>Main Water Wheel</u>, will require New One, if will give word [J.Cooke crossed out] and saw it up at the Mill and give 1 man to hand Saw the broad Planking against Cook's man – Jas.Cooke will do all other warmanship – except a few new Bolts, and old ones lengthening & repairing Jas.Cooke is wishfull to purchase By a valuation all the Paper Making Machinery in the inside of Mill on ground floor. So as he may alter it to his mind.
> Main Wheel, Arms. 12 each side = 24 (?), 15 feet long each of Larch, say 12 inch by 5 in
> Main Wheel all in Elm
> Circular Shelving, 12 inch deep and 100 feet circumference boards 2 inch thick for each side, making 200 feet of 2 in thick and fillies Round each side of inside of shelving say fillies each side 5 inches by 4¼" making about 34½" fit shelving, 31" fit fillies.
>
> American for Lining & Buckets of (shelving ? crossed out) Wheel
> Diameter of Wheel to be 34 feet (old one is 26 feet)
> lining 1½" boards 300 feet,
> Buckets 1 inch board – 600 feet
> Say 100 Solid feet 1/9d = £8.15/-

Supposed Wood	
American 100 cubic feet @ 1/9d p.foot	£8 15s 0d
Elm 65 " " @ say 1/- p.foot	£3 5s 0d
Larch for Wheel Arms 110 Cubic feet @ 1/-	£5 10s 0d
Do. for Water Course 75 " " @ 1/-	£3 15s 0d
total	£21 5s 0d[43]

A revision of the Tithe Apportionment in 1847 added a Waygoing charge of £7 3s 2d and a small tithe of £1 8s 7d[44] This added to the commercial problems of a small mill like this that only survived while cheap, raw materials, rope and canvas were available from the nearby port of Sunderland. (Shorter 1971: 131) Once steam-driven papermaking machinery had been introduced only larger mills could continue: 'The advent of steam was the death-blow to the papermaking industry in the villages ... and the pretty old wheel [of Tudhoe mill] came to a standstill'. (Dodd 1899: 96) Excise letters of 20 May 1851 note the occupation of Tudhoe as having 'left off', and Fordyce commented, that by 1855 Tudhoe was a 'paper mill for some time discontinued'. (Fordyce 1855: I, 437) From a history of Spennymoor, written in 1899, we learn that Tudhoe paper mill had closed forty seven years before when the tenant was James Cooke, 'a man still hale and hearty, though greatly advanced in age'. (Dodd 1899: 96)

By 1857 Tudhoe was being used as a saw mill, but had fallen in to disuse by 1879 and was finally demolished in 1898. The stones of the demolished mill were being used in 1968 to build new farm buildings nearby. The nearby two-storey, stone farm house with a pantile roof, possibly seventeenth century, had been the miller's house. (Kirby: 1968) All that remained of years of papermaking activity by 1925 was 'the cut from the Mill dam to permit the escape of superfluous water'. (Surtees 1925: 9)

Urpeth Mill[45]

Urpeth Mill was at Mount Escob, near Beamish, three miles north west of Chester-le-Street, in Tanfield parish on Urpeth Burn on the south bank of the River Team for the manufacture of paper (Fordyce

1857: II, 622) and one mile west north west of Trinity Church at Pelton.[46] Paper from Urpeth Mill in 1792 with the watermark Ord is evidence of the mill working by that date, but no record of previous paper manufacture has been found. (Maidwell, 1987: 15) A boundary survey of 10 November 1840 shows the dam and the millrace at Urpeth.[47] In a topographical dictionary of 1849 by Lewis (1849: IV, 425) comment was made on the occupations carried on at Urpeth, in particular iron forging and a linseed oil mill, 'likewise a paper mill and a corn mill'.

The paper maker, Archibald McKinlay, born in Govan, Scotland c1745 married Ann Grey on 20 February 1786. The baptism of his children was also noted in Tanfield parish registers; Margaret in 1792, and Ann in 1795, when Archibald MacKinlay was described as of Lintzford. When his daughter Jane was buried in 1799 MacKinlay was recorded as of Urpeth Paper Mill, similarly at the baptism of his fifth daughter, Jane, in 1803.

The baptism of children of two other paper makers of Urpeth, possibly employees, was noted in Chester-le-Street parish registers: Elizabeth the daughter of Simon Girling of Norfolk on 2 May 1802, and John the son of Thomas Beckett from Cheshire on 31 October 1802. Three other people related to paper makers of Urpeth were also recorded in the Chester-le-Street burial registers: Margaret, wife of Thomas Burdon aged 29 on 2 February 1810; James son of James Moore of Richmond, Surrey and Susanna Barker on 2 June 1810; Margaret daughter of Thomas Holdin of Maidstone and Alice Brest of Brancepeth on 15 December 1811.

Paper Made at Urpeth

Paper made in 1797 watermarked A M, and paper of 1802, could have been made by Archibald McKinlay at either Urpeth Mill or at Lintzford paper mill. (Maidwell 1987: 11) Watermarked paper suggests that good quality paper was being made at Urpeth at this period, but there is some uncertainty about this. (Shorter 1957: 161) Fordyce (1857: II, 611) stated that Urpeth Mill produced 'brown paper, [and] is worked by the Messrs. Hudson of Newcastle who, during the last twelve months, have introduced extensive alterations and improvements'. Contrary to this, Atkinson (1974: I, 180) stated that Urpeth Mill produced white papers. He also commented that most mills in County Durham in the early ninteenth century were noted for their brown paper but Urpeth was one of the exceptions. It is possible that both sorts were made here, whether at the same time or, perhaps, the mill produced white papers initially but changed to brown papers at a later stage for commercial reasons.

Archibald McKinlay & Co was the title of the firm of proprietors owning Urpeth in 1802, (Shorter 1957: 161) but that partnership of Archibald MacKinlay with John Gray, Joseph Gray, Thomas Gray, and Ralph Elerington was dissolved and the details published in the *London Gazette* on 12 January 1802. Archibald McKinlay must have continued the company because, six months later, he represented the firm at a national meeting of Master Paper Makers at the George & Vulture, Cornhill, London.[48] The three Gray partners were noted at Urpeth beyond 1802, but whether or not involved in the company is not known: Thomas from 1799 until 1806, Robert also from 1799 but until 1812, and John from 1802 for eight years more. (Wallis 1981: 3) Anthony Simpson, a paper maker of Ewhurst Mill, appeared at different dates in Tanfield parish registers at his children's baptisms, but he was specifically noted at Urpeth Paper Mill when his son Anthony was baptised there in 1803. He may have been in partnership with MacKinlay, or been his tenant. MacKinlay died in 1807 aged 62 and was buried locally near Urpeth. In that year Edward MacKinlay, possibly his son, was noted in connection with a half year's Land Tax and a Window Cess for Urpeth, totalling £4 8s 7d.[49]

The next reference to paper manufacturers at Urpeth Mill occurred in an Excise listing of 8 October 1816 that noted John Miller & Co at the paper mill working under Excise no. 243. There were paper manufacturers with the company name Miller & Co at Pipewellgate, Gateshead in 1811, possibly a registered office address,[50] but whether or not they were connected is purely surmise.

Wallis (1981: 3, 4) placed two other paper makers at Urpeth in the first quarter of the year; Joseph Harker from 1803 until 1814, and Thomas Gledstone from 1810 until he died in 1828, but their particular involvement is not known. They were also shown at Chopwell Paper Mill. During this period the Excise authorities listed different paper makers in occupation: John Glidstone in 1824; John Wardell and William Hartley in 1825.[51] By 1826 Matthew Graham, Tailor, Dealer in Old Clothes, Innkeeper and Pig Jobber, was a nominal partner in the firm of Wardell, Hartley & Graham paper manufacturers; he became an insolvent debtor in 1826.[52] The firm subsequently continued as Graham & Hartley. In 1827 'the Representatives of J. Gledston' paid Land Tax of 15s 6d for 'paper mills & land'; he was probably the owner but may have been a tenant.[53] Considerable genealogical and family history research would be needed to be more certain of the relative status and relationship between these men.

The Telford and Hudson Families at Urpeth

The Telford family appear to have taken over the mill in 1822 when William Telford paid Land Tax of 15s 6d; his continued tenancy is confirmed by an entry in Parsons & White trade directory of 1827and Excise correspondence of 3 May 1827 that names William Telford as the paper manufacturer; he is so listed in Kelly's directory of 1828. It will be shown that the Telfords were in occupation here until 1855. Telford's rent in 1829 was £55, but he was already in arrears of £55.[54] William Telford was further recorded when he paid Land Tax at Urpeth of 15s 6d in 1828, the proprietor named as Mrs Margaret Bewick,[55] also when he paid tithes between 1833 and 1835.[56] Simmons placed him there still in 1834, (Simmons: nd) and he was listed at Urpeth in Pigot's trade directory of that year. The mill's existence as a paper manufactory under W. Telford in 1832 is referred to in Excise correspondence,[57] and in 1834 it is recorded in a history of the area: 'At Urpeth is a mill for manufacturing paper'. (MacKenzie & Ross 1834: L 145)

By 1839 William Telford, junior, was in place as the manufacturer, but only two years later a Robert Telford became the occupier.[58] Four beating engines were recorded at work here at Urpeth Mill in a survey of 1851.[59] Slater's trade directory refers to the firm as Wm Telford & Sons in 1853 and 1855, but no mention was made of their products or the number or size of machines.

Although Wm Telford & Sons was listed as such until 1855 in trade directories, it was Henry Hudson who was noted as the occupier in 1850.[60] Messrs Hudson of Newcastle succeeded the Telfords at Urpeth Mill and had 'introduced extensive alterations and improvements' to the mill by 1855, manufacturing brown paper, (Fordyce 1855: II, 622) but it was a James Hudson who was named in 1860 and 1868 as the paper maker.[61] The evidence of occupation by the Hudson family in papermaking at Urpeth Mill is piecemeal. James Hudson was shown at Urpeth Paper Mill by the entry in Slater's directory of 1864, and at this mill number in 1866, but with a Newcastle address, perhaps an office address, and noted as making small hands.[62] Mercer & Crocker's Directory listed Hudson & Co at Urpeth Paper Mill in 1868, and Craig's directory in 1876 listed James Hudson again, making browns on one 45 inch machine. The business seems to have been progressing well for it was well-known that 'Messrs. Hudson believed in cash payment, and almost daily, said Mr English of Beamish Colliery, I received a £5 note in payment for coals supplied.'(Wade 1968: 143)

It would appear that the Hudsons either sub-let the mill at certain times or were in partnership with other paper makers for there are apparent duplications of occupier at particular dates. Simmons (nd) considers William Elliott to have been the paper manufacturer at Urpeth from 1856 until 1865, and he appeared under the name of the mill in trade directories of 1856, 1857, 1858 and 1861.[63] However, another entry in Whellan's trade directory of 1856 suggested that H. Hudson was then at Orpeth (sic) paper mill and also listed him as a marine store dealer in Newcastle in that year. By 1878 the mill had been listed as 'given up',[64] no doubt the victim of severe competition from large concerns. Urpeth Mill did not appear in any subsequent trade directories.

By 1988 Wade recorded that 'One building still stands, now altered for use as stable. Stone wall survives on Burn side, and foundations of other walls can be traced. Mill race largely intact, although broken near site of mill dam. Tail race still visible.' (Wade 1968: 143)

Cornforth Mills[65]

The mills called Cornforth, sometimes spelt Cornfourth, were in Bishop Middleham parish and named after the place of Cornforth, a name that itself may be derived from the original use of these mills for grinding corn. (Simmons: nd) Originally the manor corn mill, at some point Cornforth had become a corn and paper mill, then a second mill, a paper mill had been added. (MacKenzie & Ross 1834: II, 320) A county history notes that the 'mill of Cornforth is north east of the village, on a little stream called Cornforth Beck'.[66] These mills were situated on the left bank on an undulating hillside above a ford; they were fed by a leat 850 feet long, which also fed a dam that served the paper mill. (Kirby, 1968) Listed as Excise Mill numbers 80 and 81, the former was originally a water corn mill that belonged to the local Lord of the Manor and served his territory. (Simmons: nd) These seem to be small mills that were casualties of increasing competition from larger or newer, more strategically placed mills of the first quarter of the 1800s.

The first mention of a paper maker at Cornforth Mills occurred in 1793 when William Phillip took out a marriage bond in Durham and swore an allegation that he was free to marry in order to obtain a licence, but it is not certain to which Cornforth Mill he was attached, or even if he might have been connected with both mills. (Shorter, 1957, 163)

Mill no.80

By 1803 until at least 1841 Thomas Eggleston(e), a Master Paper Maker, was at Cornforth Mill, Excise no. 80. This is confirmed by various sightings of him. (Wallis 1981: 3) Eggleston attended a meeting of Master Paper Makers of Great Britain at the George &

Vulture Tavern in Cornhill, London on 13 June 1803 to discuss what action could be taken to combat the demands for an increase in wages by the combination of journeymen paper makers, the craftsmen of the trade.[67] Eggleston was listed under mill no. 80, Cornforth in an 1816 Excise listing of 8 October within the Durham Collection of paper mills, and as a paper manufacturer and corn miller in Parson & White's trade directory of 1827. On 28 November 1832 Eggleston was again noted as a paper manufacturer at Cornforth Mill, no. 80, in Excise correspondence. Simmons (nd) found evidence of Thomas Eggleston in 1828 and 1834, not only as a paper manufacturer but also as a corn miller; he appears in Pigot's 1834 trade directory as a paper maker here at Cornforth Mill. Wallis (1981: 3) noted him just as a paper manufacturer in 1841, but not in relation to a particular mill.

The Tithe Apportionment of 1839 shows Thomas Eggleston as owner and occupier at Mill Garth and the mills are depicted on the Tithe Map as two separate sets of buildings.[68] An Excise letter written on 28 June 1848 noted that the occupier of Cornforth Mill no. 80 (not named) had 'left off' business. There is no indication as to whether or not the last paper manufacturer there was Thomas Eggleston. In 1813 John Eggleston died aged 53 years; both he and Thomas are noted in a family monumental inscription at St Michael's, Bishop Middleham.[69]

Mill no.81

In his Will, proved in 1807, James Cooke, paper manufacturer of Hett Mill and at Cornforth Paper Mill (no. 81), left the mill to his son, also James Cooke.[70] John (Jno) Pearson was named as Master Paper Maker at this Cornforth Mill; he has been located there from at least 1803 until 1829. (Wallis 1981: 6) With Thomas Eggleston of the other Cornforth Mill, he attended the meeting of Master Paper Makers of Great Britain in London in 1803.[71] John Pearson appeared in the Durham Collection of the 8 October 1816 Excise listing of paper mills and paper makers as of Cornforth Mill no. 81. By the 17 February 1829 John Pearson, the paper maker, had discontinued business. (Simmons: nd) He died six years later at the age of 88, just over a year after his son John Pearson junior had died at the age of 47.[72] By 1832 it appears that a Thomas Lightfoot was at this Cornforth Mill but, later that year, an Excise list of 28 November 1832 shows that number 81 has been allocated to a mill elsewhere. This suggests that papermaking may have been discontinued during that year and the mill may have reverted to corn grinding.

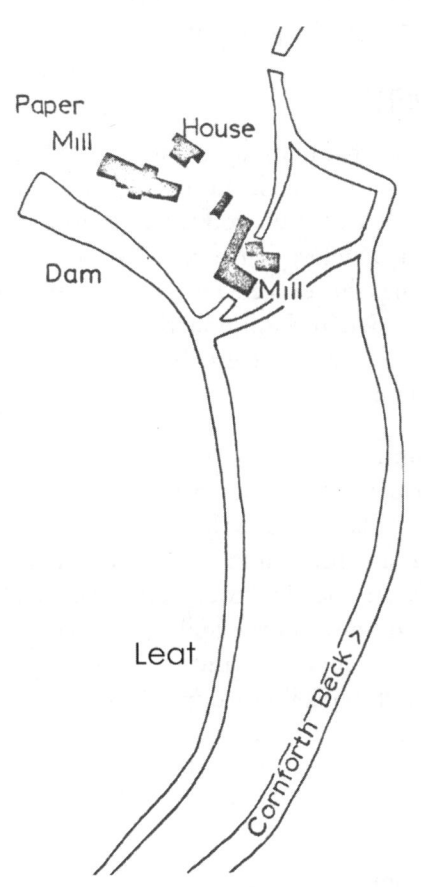

Plan of Cornforth Mills

Conversion of a Mill

A local newspaper, the *Northern Echo* of 16 October 1991, published a photograph of the mill wheel, and of a restaurant, The Olde Mill, that was described as 'once a paper mill'. It was referred to as West Cornforth, known locally as 'Doggy', and situated by the London-Newcastle railway line at the Metal Bridge near Ferryhill. It had become a Working Men's Club between 1918 and 1988, but no mention was made of the period before 1918.[73]

Butterby Mill[74]

Kirby (1968) notes that Butterby, originally a fulling mill established before 1739, came in to the hands of the Salvin family of Croxdale Hall in 1820.[75] It had been converted in to a paper mill about 1795 by William Lumley; that it remained a paper mill for nearly seventy years may have been partly because it was eventually sustained by the Salvin family on their estate. Fortuitously, the survival of detailed estate records help with piecing together the history of this mill.

William Lumley, who had been in partnership with John Lonsdale, the elder, at Croxdale Mill, Sunderland Bridge for less than a year when that partnership was dissolved, moved to set up Butterby Mill as a paper mill in 1795.[76] A letter of 7 August 1801 from Mr Thos Hopper includes details of a valuation by Mr Mowbray and Mr Taylor of the mill at Southeron Close at £975.[77] An undated document noted the rent for the mill as £180 per annum, £52 for the premises (unspecified) in Sunderland Bridge, with £14 due for the Dam based on a rate of £2 per annum.[78] The amounts mentioned, compared with the rent agreed in the lease of 1858, could imply that these were overdue payments.

The Mill's Situation

The mill stood on a level terrace four feet above Croxdale Beck in a narrow gorge. A 1600 yard leat brought water to the mill and fed a high breast shot wheel four feet by twenty feet. Remains examined in 1968 revealed only extensive concrete flooring, much tumble and the remains of pantiles that suggest the mill was of stone construction with a pantile roof. (Kirby 1968) Only an end wall was still standing when Atkinson (1974: II, 272) inspected the site in 1974.

The Lumley Tenancy

No evidence has been found to suggest that William Lumley's paper manufactory at Butterby was anything other than successful, until he was declared bankrupt in 1822. (See below) He featured as of Butterby Mill in a list of Durham Marriage Bonds taken out in 1801, and still held the mill in 1815, but disaster was about to befall him. Fire and flood were particular hazards for paper manufacturers but William Lumley was to suffer from gale force winds on the night of 29 December in 1815, gales that destroyed Butterby:

> About 3 o'clock on Saturday morning, the paper mill of Mr Lumley, situate at Butterby, about three miles from the city [Durham] was blown down. The building extended across a valley, and was in length about 100 feet, the upper part being constructed of wood and brick pillars, the lower or ground floor of stone.
>
> The wind, sweeping along the vale with irresistible force, had taken the building at its broadside, and tore away the entire roof and the whole of the upper story, or drying rooms; in fact, nothing remained standing but the two gable ends, and the walls of the lower rooms. The falling of the roof forced in the floors of the drying rooms, breaking some massy beams, and involving in the general ruin a quantity of paper in an unfinished state, all the vats, and various utensils etc. used in the mill.[79]

The mill was subsequently rebuilt, and continued to be used as a paper mill until at least 1855.[80] William Lumley continued at Butterby under mill number 78 and he is so listed on an Excise list of 8 October 1816. Gooch (1989: 52) noted a record of sale from which it is clear that the ownership of the Butterby estate, including the paper mill, changed in 1820 from Robert Ward and George Head, Southeron Closes by sale to W. T. Salvin under the name of Southeron Closes Mill at Butterby.[81] No further mention of William Lumley's involvement in the mill has been found until he appears at the Kings Bench Court as a bankrupt tenant of Butterby in a valuation for bankruptcy of 7 March 1822,[82] then again as an insolvent debtor in 1825.[83] No evidence of William Lumley functioning as a paper maker has been found after 1825; he may have retired at the age of 69 in that year. He died on 16 October in 1836 aged 80 years.

The Mill Leased to the Teasdales[84]

Excise correspondence of 17 June 1825 indicates Robert Teesdale snr and Robert Teesdale jnr to have been tenants of Butterby Mill at that period. Albeit, only a year later Robert Teasdale snr, late of Stonebridge, and Robert Teasdale jnr, late of Croxdale, partners in the firm of Robert Teasdale & Son at Stonebridge, Croxdale, Butterby and Whitehill paper mills, were found to be insolvent debtors at Durham.[85] A James Teesdale appears in Excise correspondence in 1827, then a Joseph Teesdale the following year,[86] and as a paper manufacturer at Butterby Mill in a trade directory of 1828, but no other record mentions either James or Joseph.

When he was declared an insolvent debtor at Portugal Street, London in 1832, William Teesdale was said to be a paper manufacturer of Butterby Mill, formerly of Dowgate Wharf, Upper Thames Street and Furnival Inn, London; then of Turnpike Gate, Vauxhall Bridge, South Lambeth and, lastly, at Seymour Street, Somer's Town, London, but subsequently out of business.[87] One other Teesdale, a Robert, was mentioned in Excise correspondence as having been at Butterby Mill between 1832 and 1837.[88] In the 1834 edition of Pigot's trade directory, Joseph Teasdale is recorded as the paper maker at Butterby. A Robert Teesdale, paper manufacturer of Sunderland Bridge, appeared in a list of subscribers to the MacKenzie & Ross' (1834: I, viii) history. The relationship between these Teesdales is not known.

The Martins and the Rotary Steam Engine

The Martins, father and son, both called Robert, were at Butterby Mill as tenants of the Salvin family by 1837.[89] Robert Martin, senior, had been in correspondence with the Ruthverd Patent Press

& Steam Engine Manufactory in Edinburgh concerning a rotary steam engine that is described in a letter from the company dated 25 December 1837:

> By means of a hollow axle, on which are two hollow arms, placed in to a cast iron case, and the steam being conveyed by a pipe in to the axle, through which it passes in to the arms, and discharged by an aperture at each end, producing a rapid rotary motion, a power direct from the steam in the Boiler without cylinder, piston, valves, cranks, fly wheels, etc, etc. and thus all the power lost in the piston engine by these movements, and which is considered to be four tenths of the power, is saved in this Rotary Engine … from its simplicity, and where a uniform revolving power is required it is invaluable. Much depends on the quality of the fuel used as to quantity, but it may be stated as greatly less than any other engine.[90]

Robert Martin senior was sufficiently interested to journey to Edinburgh to inspect this rotary steam engine and asked his son to write to William Thomas Salvin Esquire to make a business proposal. In his letter of 21 April 1838, Robert Martin junior enquired whether the Martins might put up a steam engine, and explained that his father had seen a rotary engine in Edinburgh, invented by John Ruthverd, inventor of the letter copying machine, that could replace the conventional waterwheel. Martin gave Salvin details of the device, of costs and its advantages:[91]

> It is simple and takes up half the space of previous engines. One six horse power and a twelve horse power boiler would cost about £100, that with a new chest, building shafts etc would not be more than £250. My Father … says I Might offer six per cent as an inducement for you to lay out the money. He suggests these arrangements be put in to the lease and me to leave that value at the end of the lease. He says he could not finance himself at present.[92]

In a subsequent letter of 14 May 1838 Robert Martin reassured Salvin that the cost of the chest pipes and rollers would be within the total cost of £250. He, Martin, would keep the whole in good repair at his own expense, but he asked to be allowed stones for the walls, wood for the uprights and the roof, yet he would cover the expense of casting them. 'I hope and trust you will never have occasion to repent it'.[93] Salvin seemed pleased with the proposition. He agreed to this modernisation and suggested an eight-horse power engine that would allow for expansion. Writing again to Salvin on 2 June 1838 Martin reported that his father was busy putting up the machine and reassured him that it should be working within a month, by which time it would be possible to evaluate its performance.[94] Dr Hills commented that 'the rotary engine by acting directly didn't need all the moving parts of the other. While the theory was good, sealing the steam was its downfall'.[95]

How well the machine functioned, whether or not it was efficient or cost effective, is unknown for no further records concerning that rotary steam engine seem to have survived. By 1841 another father and son partnership held the mill, that of Ebenezer and William Martin. It soon became clear that repairs were needed and finance was scarce, for Ebenezer Martin reported to Salvin on 15 May 1841 that the Bank was not being helpful with financial arrangements and considered his interview there to have been in 'such unpleasant circumstances'. Wood was needed to repair the waterwheel, a job his son William could manage, he reassured Salvin, then the mill would be working again and spring water could be introduced.[96] Father and son, Ebenezer and William Martin, were still listed at Butterby Mill in November of that year but the mill is noted as having 'left off' by the beginning of December 1842.[97] As a Robert Martin, paper manufacturer of Butterby Mill was declared an insolvent debtor in 1842, but failed in his petition and was incarcerated in Durham gaol, presumably he had also been involved in the mill's management with William and Ebenezer Martin.[98]

The Cooke Family at Butterby

By 1850, and until at least 1855, James Cooke can be found listed at Butterby in trade and paper makers directories, and he is recognised as the tenant there by the Excise authorities in 1851.[99] Maidwell (1957: 24) comments that the brown paper trade was the main business here, Cooke concentrating on producing wrappings. A Parliamentary Survey of 1851 indicated that the mill had two beating engines and both were working.[100]

A letter written from Moorsley Bank Mill by J. Cooke on 25 January 1857 to Mr Fleming at Tudhoe Paper Mill, contains an inventory of papermaking implements and machinery at Butterby Mill.

> One Paper Machine 54 inch wide
> Consisting of Whire Frame & Rolls
> Couch Rolls
> 2 Lots of Press Rolls
> 4 Steam Drying Cylinders
> Curculer Knifes, Reels & Cutting Benchis
> Callinder Rolls, Setters Vacum Box & Lifters
> Large Pulp Chest and 16ftt over Shot whater wheel and all other necessary gear for Driving Machine
> 3 Rag Beating Engins 11ft x 4ft 10in x 2ft deep
> 1 Rag Boiler
> 1 Chopper with 4 Knifes
> 1 Cone w/melloew (?)
> 3 Rag Lettaces
> 3) ? & Size Boilers
> Steam Boiler 24ft x 4ft
> D. D. 27 x 2½ ft
> Steam & Water Pipes & T/ L? J? ape one of the Rag Beating Engins & Steam Boiles 27 x 2½
> I praporea having them over to Moorsley but if any person wishes to have them bursy they are fit up they can do so one waterwheel 18ft deameter overshot withe first & second motions belongs the Place allso 2 dry Pressis for Presng Paper one Pres is mine but as it is not of great importance I have not entered it with the other things on the other side [of the letter] hoping this will do for what yew want and hope you will get a tenant
> Yours Respetfully
> J. Cooke[101]

In 1857 Butterby, a water power paper mill, was advertised in *The Times* to let and described as 'well adapted to the brown paper trade with overshot water power ... machinery complete, two beating engines ... and may be had at valuation'.[102]

However, the mill seems to have remained in the Cooke family's occupation for, Messrs Cooke (ie. Robert Cooke of Cornforth, paper maker; Lane Cooke & Matthew Cooke, stationers, in the City of Durham) leased Butterby Mill from Marmaduke Charles Salvin Esquire in 1858. The indenture of 6 September reads:

> I grant and devise to these three all those erections & buildings situate at Butterby, lately occupied by James Cooke, used by him as paper mill together with the waterwheel attached thereto and a stable near the same.

The lease excepted the cottage, garden, and byre occupied by Mr George Nelson and reserved the right of M. C. Salvin to the entire use of the premises one day per week for working the saw mill nearby. Messrs Cooke were to yield and pay the clear rent or sum of £30 by three equal payments on 13 November, 13 February and 13 May; also they were to discharge all rates and taxes due on the said premises and maintain the interior and waterwheel to its existing standard.[103]

The End of Papermaking at Butterby

The business of L. & M. Cooke was listed in a paper makers directory at Butterby in 1860, however, in the 1861 census return it was noted that the mill was uninhabited, and by 1862 was said to be 'not in work'.[104] Dodd (1899: 96) suggests that the advent of steam was the reason for papermaking ceasing here, presumably the firm unable to adapt the mill. Another possible cause of closure might have been that the water in Croxdale Beck was becoming polluted by the coal washing process upstream.[105] Butterby Mill had disappeared from trade directories and other likely records by 1866. According to Kirby (1968) at a later stage of the 1860s it was said that the mill had been converted and used for the manufacture of worsted yarn, and continued in use until at least 1915. By 1974 'only the end wall of this paper mill still stands' reported Atkinson. (1974: II, 272)

Ewhurst Mill[106]

Ewhurst Mill was situated in Tanfield Parish, one mile south of Lintzford Mill. A paper mill is shown on the Ordnance Survey 1" map one mile south of Lintzford on a tributary of the Cong Burn, possibly Red Burn. (Maidwell: 1987, 12)[107] It is sometimes referred to as Lintz Old Paper Mill and is shown as such on an Ordnance Survey map 1:25,000. Shorter (1957: 162) suggests the mill on the 1inch to the mile Ordnance Survey map could well be Ewhurst paper mill and does not refer to Lintz Old Mill at all. Whether Ewhurst is a change of name, with or without a change of use, or was built on the site of Lintz Old Mill cannot be established, as no records of Lintz Old Mill have been found.

Paucity of Records

Relatively little is known about Ewhurst Mill. While a probable proprietor and a succession of tenants can be placed at Ewhurst, no evidence has been found of the type of paper made, nor if papermaking machinery had been installed. It is likely that this was a small mill making only inferior paper because iron in the water locally caused discolouration, and the concern closed down when no longer able to compete in the paper trade, as many other small mills at the same period. No record has been found before 1797 to suggest when it might have been built or converted to use for making paper, nor to indicate the reason for the mill's closure by 1838. (Shorter 1957: 162)

The first reference to this mill is found in the *Newcastle Courant* of 15 April 1797 when it was advertised for sale by auction. Offered in two or three lots, the property comprised:

> All those FREEHOLD FARMS, and capital PAPER MILL ... known by the Names of High Ewhurst, Middle Ewhurst and Ewhurst Paper Mill, and Low Ewhurst, containing together 147 acres or thereabouts of arable, meadow and wood land. ... A Branch of the Turnpike Road ... passes very near them, [farms] by which the Manufacture of the Paper Mill is early brought to market.

From this, and a subsequent issue, 22 April 1797, we learn that the paper mill:

> 'together with 13 Acres of Ground as now let to Messrs. Surtees and Jobling upon Lease, 31 years of which were unexpired on the 5 April instant'.

Changing Tenancies

For the period of papermaking at Ewhurst Mill, several changes of tenancy have been noted, some tenants working the mill for only a very short time. One of those in longer occupation was Anthony Simpson, who married Sarah Summerson in 1796; their first child, Thomas, was baptised at Lanchester the following year.[108] Anthony Simpson was shown as 'paper maker of Yewyhurst', perhaps tenant, in Tanfield Parish Registers at the baptisms of his children between 1800 and 1811. Reference to the baptism of Anthony, son of Anthony Simpson of Urpeth Mill in 1803, also in Tanfield parish register, begs the question — is this the same Anthony Simpson? Maidwell indicates that another Simpson paper maker, Henry, was also at Ewhurst in 1800 and in 1816. Further investigation is needed to establish whether or not they were related. From 1797 Maidwell (1987: 12) considers the proprietor to have been Ann Ord; she was described as the paper maker at Ewhurst in an Excise listing of 1816 under mill no. 238.[109]

Richard Pearson had become the tenant by October 1817, but no further record refers to his tenancy.[110] Joseph Gray, Thomas Ord, and James Wilson Gray were trading at Ewhurst Mill as Joseph Gray & Co by 1824,[111] and until their partnership was dissolved on 11 May 1826, when it was recorded that Joseph Gray was to make arrangements to settle; no details of that settlement appear to be extant.[112] By 1827 a Thomas Ord was listed at Ewhurst Mill in Parsons & White trade directory.

Mention of Ewhurst Mill, with Archibald MacKinlay as tenant, occurred in Excise correspondence in 1830,[113] but it is Edward MacKinlay who appeared as tenant there by 1832.[114] No further details of tenants, or even that the mill continued to function after that date, have been located, but the mill had ceased to make paper by 1838 according to correspondence in Excise archives.[115]

Moorsley Banks Mill[116]

This mill near Brancepeth is on a low and level terrace four feet above the 1868 level of the River Browney, and cut in to the steep valley sides of the 30 feet high Moorsley Banks from which the mill's name is derived. A 160 yard leat conducted water from the Browney above a six-foot masonry dam to supply the mill. The mill has been variously referred to as Morsley, Moresley Bank(s) and Moorsley Bank mill. Once a fulling mill used by monks at Finchale until 1580, Moorsley Banks was termed a water-corn-fulling mill when it was separated from the Aldin Grange Estate in 1779. (Kirby: 1968)

Uncertain Beginnings

When Moorsley Banks first operated as a paper mill is not known, and men who appear in the registers of the local Durham parish, St Margarets, noted as paper makers, could be of Moorsley Banks, Relly or Stonebridge mills. Even then, we cannot be sure if they were proprietors, tenants, craftsmen or paper mill workers. These men were Thomas Wennington noted in 1798, Henry Lacey, Robert Smith and John Graham all appearing in the registers in 1799, and a Joseph Douglas in 1800. (Shorter 1957: 163) The first record that confirms the existence of a paper mill here occurs in Excise records of 1816 that list Moorsley Banks Mill under no. 77 and give the paper maker as Benjamin Ord.[117]

On the 4 January 1822 the:

> paper mill of Mr Ord took fire owing to that part of the machinery which is called 'the Devil' and is used in tearing up rags preparatory to their being converted in to paper, having, from the great heat caused by its rapid motion, become ignited. Mr Ord and his workmen who resided on the premises, having been roused from their beds, proceeded to arrest the progress of the flames, and, after considerable exertion, succeeded in getting the fire under, [control] but not until considerable damage had been done.

The alarm had been raised by a Mr Miller, an old man guarding the mill, but he died of injuries received while trying to extinguish the fire before others arrived to help. (Sykes 1866: 156)

Ord, the Smiths and Other Occupants

We learn that Benjamin Ord was not always the sole occupant of the mill as he was cited with John William Addison as late partners at Relly Mill and Moorsley Banks Mill, who had traded as Ord & Addison, but had become insolvent debtors at Durham in 1826, their petition heard on 18 July.[118] A year later John Ord is noted here, Benjamin Ord alone in 1828, then with John William Addison four years later.[119] If the Ords were tenants in chief this might explain the listing of Ralph Crozier by Excise authorities in 1831 and 1832, then William Crozier in 1839, presumably as sub-tenants, who became tenants in chief during 1832.[120] Ralph Crozier, paper maker, appears in Pigot's trade directory of 1834 but at Silver Street in the City of Durham; there is no mention of his connection with a particular paper mill. It seems that from 1827 until 1860 bankers Jonathan and James Backhouse financed Moorsley Banks Mill. (Kirby 1968: 80)

Subsequent sightings of Moorsley Banks Mill are occasional. From the Tithe Apportionment of 1838 we learn that Ralph Crozier was the occupier who leased the mill from the Dean & Chapter, of Durham, covering one acre, one rod and seventeen perches, also a garden, a house, a garth and an orchard.[121] By 1841 Anwick Smith and John Smith were known to be paper manufacturers at Moorsley Banks.[122] Paper was being made at Moorsley Banks in 1851 when three beating engines were recorded as working,[123] and the company was also recorded in a trade directory of 1853.[124] However, the firm of Anwick Smith & Son was no longer involved here by 1860.[125]

Rapid Management Changes

Moorsley Banks Mill was about to experience a fairly rapid change of management: James Cooke & Co had taken over the mill by 1860, but it was not working during 1862, perhaps as a result of a boiler explosion in 1860 to which only Maidwell (1957,21) refers; no other references have been found to this incident. John Davison was subsequently listed here in directories for the two years of 1864 and 1865.[126] Matthew Cooke was certainly one of the family here in 1861 because he was noted as paper manufacturer employing 20 men, 20 women and 3 boys in the census return.[127]

A further change is suggested by an entry in a Paper Makers Directory of 1866, and in a subsequent entry of 1867, in which Robert Armstrong was listed at Moorsley Banks making browns and small hands. An undated document refers to small hands being made here on a 60 inch machine, and rope brown paper in a small way. (Maidwell 1987: 7) Armstrong, formerly of Beamish Forge, was subsequently declared bankrupt on 1 June 1867 but discharged on 12 August 1867.[128] As Armstrong was described as an Engineman rather than a paper maker, that may suggest he did not have sufficient papermaking expertise to be successful; equally, the problems for any manufacturer competing in a strongly competitive market within the limitations of this particular mill, were probably overwhelming as the rapid change of occupier may indicate. The next ill-fated manufacturer at Moorsley Banks was George Bond aka Frederick Bond, trading as George Bond & Co, making brown paper and cardboard, which was also declared bankrupt only a year later.[129]

The Last Years

Paper Makers directories complete the history of this mill. A concern was formed entitled Moorsley Banks Paper Co that maintained production for two more years, but the mill was not working in 1871. John Millwood seems to have been the occupier in 1872 but was succeeded only two years later by John Binns. A trade directory of 1873 noted that Cap Papers were being made here under John Binns; he remained at Moorsley Banks until 1876, only to be followed by Mrs Ellen Binns of Croom; she was listed for the next three years.[130] No further entries were included for Moorsley Banks Mill. A trade journal for 1887 included an advertisement that 'announced the sale of the Moorsley Banks Paper Mill, situated on the River Browney, near the City of Durham'.[131]

The mill's subsequent history is unknown but the problems of sustaining a business, tried by a succession of occupiers, suggest that the mill could no longer compete with large-scale concerns using a range of machinery. By 1968 little remained of the mill, only some cottages that had been attached to the mill and the remains of the stone weir, but virtually nothing of the paper mill. (Kirby 1968)

Stone Bridge Mill[132]

During the early days of papermaking in this area it is difficult to distinguish which paper makers were associated with Stone Bridge Mill on the River Browney just west of Durham City. In the parish registers of St Margaret, Durham there is mention of paper makers Thomas Wennington in 1798, Henry Lacey, Robert Smith and John Graham in 1799 then of Joseph Douglas in 1800, but no information that refers to their status as owner, tenant or employee, nor to which paper mill they might belong, whether Stone Bridge, Relly or Moorsley Banks. (Shorter, 1957, 162)

First Known Tenant

Ralf Gray (1783-1826) who married Elizabeth Rontree, was originally apprenticed in the ropemaking business and became a member of the Guild of Ropemakers. As a young businessman he soon turned his attention to papermaking. By 1811 he can be placed at Stone Bridge Mill for he had asked the Excise authorities to reduce a fine of £700 imposed on his business. The reason for the fine is not known, although probably for underpayment or non-payment of duty, but his appeal was refused.[133] He continued to make paper there at least until 1816 because he was listed at Stone Bridge Mill no. 83 by the Excise authorities at that date.[134] Two children of a William Grey, Papist of Sunderland Bridge, were buried at Croxdale Chapelry, his daughter Mary in March and his son George in November 1872.[135] It is possible that this William may have been related to Ralph Grey and held the mill at an earlier date.

Teasdale Family at Stone Bridge

Following Ralf Gray, the Teasdale family occupied Stone Bridge Mill from 1817, Robert Teasdale alone in 1817. A James Read was noted here in 1818, perhaps as a sub-tenant, but both Robert Teasdale, senior and Robert Teasdale, junior were recorded at the mill in 1824.[136] Witnesses at a Poor Law Settlement Examination in 1835, including Ralph Gowland, paper maker, who had worked at Stone Bridge Mill during the Teasdale's occupancy, confirmed that Robert Teasdale had held the mill between 1823 and 1825. Gowland stated that the appellant's husband, William White, had completed his apprenticeship at Stone Bridge Mill between 1823 and 1825 under the occupier, Robert Teasdale.[137]

That it was advertised for sale with vacant possession in a local newspaper in 1826 perhaps foretold the fate of this mill. It was described as 'Spacious premises, Paper mill, dwelling house, workman's cottages and outbuilding and three acres of land late in the occupation of Robert Teasdale. Buildings requiring waterforce, and 19 acres of arable land and grazing land'.[138] Only a month later Robert Teasdale senior and Robert Teasdale junior, late of Stone Bridge and Croxdale, trading as Robert Teasdale & Son, paper manufacturers at Stone Bridge, Croxdale, Butterby and Whitehill Mills, became insolvent debtors at Durham in 1826.[139]

Early Closure

Excise papers confirm that Stone Bridge Mill had closed by 1832.[140] It was advertised for sale three years later,[141] but the mill number 83 had been transferred to Ford Mill by 1838.[142] It was, therefore, unexpected to find that the Tithe Apportionment of 1838 listed Stone Bridge Paper Mill (schedule no. 94) and showed its extent to be '1r 32p with a Tithe of 16s.6d' payable to the clergy, and noted Ralph Hampson as the owner, with the occupier Bartholomew Robinson, possibly a paper maker.[143] Presumably, either this tithe map depicted the defunct paper mill as a building but its use was not recorded correctly on the apportionment, or the mill had been reopened for papermaking for a short period before finally closing.

Atkinson (1974:II, 279) noted what could still be seen in 1974: 'the few remains of a paper mill; part of the foundations and one outbuilding'.

Snowden Hole Mill[144]

Snowden Hole Mill was in the parish of Heworth, downstream from Felling Burn, and shown on a plan of Heworth Shore in 1764. (Bennett, Clavering & Rounding 1990: II, plan8)[145] Surtees (1820: II, 85) informs that it stood 'on the scite of the ancient manor-mill of Heworth'.

The Tenants

It is difficult to be sure exactly who were the tenants at Snowden Hole at some dates. Several men who were paper makers appear in the parish registers of Heworth, or are known to have been involved in papermaking but, either without specifying their status or without specific reference to Snowden Hole Mill. For instance, paper maker Richard Blenkinsop appeared in Heworth parish registers in 1798 and 1809; similarly, David McLeod a paper maker is noted by Wallis (1981: 5) in 1798 and in Heworth registers in 1800. (Shorter 1957: 160)

Thomas Sill was the tenant of a corn and paper mill here in 1807 and 1814,[146] and was confirmed as the paper maker at mill no.246, Snewdensholl, [sic] in Excise records of 1816.[147] Four years later Robert Surtees (1820: II, 85) wrote:

> At Messrs. Sill & Bourne's [Thomas William Bourn] Mills, which are worked by water and steam, and stand on the scite of the ancient manor-mill of Heworth, large quantities of wheat are ground and dressed; also the materials for making brown paper and fire-bricks, both of which articles are extensively manufactured here.

Shared Uses

As the proprietor or main lessee of a steam corn mill being partly used as a paper mill, Thomas Sill, of Kirton Gate near Gateshead, advertised it as available to let in 1818.[148] During the following year the firm of Sill & Bourn was trading as paper and firebrick manufacturers at Snowden Hole Mill. During their occupancy the partners had 'improved the performance of the mill by building two new dams and a more efficient system of sluices. (Hewitt nd: 47) However, the partnership of Thomas Sill and Thomas William Bourn failed and was soon dissolved.[149]

By 1822 Thomas Sill was also offering to sell his share (Shorter 1957: 160) from his partnership with Joseph Robson[150] in a paper and brick manufactory; he clearly felt it was necessary for someone with papermaking expertise to join the partnership as he advertised for 'a person who can take the managing department in the paper manufactory [so] will have a preference'. Perhaps this was in the hope of avoiding bankruptcy. He did not succeed for, later that year his creditors were advised officially that he was bankrupt as a paper maker and that they should make their claims forthwith.[151] Ten years later, Thomas Sill was again listed by the Excise authorities at Snowden Hole Mill manufacturing paper.[152]

Thomas Lightfoot can be located at Snowden Hole Mill in 1824 from a trade directory entry but, as he is described as a paper mould maker, he may either be renting part of the premises for his work or have a financial interest in the concern. A paper manufacturer named William Ridley, who also had a marine stores in Gateshead, was listed in 1824 in Gateshead, but not specifically at Snowden Hole Mill.[153]

The only other references to this mill relate to Thomas Lightfoot. On 7 November 1835 a fire was discovered in the drying house attached to his paper manufactory that resulted in the whole property, contents and buildings, being consumed before fire engines could arrive. (Fordyce 1867: 46) As no further record of Thomas Lightfoot has been located until he was declared insolvent, five years later, we may assume that he was unable to rebuild the mill, or unable to produce paper satisfactorily. An order was made against him by The Court of Common Relief of Insolvent Debtors for insolvency in 1840, his petition was heard, but before the end of the year he was incarcerated in Durham Gaol for debt, when he was described as late of Snowden Hole, Heworthshore, paper manufacturer, previously of Bridge Street, Gateshead, Linen Draper.[154] Further detailed investigation would be needed to confirm whether or not this is the same man as the Thomas Lightfoot found at Blackwall Mill in 1825. At this period the mill was working with 'a 58 inch papermaking machine, two drying cylinders, two beating engines, a chopping machine and screw presses'. (Chapman 1977: 18)

Paper production had ceased by 1841 according to Excise correspondence.[155] A list of 1853 shows Excise number 246 to have been allocated to a paper mill in Nottingham, indicating that papermaking had not been resumed on that site, or not as a continuing business.[156] By the 1860s the mill site had become Cargey's cement works, and by the 1890s it was described as a 'bat-infested ruin'. (Hewitt nd: 47)[157]

Thinford Mill[158]

The first indication of papermaking at Thinford Mill on the Thinford Beck off the River Wear, near Bishop Auckland, is from a list of Master Paper Makers who attended a meeting at the George & Vulture Inn, Cornhill in London on 13 June 1803. They met to discuss how to counteract the demands of the journeymen paper makers combination or trade union. Robert Moon attended and was listed as the master paper maker at Thinford Mill.[159] He was also noted as the paper maker at Thinford Mill, Excise no.82 in Excise correspondence in 1816,[160] but in 1820 the paper maker shown as the occupier at Thinford was named Thomas Moon.[161]

Thinford Mill stood on a terrace four feet above Thinford meadows, that themselves are two feet above the 1868 level of Thinford Beck. Water was conducted by a 740 yard leat from Thinford Beck, around a shoulder of rising ground against which the mill stood, to what must have been a breast shot wheel within the mill. All three floors of the mill were accessible from the outside. (Kirby 1968) The situation of the mill in the 1820s was described as 'shaded by a clump of sycamores'. (Surtees 1823: III, 14) It was 'worked by the same stream [Cornforth Beck] and stands near the western boundary [of the village] and is not mentioned after 1857'.

Uncertainty of Business

John and Thomas Anderson were the paper makers in occupation at the mill in 1825,[162] but both John Anderson senior and Thomas Anderson senior, stated as partners at Thinford Mill, were declared insolvent debtors at Durham during the following year.[163] John Anderson the elder, described as late of Tudhoe paper mill, Brancepeth, also of Thinford Mill, Bishop Auckland, paper manufacturer and late partner with Thomas Anderson, paper manufacturer, had been appealing at the Court House in Durham, petitioning as an insolvent debtor.[164] Later that year another Anderson paper maker, James, was in occupation at Thinford.[165] However, the concern was clearly not profitable for, within a few months in occupation, James Anderson's business was discontinued.[166]

Parsons & White (1827) trade directory still noted Thomas Anderson at Thinford in 1827, and Simmons (nd) noted a Thomas Anderson, paper manufacturer here with John Moon, a corn miller in 1828, but this arrangement does not seem to have been any more successful than the previous attempts at the papermaking business at Thinford. Subsequent occupiers appear to have managed to sustain manufacture for a longer period. Excise correspondence confirms George and John Oates as paper makers in occupation at Thinford by 1830, until 1832 from when John Oates was noted there alone but, by 1834, a George Oates was shown alone until 1841 when it was recorded that 'the occupier left'.[167] There is uncertainty here because a Mr Gates is shown as the paper maker at Thinford Mill in 1843 by an entry in Pigot's trade directory.

According to the Tithe Apportionment of 1839 John Moon was both owner and occupier of the paper mill that included the mill heading and the mill dam. The paper mill is outlined and marked 'paper mill' on the Tithe Map.[168] Subsequently, Excise records listed James Clark as the occupier of a new paper mill at Thinford in 1842. Presumably the mill had been rebuilt to modernise it, or had been damaged by fire or flood, although no evidence has been found to explain why there would have been a new mill at Thinford at this date.[169] Clarke suggests the mill may still have been used to produce paper until 1844,[170] but no further information has emerged about this mill in relation to papermaking.

Reversion to Corn Milling

It may reasonably be assumed that papermaking could not be sustained here as a profitable business as Thinford reverted to being used as a corn mill at some stage after 1844; in 1857, the occupier was John Moon, corn miller and farmer. (Kirby 1968) A document of 1 January 1871 concerning the mill site indicates that it was then sold for the value of the coal seams running beneath the site.[171]

Chapter 4

Paper Mills Established 1814 to 1838

In this short period several businessmen ventured in to papermaking but some concerns were too small and poorly situated to contend with increasing competition from larger and more highly mechanised paper mills in the long term. Four of the seven new mills discontinued business within eight to twenty four years. Two mills were in business for three quarters of a century, but one mill proved to be exceptionally successful, mainly because its proprietor developed the use of esparto grass as a furnish.

Washington Mills[1]

The mills on the River Wear known as Washington White Paper Mills produced good quality paper. They were listed under Excise no. 86, but later appear to have been given a second number 551, perhaps to distinguish them from each other. There is no record extant before 1814, but the description of the mills at that date in an advertisement suggests that paper had been made at Washington recently, possibly for a short time only as the machinery is described as 'new and of a very superior kind':

> To be disposed of by Private Contract ALL those two capital Overshot Mills, furnished with Sizing House, Ware Room, Foreman's Dwelling, Workman's(sic) Cottages and every requisite convenience and accommodation for carrying on the
> manufacture of white paper with five acres of excellent land, held

on a seventeen year lease unexpired. These Mills each work one Vat and are supplied with a constant and plentiful stream of driving as well as superior washing water, situate in the midst of the populous districts of the Tyne and Wear, Sunderland, the great ports of North and South Shields, Newcastle and Durham. They command a well selected and widely extended country shop connection and from bordering on the navigable River Wear possess the great advantage of connecting by boat to Sunderland - from which rags are secured and paper shipped at very trivial expense. The machinery is new and of a very superior kind. From the above and other local advantages conjoined this concern will be found worthy of the attention of manufacturers.

APPLY Mr Hutchinson at Durham or Mr Cruddas at Newcastle.[2]

Wallis (1981: 4), noted Ralph Hutchinson as paper maker at Washington from 1816 until 1823. He was listed at Washington under mill no.86 by the Excise authorities in 1816 but,[3] in the same year the dissolution of his partnership with Matthew, or Matthias, Dunn by mutual consent, with any debts to be paid by the agent, Michael Bellerby, was publicised in the *London Gazette*.[4] Excise correspondence referred to Matthew Dunn as the occupier in 1818.[5] Two years later the tenants listed at this mill were the paper makers John Johnson and William Telford.[6] By 1823 Excise listings clarify the situation: John Johnson is listed as occupying mill no. 86 and William Telford the tenant in what is described as a new mill, working under Excise no. 551.[7]

We find from trade directory entries that in 1827 and 1828 John Johnson also had an address at 51 Pipewellgate, Gateshead, but it is not clear whether this was his home or an office, or even if this was the address of his paper warehouse. (Parsons & White trade directory 1827) [8] Excise letters confirm his continued occupation of mill no. 551 in 1828, and Matthew, or Matthias, Dunn occupying that mill in 1830, by which date a mill numbered 86 is in another county, therefore, it is reasonable to presume that only one mill was by then working at Washington.[9] By the following year Edward Savage, a paper maker, was the tenant at Washington.[10]

According to a county history, (Mackenzie & Ross 1834: I, 74), the mill was still working in 1834 but, as it was no longer listed by the Excise authorities on 28 November1832, it seems the research for the Washington area may have been completed before 1832 and some time before the history was published. No further evidence of this mill functioning after 1831 has been found.

Aycliffe Mill[11]

The paucity of records that mention Aycliffe Mill suggests that papermaking activity here was short-lived but, with little more than a few references in Excise correspondence, it is difficult to be precise about its history, or to be sure of the reason for its demise.

Lewis (1849: I, 119), in his typography described the village of Aycliffe as 'pleasantly situated on the road from Darlington to Durham, and on the west bank of the River Skerne, on which are a spinning mill, and a mill for the manufacture of brown paper, but not now in use.' He added that the River Skerne frequently overflowed, but did not make clear whether or not this flooding affected the paper mill on the east side of the village.

Although Lewis description helps locate the site of the paper mill, there is no record extant that named the proprietor or the occupant until William Harvey was recorded in Excise correspondence of 1822 at Aycliffe Paper Mill, Excise no. 381.[12] Three years later we find Nicholas Phillips in occupation,[13] and William Phillips subsequently became his partner in this papermaking enterprise. This joint business clearly failed as Nicholas Phillips was declared an insolvent debtor of Durham on 20 March 1830, and the late partner of William Phillips, trading as Nicholas & William Phillips and late of Great Aycliffe.[14] Correspondence among Excise records confirms that papermaking at this mill had been discontinued during 1830.[15]

MacKenzie & Ross (1834: II, 157), refer to the paper manufactory here at Aycliffe in their history published in 1834 but the work was probably prepared over several years and the mill closed after the information had been noted.

Blackwall Mill[16]

The frequent collapse of partnerships at this mill is fairly typical of smaller concerns at this period of the early 1800s, struggling to finance papermaking machinery, find reasonably priced sources of raw material, and compete in the same market as much larger concerns. That the business of papermaking at Blackwall Mill was short-lived is therefore not surprising.

In 1825 a new paper mill situated near Gateshead on the River Tyne was given Excise no.578 by the authorities concerned. The occupiers were noted as Thomas Lightfoot, George Lamb, and Joseph Harvey.[17] By August that year this partnership, trading as Lightfoot & Co at Gateshead Mill, seemingly Blackwall, was dissolved.[18] George Lamb and Joseph Harvey appear to have continued the business with the addition of a partner named John Nichol and, at some stage, also a George Ward, trading as Lamb, Nichol & Co. (Parsons & White trade directory 1827)[19] However, in other trade directories they were listed as George Lamb & Co. until 1830. (Wallis 1981: 5)

In the early 1820s Robert Stephenson's company in Newcastle, making locomotive and stationary steam engines, diversified in to more general engineering work, especially to build new types of machinery that included paper drying and handling machines. Among the first customers was George Lamb & Co of Blackwall Mill for whom Stephenson made 'two small rollers, a small paper frame and several incidental components' between February and May 1828 at a cost of £36. (Bailey 1990: 3, 10, 19)

Changing Partnerships

In 1830 this partnership of four assigned the business to Thomas Cummings Gibson, merchant of Newcastle upon Tyne, and Robert Scott, timber merchant of Gateshead, on 10 April 1830.[20] These proprietors appear to have let Blackwall Mill to yet another partnership of paper makers: Archibald MacKinlay, John Cox snr, John Cox jnr, Hannah Cox, and Will Reed.[21] By 1832 John Cox jnr appears to have been replaced by a William Fryer.[22] That the mill was working subsequently is confirmed in a description of this concern in 1834 as 'a paper manufactory carried on by Messrs. Cox & Co. on the banks of the river' near Gateshead. (Mackenzie & Ross 1834: I, 102)

The Archibald MacKinlay mentioned here may be the son of Archibald MacKinlay of Urpeth Mill who died 1807, but it has not been possible to prove this. By 1835 Archibald MacKinlay was not named in the *London Gazette* when the dissolution of the partnership of John Cox of Crookhill, Ryton, Hannah Cox of Scotswood, Northumberland, John Cox of Blackwall and William Reed of Blackwall, paper manufacturers at Blackwall Mill under the style of John Cox & Co, was reported as having been dissolved on 18 November 1835. All four were subsequently declared bankrupt during the following year. Five years later a George Harvey of Blackwall Mill was listed as an insolvent debtor, and it was noted that he was to petition on 1 March 1841.[23] It is possible that a William Harvey, noted as a paper maker and grocer of Gateshead, had a financial interest in this mill c1845. (Wallis 1981: 4)

Wallis considers that from 1837 until 1841 William Fryer, paper maker, was in occupation but no source is given for this deduction. (Wallis 1981: 3) Certainly a paper makers directory of 1847 lists William Brown Fryer and William Fryer at Blackwall Mill. However, it has not been possible to establish any further changes or developments at Blackwall, only that Excise correspondence revealed that the mill had 'left off' business by 1849.[24]

White Hill Mill[25]

White Hill Mill is situated at Pelton Fell, Chester-le-Street on Cong Burn, a tributary of the River Wear, just east of White Hill Hall, and is approached from a lane off White Hill Lane.[26] The mill functioned under the Excise number 531, but no history has been established before 1823 when it appeared in Excise correspondence listed as White Hill Mill with Christopher Ord in occupation, then with Robert Teesdale senior and Robert Teesdale junior as occupiers in the following year.[27] In 1826 when Robert Teesdale, the elder, paper maker, petitioned the authorities as an insolvent debtor,[28] he was described as late of Stone Bridge, late partner with Robert Teesdale, the younger, in the firm of Robert Teesdale & Son at Stone Bridge Mill, Croxdale Mill and Butterby Mill, all in the parish of St Oswald, also at White Hill Mill. Then followed a partnership at White Hill between Simon Gallon and George Moore trading as Simon Gallon & Co in 1827. (Parsons & White trade directory 1827)[29]

At a Special Sessions for the Highways at Chester-le-Street on 21 March 1833 there was consideration that a public footpath 'leading from Chester-le-Street to or towards White Hill Paper Mill … and extending thence two thousand four hundred yards westwards … may be diverted, turned or stopped up so as to make the same more commodious for the public'. Appeals had been received that mentioned 'a dangerous bridge at White Hill Paper Mill' and other obstacles.[30] This route would have taken the footpath through John Cookson's grounds, then east past the flint mill. No mention is made of Cookson's occupation but, later, a Daniel Cookson was in partnership with James King at this mill, a partnership that was dissolved in 1850. Might John Cookson have been at White Hill Mill in 1833?[31] The Cookson family appear to have owned the White Hill estate from about 1740 and been particularly concerned with iron founding, including erecting a blast furnace there. (Armstrong 1864: 84)

Tracing the Paper Mill

The paper mill 'seems to have been superimposed on to an old coal mill. There is a mile-long millrace engineered in to the hillside; it reaches a dam or header tank on a bluff above the burn'.[32] White Hill Mill 'is a brown paper manufactory belonging to Messrs. Gallon & Co.'. (MacKenzie & Ross 1834: I, 123) Little is known of the paper mill itself, although it is mentioned in Excise correspondence of 1832,[33] nor of the people who were proprietors or tenants. What little information there is comes mainly from trade directories and the *London Gazette* when bankruptcies or the dissolution of partnerships were published. By 1828 and 1829 the manufacturers appeared to be Gallin & Moor, Gallin being a poor transcription for Gallon.[34] Joined by Mary Gallon, Thomas Gallon and George Moore, trading as the firm of Simon Gallon & Co, were listed at White Hill Mill as paper manufacturers in 1832 in Excise records, and again in 1834 in paper makers directories.[35]

In 1838 Edward MacKinlay, (possibly a son of Archibald MacKinlay, and brother of Archibald Mackinlay, paper manufacturers associated with Lintzford, Shotley and Urpeth mills), with Roger Patterson MacKinlay, was at White Hill Mill, then Edward Mackinlay junior in 1839.[36] A Mr Scales was also mentioned at a paper mill, unspecified, near Chester-le-Street in 1839, probably the William Scales, a paper manufacturer, who continued to be mentioned in connection with this mill until 1864, with a period of shut down about 1850 as the mill was then noted as 'left off', but working again in 1851.[37] In the middle period of his tenure Scales clearly had financial difficulties for a petition of bankruptcy was lodged against him in 1853, and it was not until 1856 that he finalised the repayments of the petition.[38]

To confuse matters, James King, a paper maker, was noted at Chester-le-Street in 1841 (Wallis 1981: 5) but, eventually, the dissolution of his partnership with Daniel Cookson, as James King & Co, was published in the *London Gazette* in 1850.[39] Perhaps King was a sub-tenant of Scales or the mill had been divided in to two. There were two beating engines at work in 1851 when a countrywide survey was carried out.[40] In 1864 a W. Brough was mentioned as a paper maker at White Hill, but the mill did not appear subsequently in any directories.[41]

Situation of the Mill

Fordyce (1855: II, 608), in his history, referred to White Hill as a brown mill and commented on 'ochre, used in the manufacture of brown paper', being found on the ground adjoining the mill. Shorter (1971: 145) also referred to it as a brown paper mill using rope from Sunderland as a furnish, common in the north east.

When Alan Stoyel visited the site in 1965 he found the mill to have been built on a causeway, on the west bank of Cong Burn, between a fairly large pond to the west and a stream to the east. It had been built of stone with some bricks, its walls 17 inches thick, with a wheel that was either external or in a pent house on the northwest side. 'The interior dimensions were 18ft northeast to southwest and 15ft 6" northwest to southeast. The head of water was approximately 6ft.' Nine years later Atkinson (1974: II, 275) was to comment that 'the only traceable remains of this paper mill are the wall foundations'.

Tyne Mill[42]

In a history of Gateshead, Manders (1973: 53) considers manufactories adjoining the River Tyne. He describes a route 'down the winding cart road (from the Windmill Hills to Redheugh), a little east from the end of which, adjoining the river, at the bottom of a lofty precipice, stands a Paper-Mill built in 1828'. He is probably referring to Tyne Mill having been rebuilt after severe damage from flooding in 1828, for the first reference found to a paper mill here occurred in Parsons & White trade directory of 1827.

This mill was generally known locally as Muschamp's paper mill before 1849, but in later years it was sometimes referred to as New Stourbridge Mill because of its location. (Maidwell 1987: 11) It was situated at Pipewellgate, Gateshead, near the Redheugh Bridge and was worked under Excise no. 241, but it was also listed as Excise no. 667 in 1855.[43] There may eventually have been a second mill on the site, or the mill had been renumbered after being rebuilt in 1828, or the premises subsequently divided; this might explain the apparent duplication of occupiers from the 1840s.

In the Parsons & White trade directory of 1827 John Johnson was noted at Pipewellgate and at Washington Paper Mill, as well as at a paper warehouse in Gateshead. A year later in 1828 the landowner, Cuthbert Ellison Esq, agreed that his tenant, Mr George Sowerby, might sublet specified land and premises to Mr John Jefferson Harrison, Paper Manufacturer, and this was duly documented on 18 April 1828. A lease of 19 April 1828 between Sowerby and Harrison referred to the parcel of land in the Parish of Gateshead in more detail; it included a quay and the surrounding property owners were named and located. The sub-tenant, Harrison, was to be allowed 'with full and free liberty Power and authority ... to make erect and Build all and every such Quays, Wharfs, Dwelling and other Houses Erections and Buildings' as he wished, and to carry away stone to use in the building. Conditions applied in relation to existing tenants rights, public highways and bridle paths, also to the owner's rights to minerals and other deposits. Unusually, perhaps, Sowerby had to undertake not to manufacture paper on his adjoining premises. As Sowerby was not known to have been a paper maker, presumably this stipulation was to prevent him from leasing adjoining land to a competitor of Harrison. This twenty-year lease applied from 1 May 1828 and specified an annual rent of £40.[44]

Storm Damage, Rebuilding and Financial Difficulties

In July that year (1828) rebuilding continued but very heavy rain was followed by severe flooding in the northern counties of England, particularly from the overflowing River Tyne, its waters increased further by Spring tides. During the storm of the previous Sunday, (13 July) it was reported that 'The gable of Mr Harrison's paper mill, now erecting at the head of Pipewellgate, Gateshead, was thrown down by the water running in to the building, thereby swelling the clay, which burst away the foundation'.[45]

Extensive rebuilding and repair work, and inevitable loss of trade during rebuilding, left Harrison in financial difficulties by 1830. He was forced to borrow from widowed Catharine Harrison the sum of £2300 at £5 interest per £100 each year. Details were recorded in an Assignment of 27 January 1830. Had Harrison been unable to repay this loan he would have had to forfeit his machinery, engines and other property.[46] However, John Jefferson Harrison was listed at New Stourbridge Mill no.667 by Excise authorities between 1829 and 1833,[47] and he continued there until 1839, (see below) so he must have overcome his financial problems.

Considerable rebuilding and repair work must have taken place because, by 1834, Tyne Mill situated at New Stourbridge, Gateshead was described as 'the new and extensive paper manufactory of Messrs. J. J. Harrison & Co.'. (MacKenzie & Ross 1834: I, 103) An Alexander Annandale was recorded by Wallis (1981: 1) at Tyne Mill in 1830, but there is no other indication of an Annandale family involvement. There were several men in the papermaking fraternity with this name, so it may have been one who had been apprenticed there managing the business, or perhaps advising a fellow paper manufacturer on the rebuilding of his mill.

Closure and Reopening

An indenture of 12 March 1839 and one of transfer on 30 May 1839, as well as a transfer of mortgage in 1839 seemed to herald Mr Harrison's departure from Tyne Mill.[48] By 1841 the mill was said to have 'left off' working, and an official notice informed the public that J. J. Harrison of Gateshead, paper manufacturer, had been declared bankrupt on 25 November 1840; this no doubt explains the closure.[49]

The mill, under Excise no.241, was being worked again by 1842, but by Daniel and Joseph Robson with a John Sowerby, the latter possibly a financial partner.[50] They remained at the mill for several years but, by 1847, a trade directory recorded new occupiers, Wm Harvey of Tyne Mill and Redheugh, also James Vint & Co at Redheugh.[51] A further change of occupier was indicated in Excise correspondence that refers to John Rymer and John Tweddell at Tyne Mill in 1848.[52] This reference to the earlier Excise number suggests that the mill may have been divided in to two establishments for making paper or that there may have been a second paper mill here.

In 1849 Mr F.Anderson acquired the mill, (Maidwell 1987: 11) but W. Muscamp (sic) appeared in a paper makers directory of the following year.[53] Ward's trade directory listed Vint & Co at Tyne Paper Mill, New Stourbridge also in 1850, and James Vint was listed with Jno. and William Muschamp at Tyne Paper Mill Co in 1855.[54] In 1851 notice was given that the partnership between James Vint and John Rymer of Tyne Paper Mill had been dissolved, but John Rymer was to settle outstanding matters and continue alone at this brown mill.[55] Four beating engines were listed at work in an 1851 survey under the mill name of New Stourbridge so the firm appeared to be reasonably busy with orders.[56]

However, this business did not fare well and John Rymer, paper manufacturer of Gateshead, as so many others, became a declared bankrupt in 1852.[57] The following year he appeared at Tyne Mill in two entries with different Excise numbers, and once in 1855 as John Rymer & Co, (Maidwell 1987: 11) so, presumably, had arranged further financial backing for his papermaking enterprise. James Vint was recorded as having left the company on 14 March 1855, leaving William and John Dover Muschamp to continue.[58] In the same year a Mr Muschamp was cited as the proprietor of this brown mill near Redheugh. (Fordyce 1855: II, 785)

A Schedule of Deeds and Writings, drawn up in 1860, 'of the Title of Mr Emerson Muschamp Bainbridge to a Paper Mill at Gateshead in the County of Durham and in Mortgage to Mrs Mary Burn and Mr John Dixon for securing £1000 and Interest', reflects the change of mortgage arrangements and assignments of tenancy. In this schedule of documents covering 1859 and 1860, the name of Emerson Muschamp Bainbridge appears with that of William Bainbridge, and Henry Jefferson.[59]

Confusion between Occupiers and the Mills

These apparent changes of occupier are difficult to disentangle. They may indicate that there were two mills on this site, or there may be confusion between owners and tenants. The uncertainty continues. From 1860 until 1871 the concern was listed as the Tyne Paper Co,[60] with James Vint and John Rymer again together here by 1865.[61] Proprietors in 1871 were recorded as W. & J. B. Muschamp, but in 1872 the company name was changed to Tyne Paper Mill Co.[62] Two years later the company became known as the Tyne Paper Mills & Patent Rivet Co at Redheugh where Wm Harvey, paper merchant, was placed in connection with this company, perhaps as a financial partner, a situation that was common with men in related trades as the papermaking industry expanded. William Muschamp was the proprietor.[63] Once the firm had become the Tyne Paper Mill Co, a John Muschamp was appointed Managing Director.[64]

Papers produced at this mill were browns and glazed browns that were promoted by a London agent, J. B. Muschamp, later by W. E. Muschamp. More specifically, by 1894 the company was producing rope browns, glazed rope browns, glazed backings and cotton samplings.[65] A particular paper being sold in 1900, Golden Leather Brown, was described as a tough sheet of paper; its specification '- s/o DC 22lb @ 4s 3d per ream 480s'. These papers were being made on a 68 inch machine that Maidwell (1987: 11) describes as a very early largely wooden version of a papermaking machine but, whatever the quality, such a relatively small, single machine mill could not match the competition from large-scale production, (Shorter 1971: 155) so the mill closed. The last reference to the firm in paper makers directories appeared in 1901.

Wearmouth Mill[66]

The firm of Vint, Hutton & Co bought an old saw mill in about 1826 and converted it in to a paper mill there making rope browns, glazed backings and samplings, especially from old sails, cordage and other redundant, and abundant, raw materials from the old wooden sailing ships of those days. This was Wearmouth or Deptford Paper Mill near Ayres Quay, just north of Sunderland, that worked under Excise no. 170 and was situated two miles east of where Ford Mill was later to be built by the same concern. Cornett (1908: 161) comments that this mill was to develop a good local reputation for the excellent quality of its brown papers made on their one 68 inch machine from the rope and sails, abundant raw material in those days of wooden sailing ships. Simmons (nd) considered this mill to have been the cradle of the paper industry in Sunderland.

According to Chester (1976: 2) the brothers, James and Robert Vint, were not paper makers but Robert Hutton had served an apprenticeship with Henry Cooke, paper maker at Egglestone Abbey paper mill so he understood the craft and the technical side of papermaking. Robert Hutton (1799-1865) had nine children including two sons, one of whom also became a paper maker. (Richardson 1908: 178) The Excise authorities listed those three, James and Robert Vint with Robert's son, and William Hutton as the occupiers on 1 January 1835 in 1835, and again on 30 November 1841, except for Robert Vint jnr, but with the addition of a Thomas Harden and John Blackwell. A year after the dissolution of the partnership of Robert Vint, Robert Sutton, James Vint, William Hunt, John Blackwell and Thomas Fletcher, trading as Vint Hutton & Co. at South Southwick, Claxheugh, because Robert and James Vint had left on 21 March 1844, the list of people working this mill comprised Robert and William Hutton, Thomas Fletcher, John Blackwell and John Brunton Falconer.[67]

Destruction by Incendiary

In 1845 there was a widespread strike among paper makers (the craftsmen trained to make paper by hand) that affected every county north of Derby. The main cause was that the customs upheld by their trade union, The Original Society of Papermakers (OSP), had not been adapted to the machine trade and employers were not conforming to the long-standing customs of that union, previously accepted by employers and the OSP members alike, customs that concerned the ages at which boys were to be employed or apprenticed.[68] The workmen at Wearmouth Mill went on strike in 1846 and a fire broke out while the mill was shut down. (Maidwell 1987: 7)

The words 'Destruction of a Paper Mill by an Incendiary Fire' headed a report in a local newspaper:

> The Brown Paper Mill of Messrs. Hutton, Fletcher & Co. ... was discovered to be on fire [on 6th February]. Some parties passing to their work, between 5 and 6 o'clock in the morning, discovered a strong light in an apartment of the mill, and immediately gave the alarm. In 35 minutes the floating fire engine was alongside, the engine belonging to the Patent Ropery, and the Bishopwearmouth parish engine, [so] a torrent [of water] was speedily brought to bear upon the fire but ... in about an hour the floors of the building gave way, and precipitated the mass of ropes[?] etc. upon the valuable machinery on the ground floor. The roof speedily followed, and the flames shot up in to the air with prodigious fury, threatening the destruction of the neighbouring ship-yards. The Machinery and stock ... are insured in the Leeds & Yorkshire, and the buildings in the Globe.[69]

Because the workmen had been on strike there were suspicions that a fire had been started deliberately. The newspaper reporters comments went beyond suspicion:

> What makes this calamity more distressing is, the certainty that it has been occasioned by an incendiary. ... The fire, when discovered, was confined to the beating engine-house — a place the least likely, in all the manufactory for a fire to occur by accident. The proprietors, in common with other manufacturers in the district, were determined to resist the dictation of the Paper Makers' Union, the headquarters of which is at Maidstone in Kent, and the secretary of which has been in the neighbourhood just previously, advising the workmen.[70]

The night before the fire, the workmen had learnt that the proprietors had engaged some non-union men from Scotland to start the next day. The report continued:

> There can be no doubt whatever, that some miscreant, seeing the hopes of the Maidstone Union [OSP headquarters] thus frustrated, has resorted to this diabolical means of revenge. A reward of £100 is offered by the proprietors for the discovery of the offender, and application is made to Her Majesty's Government for a free pardon to any but the actual perpetrator of the deed. [71]

Union records are not now extant for this period, but notes compiled by a previous OSP Secretary in the 1950s from such records as had then survived, with family records and oral history passed on through generations of paper makers, refer to such an incident:

> The strike [in most northern counties in 1845/1846] was a violent one, [unusually so for the non-militant OSP] and a spirit of great mischief was abroad. The Secretary of the Society [OSP] was sent down at the request of the men out of work. He addressed them in very inflammatory language and, it was alleged, incited them to burn a mill down. It was burnt down, and the owners wrote to his employer and he was at once discharged ... and removed from the union.[72]

The mill in question was not named but the circumstances and the year parallel the events at Wearmouth Mill. Nothing was saved but the boilers, a steam engine and a stock of paper. (Cornett 1908: 161) Without a means of making paper the partners had to arrange to have their orders fulfilled at Scotswood Mill in Northumberland. (Maidwell 1987: 7) William and Robert Hutton retired on 3 November 1847, so their partnership with Thomas Fletcher, John Blackwell and John Brunton Falconer was dissolved and reported in the *London Gazette*.

Wearmouth Paper Co and the Richardsons

By February 1848 Robert Hutton and W. H. Richardson of Jarrow were in partnership,[73] had acquired the lease and rebuilt the paper mill. (Maidwell 1987: 7) The mill reopened on 19 August 1848 (Walker 1984: 49) and two years later W. H. Richardson was noted as occupier in a paper trade directory. At that time Robert Hutton was the manager of this mill and living in Millfield House in 1850 according to Ward's trade directory. From the time of the fire and until closure in 1902 the Hutton family and W. H. Richardson were mainly in control of the mill. (Millburn & Miller 1988: 29)

The firm changed its title to the Wearmouth Paper Company and were making wrappings. In 1851 the product had developed to the point that Messrs Venables of this concern were exhibiting samples of 'Fine Brown Paper Glazed in the Long Length'; very true rollers were needed to achieve this.[74] Five beating engines were working that year but the firm was listed as Ayre's Quay, a place rather than the company name,[75] but it was still listed in trade directories as Wearmouth Paper Co in Bradshaw's Directory of 1853. Cornett (1908: 163) says that during 1848 Michael Hutton had taken over management of the mill from his father, Robert, who died in 1865.

A paper makers directory of 1860 confirmed W.H.Richardson as still the proprietor of this mill and the business was listed as the Wearmouth Paper Mill Co, but the mill was then being worked by Michael Hutton, son of Robert Hutton. (Maidwell 1987: 7) W. H. Richardson was still listed by the Excise authorities in 1862 however, as manager in 1868 rather than proprietor, and in paper makers directories from 1864 to 1871 and noted as making rope browns; by 1871 these were being produced on a 72 inch machine. Simmons (nd) noted that H. Y. Richardson was the proprietor at this mill in 1867. Apparently he had bought the mill and traded as H. Y. Richardson & Co from 1868 to 1871. It seems that the brothers Henry Yarker Richardson and Edward Richardson were in partnership, trading as H. Y. Richardson & Coy, Sunderland, paper manufacturers, and as Richardson Bros, Newcastle upon Tyne, Iron & Commission Merchants, the latter partnership dissolved in 1868, and noted in the *London Gazette* of 28 November and 4 December 1868. Henry Yarker Richardson no longer featured in papermaking after 1870 for he was killed in a tragic railway accident on 6 December 1870 at the age of 51. His career had begun in engineering, working with Robert Stephenson in Newcastle but he was considered to be 'possessed of a rare wisdom and a practical ingenuity ... [a] proprietor of a paper manufactory which flourished rapidly in his hands'.[76]

The Hutton Family

By 1870 M. Hutton & Co had become the proprietors of Wearmouth Mill (Cornett 1908: 163) making rope browns and glazed browns from 1872-1891 and were so noted in paper trade directories. This continued until Michael Hutton died in 1874; then his widow took over the business with Alderman Johnson, an ex-clerk of the mill and a much-respected figure locally. (Richardson 1908: 178) In due course Mrs Hutton's brother, Mr Shillington Scales, a chemist, joined the company but disagreed with Johnson; he, Scales, considered he could make rope browns without rope, perhaps foresaw the possible use of wood pulp and experimented with such a furnish. (Maidwell 1987: 8)

M. Hutton & Co was listed at Bishopwearmouth, Sunderland, in Craig's Trade Directory making best rope browns and glazed browns on a 72 inch machine in 1876, and at Ayre's Quay and at Bishopwearmouth in 1879. The firm and its products were certainly considered to have 'a first class name in the market' and could 'always command a good price, as it is known to be free from adulteration'. The paper was reputed to have been 'greatly used by hardware manufacturers in Birmingham, Wolverhampton etc for packing'.[77]

By 1880 motive steam power had been introduced, and output was increasing gradually; it had reached 17 tons a week by 1884 and 18 tons a week by 1887. (Simmons nd) Five years later the company changed its title to Hutton & Scales,[78] and this pair was in partnership with F. Shillington Scales whose role was that of mill manager. (Cornett 1908: 163) The partnership was also mentioned in 1898 in a local guide.[79] They were working on one 74 inch machine making genuine rope browns. Strong browns were added to the list of paper sorts by 1899 and agents were working in London, Glasgow and Dublin by 1901 to help extend the business; this was recorded in paper trade directories of this period.

At a time when competition among paper manufacturers was becoming increasingly difficult in the area of brown papers, Messrs. Laing & Co, shipbuilders, were anxious to extend their shipyard so the mill was closed and sold to Messrs Laing & Co in 1902. They wished to launch a particularly large ship and needed an additional, adjacent site.[80] One man who retired when papermaking ended at Wearmouth Mill was John Whittaker; he had been Foreman there for fifty years.[81] Whittaker died in 1919 aged ninety and his family was given a funeral grant by the trade union of which he had been a member for many years.[82]

Note: A reference to the Ayres Quay Mill (presumably Wearmouth) having 'collapsed' in the National Union of Paper Mill Workers Annual Report of 30 November 1891 seems to refer to the membership at that mill leaving that union rather than the paper mill having suffered serious damage. The committee had been considering amalgamation with other paper makers unions, the Modern Society and the United Brotherhood, because of 'the value of our combination for protective purposes'.[83]

Egglescliffe Mill[84]

Egglescliffe Mill, also called Eaglescliffe or Tees Mill, was situated on the River Tees at Yarm and first mentioned as a manorial mill in 1538.[85] Papermaking has been noted variously as having been 'commenced here [in Egglescliffe parish] in 1830 by Charles T. Bainbridge & Sons' in Whelan's trade directory of 1894, and, in a county history of 1928 that, at Egglescliffe 'there was formerly a paper-mill; it was built in 1832'.[86] This was on a site previously occupied by corn granaries (Dingle 1973: 13), that had presumably provided storage for the manorial mill. The paper mill was described in 1857 as 'situated near the bridge ... worked by steam-power, the property of Messrs Bainbridge and Son'. (Fordyce 1857: II, 220)

C.T. Bainbridge

C. T. Bainbridge married at Easingwold on 15 November 1808[87] and a C. T. Bainbridge was listed in Baines' trade directory as a spirit merchant there in 1823; a Chas Thos Bainbridge had a tallow chandlers business in Easingwold in 1834, noted in Pigot's tarde directory. It is not known if this is the same C. T. Bainbridge as the paper manufacturer, perhaps a relative, or a person of a different family.[88] When Bainbridge came to live in Egglescliffe he occupied a house above the paper mill. (Dingle 1973: 13) Another

Bainbridge, Richard, a rag merchant and shoddy carder may have supplied the business with inferior rags for use in making brown paper; he appeared in White's trade directory of 1840. Wallis (1981: 1) noted Messrs Bainbridge & Son at this mill in 1841 but was uncertain as to whether as owner or tenant. The firm can also be found in trade directories for Stockton or for Yarm; for example in 1840 in White's, also in Pigot's, and in Slater's trade directory of 1848.

An Extensive Fire at the Mill

A newspaper report of an extensive fire at this mill in 1846 confirms that Messrs Bainbridge & Son were in occupation at that date.

> Yesterday morning about two o'clock, the Tees Paper Mill, occupied by Messrs, Bainbridge & Son, at this town [Yarm] was discovered to be on fire. No time was lost in giving an alarm, and a messenger was immediately despatched to Stockton-on-Tees to obtain the fire engines. When they reached the scene of destruction, about 4 o'clock, the principal part of the building was nearly gutted; for, in consequence of the extreme violence of the wind, the flames spread with fearful rapidity, and not only that part of the mill in which the fire is supposed to have originated, but also a cottage and a public house adjoining, with other outbuildings, were soon reduced to a heap of smouldering ruins. By the exertions of the firemen, a considerable portion of the machinery was saved, and paper to the value of about £1,000 was also got out, being only slightly damaged. The damage to the mill and stock will not amount to less than £3,000, a small part of which is covered by an insurance.[89]

Richmond (1868: 200) records that 'nearly the whole of the mill, a large portion of the stock, the Red Lion public-house, a smith's shop and a cottage, were all entirely consumed before the flames were got under'.

The Firm of C. T. Bainbridge

It seems the mill was rebuilt as in an 1848 directory, Slater's, Charles Thomas Bainbridge was noted as the paper maker at Tees Mill; a paper trade directory of 1850 listed the concern with the same occupier, C. T. Bainbridge & Son. A national survey of paper mills in 1851 shows four beating engines all at work, although the mill was then referred to as Yarm Mill in County Durham.[90] By 1851 Charles son, William (born 1810) a paper maker and wholesale stationer, was employing 15 men and 23 women at the mill.[91] Ten years later the local census return described him as a paper manufacturer living with his wife, Isabella, and two nephews, William B. Robinson and Raper Robinson. They were both Clerks and may have worked for him at the mill until they died in 1866 and 1867 respectively. William Bainbridge had retired by 1871 and died ten years later in 1881.[92]

By 1853 Bradshaw's Directory reflected the fact that the paper mill was then known as Tees Mill at Yarm in Yorkshire. The concern was entitled C. T. Bainbridge & Son in 1864 (paper trade directory) and described as making glazed and unglazed browns and purples. 'The river water proved too coloured for finer sorts of paper and coarser kinds were cheaply made, especially a felt paper that was exported to India. This was dried in a kiln', unlike most paper that was dried on suspended lines or in drying machines. (Dingle 1973: 13) Listed as at Tees Mill, Egglescliffe, Yarm in 1876, the same company was still in occupation in 1879, according to paper makers directories.

Expansion and Closure

After considerable alterations in 1889, that 'included the substitution of a 120 horsepower horizontal engine for the old 40 horse-power beam engine, the output of paper was increased from 8-25 tons per week'. (Wardell 1957: 115) Messrs. C. T. Bainbridge & Son of Tees Paper Mills, Yarm (and of Castle Mill, Richmond, Yorkshire) was reported in 1892 to be 'now represented in London in the makes of brown directly and solely by their traveller, Mr C. Seel'. An advertisement described their products in more detail: 'glazed and unglazed browns of all descriptions, caps, casings, manilas, glazed and unglazed shops, millwrappers and carpet felt. Hand and machine-made square bottom and flat bags in all qualities'.[93] The continuence of this firm was confirmed by a directory entry of 1894 that noted the paper mill in Egglescliffe parish still carrying out its business under the title of Charles T. Bainbridge & Son, making paper and paper bags.

Although the business did not do well at first it later flourished and the firm became very prosperous, working under the Excise number 102. Eventually business declined and it was reported that the mills, 'which had been idle for some time, have been sold to a Middlesborough [sic] building firm [in 1896], who intend to erect workman's cottages on the site'.[94] Whether or not those cottages were built is uncertain for, 'after being sold twice, it was given up', (Dingle 1973: 13), some 70 years after it had been built. (Wardell 1957: 115) Comments from Cleveland Archive Service and local people suggest that the paper mill was taken over by Cecil Wren Brewery, presumably soon after the turn of the twentieth century, but possibly only for storage purposes. It has not been possible to confirm or refute these statements. As this mill was some way from other paper mills in County Durham perhaps the manufacturers were not under as much pressure from competition as those manufacturers further north in the county.

Paper Makers in Egglescliffe

In the 1881 Census of Egglescliffe several paper makers are shown to be living at Stockton Road, including Thomas Robinson, a paper manufacturer. Aged 73, he had been born at Egglescliffe, as had his son Robert aged 35. Another Robinson, John, a paper maker here, had a son Thomas May aged 15, also born in Egglescliffe. Henry Savage, appears here in this census, designated a paper manufacturer, with a 15 year old son, Alfred, also born in Egglescliffe.[95] These entries may indicate a partnership between Thomas Robinson and Henry Savage. It seems reasonable to assume that the papermaking firm was managed by relatives of Bainbridge as it continued under the C. T. Bainbridge name throughout its history.

Maidwell (1990: 20) noted that W. C. Warrell, later to become a paper maker, 'was born in the mill one winter's night, his parents having tramped from Richmond'; he offers neither date nor source for this information. A Walter C. Warrell, paper maker, appears in a list of trade union members working at Shotley Grove in 1896, but whether this is the same man has not been ascertained.[96]

Commemoration Sheet - Opening of Ford Mill 1838

Ford Mill

Ford Mill (or Ford Farm Mill as it may have been called at one time) stood on the flat ground of the River Wear's south bank adjacent to a prominent limestone cliff known as Claxheugh Rock in the South Hylton hills, near Sunderland, one third of a mile north west of Ford Hall. The site was approximately one mile down river from South Hylton and two miles west of Wearmouth paper mill. (Walker 1984: 51) This gave easy access to the keel boats that plied their trade on the water, and to a spring of good clear water close by. A tramway had been built from the mill to the river for ease of transporting raw materials from the keels, and Chester (1976: 1-2) comments on the tramway that was to be superseded in 1866 by a railway link to the Penshaw Branch Railway, while Walker (1984: 51) refers to the incline railway constructed to the mill yard. The mill's name was taken from the existence of a river ford near the site, but it eventually came to be known as Hylton Mill because of its proximity to Hylton. (Chester 1976: 1)

New Paper Mill

In 1836 Robert Vint, James Vint and William Hutton of the firm Vint, Hutton & Co began to build a paper mill here.[97]

> The mill building was of huge pitch-pine timbers, twelve to fourteen inches square and up to thirty feet long. Walls were double-cleaded up to window sill height with extensive glazing. Upper floors were of two and a half inches thick oak, caulked and pitched ... Lighting was by gas from the mill's own plant ... although work in out of the way places was done by candlelight, duck lamps or carriage lamps. (Chester 1976: 2, 15)

Ford Mill was opened on 29 August 1838; the Chairman and Manager Robert Hutton, the paper maker of the firm, with Vice-Chairmen James and Robert Vint, watching while white paper was made entirely from rags on a 70 inch deckle machine with one drying cylinder in five minutes. Thomas Marwood, a printer, had brought a printing press to the works especially, for he then printed a commemorative sheet for each person attending the opening ceremony. (Walker 1984: 49) Output increased rapidly to 16 tons a week.[98] Excise authorities allocated no. 83 to the mill, a number previously used by Stone Bridge Paper Mill that had closed in 1832.

Changes of Proprietor

Within a year or two, certainly by 1840, the proprietors appear to have been Fletcher, Blackwell & Faulkner (or Falconer), (Millburn & Miller 1988: 29) with James Vint, Robert Hutton, William Hutton, Thomas Fletcher, and John Buckwell as occupiers as stated in Excise correspondence of 30 November 1841. Although not named in this correspondence, Robert Vint was still involved in Ford Mill until 1844 when, with James Vint, he left the company trading as Vint, Hutton & Co at South Southwick, Claxheugh. This inevitably resulted in the partnership with Robert Hutton, William Hutton, John Blackwell and Thomas Fletcher being dissolved and reported in the *London Gazette* of 21 March 1844.

Further changes took place when William Hutton's retirement was noted in the *London Gazette* on 3 November in 1847 and, a year later Robert Hutton left the firm to rebuild Deptford Mill aka Wearmouth Mill in partnership with W. H. Richardson. (Chester 1976: 2) It may have caused dissention at Ford Mill and be the reason for the subsequent dissolution (Walker 1984: 51) of the partnership between W. Hutton, R. Hutton, T. Fletcher, John Blackwell, and John Brunton Falconer trading as Hutton, Fletcher & Co, details of which were published in the *London Gazette* of 2 February 1849. Robert Hutton's son, Michael, then took over the management of the mill according to Cornett (1908: 163), but two months later the mill was being advertised for sale at auction 'in consequence of the dissolution of the partnership'.[99] It is clear from these details that papermaking continued at Ford Mill yet it is not mentioned on the Tithe Apportionment of 1844, and buildings outlined on the Tithe Map are named 'High Ford' with no reference to a paper mill.[100]

Thomas Fletcher and John Brunton Falconer, paper makers of Scotswood paper mill, with John Blackwell, who had connections with the *Newcastle Courant* newspaper, (Cornett 1908: 161) were occupying Ford Mill, manufacturing paper and pasteboard by 1850, as Excise records of 16 May indicate. A trade directory of that year lists the firm as J. Blackwell & Co, with Mr Francis Blackbird as Manager, living at Claxheugh Grove and this is confirmed by Chester (1976: 2).

Boiler Explosion and Repairs

An indication of the mill's size and likely output was reflected in the number of beating engines that were at work in 1851 having been recorded in a Parliamentary survey.[101] During that same year Thomas Fletcher had been replaced by Joseph Fletcher in the partnership, leaving Blackwell still in occupation with Falconer.[102] A paper trade directory of 1851 noted that the firm of Blackwell, Falconer & Co, Ford Mill, kept a warehouse at North Quay, Sunderland.

On 20 December 1851 a boiler exploded leaving two men dead, (Chester 1976: 2) an employee and his son Oliver. (Fordyce 1855: II, 263) When the mill had been repaired papermaking was resumed. Edward Richardson became manager; (Simmons nd) in 1853 George Blackwell had joined the company. (Maidwell 1987: 4) In 1855 Fordyce (1855: II, 532) noted that Ford Mill was now trading under the title Messrs Blackwell & Co, that the mill manufactured printing papers among others and was worked by steam. Francis Blackbird had become manager in 1853, and remained so until at least 1856, living at Claxheugh Grove. In that year the company changed its title again to John Blackwell & Co. (Chester 1976: 2)

Financial Problems

Financial difficulties led to the sale of the mill by Blackwell & Co, (Cornett 1908: 163) at auction in 1860 to Thomas Routledge & Co. (Millburn & Mitchell 1988: 28-29) He was considered to have saved the mill, 'assured its place in history, and prolonged its life by over a hundred years'. (Walker 1984: 48) It was reported that the Ford Mill auction included cottages for the work people and homes for managers and foreman, 'and all the machinery and appliances suitable for manufacturing 14 tons per week of printing and other papers. Pure spring water with coals and carriage cheap'.[103] Simmons (nd) considers that John Blackwell continued at Ford making printings and music demy, at least until 1862, and certainly the firm continued to be advertised as John Blackwell & Co in paper trade directories for the next two years. It is not known whether or not John Blackwell was subsequently involved in papermaking; he died in February 1872 and his Will was proved on March 7 in the same year. John Brunton Falconer, a partner of Blackwell's, died in 1864 but one of his sons, Charles, was then still making paper in Newcastle.[104]

Thomas Routledge and Esparto Grass Furnish

From Hills (1988: 139) we read that Thomas Routledge, who took over Ford Mill in 1860, had experimented first at Eynsham Mill, Oxfordshire, with patents for treating esparto grass fibres with:

> a caustic ley, composed in the ordinary manner of soda or potash and lime, but containing an excess of lime, that is to say more lime being present than is necessary to render the alkali caustic, this being necessary to bring the gums resinous and siliceous matter (coating and cementing together all raw vegetable fibres more or less) to a soluble state.[105]

It would be followed 'by boiling and rinsing in a solution of carbonate or bicarbonate of soda'. (Evans 1955: 110) Problems of waste removal forced him to move and he chose Ford Mill where there was easy access to the River Wear for simple disposal of effluent. There was also the advantage of good transport facilities to Sunderland and Newcastle, particularly with Ford Mill having its 'own quay, where vessels discharge their cargoes of Esparto fibre in to the warehouse direct from Africa'. (Mitchell 1972: 158)

There Thomas Routledge set up a company, Routledge & Co, with [Sir] John Evans as Chairman, a son-in-law of John Dickinson and well-known in the paper trade.[106] It was Routledge who pioneered the use of esparto grass to make esparto half stuff and esparto white paper. Chester 1976: 5, 6) He is considered to have revolutionised the manufacture of fine papers in Great Britain (Walker 1984: 54-55), for esparto had properties that enabled high grade printing paper to be made. Once at Ford he refined the process that basically:

> involved the digestion of the grass with caustic soda (prepared by boiling lime and sodium carbonate together), and the economic recovery of the sodium carbonate from the spent liquor, after its concentration by evaporation and the burning off of the organic matter. The washed digested esparto was then bleached with calcium hypochlorite and re-washed. During the early part of this period digestion was at atmospheric pressure.[107]

Routledge also worked in conjunction with John Dickinson, supplying esparto half stuff for esparto paper to be made at Dickinson's mills in Hertfordshire. 'The half stuff from the Ford Works came in hydraulically-pressed round, upright canvas bales of about 3 cwt. and required to be broken small for bleaching and further working'. (Evans 1955: 111) Routledge developed the making of paper using esparto fibre as a furnish and was the first person to produce esparto paper on a commercial scale. (Chester 1976: 3) To avoid Excise Duty on paper (before Duty was abolished in 1861) Routledge made the pulped esparto in to thick sheets to sell to paper mills, but the Inland Revenue categorised this as paper therefore subject to duty, so this method was suspended. (Walker1984: 55) By 1864 the firm, as Routledge & Co, were advertising in paper trade journals and directories, offering for sale printings, news and cartridge paper made from esparto grass.

Thomas Routledge oversaw the building of this plant at Ford Mill following a custom-made specification, the first plant in the world to be fitted specifically for the preparation and use of esparto grass as a furnish. (McCord 1979: 142) This was the first fully developed plant for the conversion of esparto grass in to white paper. (Linsley 1989: 8) Although in the first nine months Routledge produced only 50 tons of esparto paper, and that suitable just for newsprint, he aimed at 120 tons of half stuff a week in the second year. (Evans 1955: 111) Routledge was sufficiently established by

1864 to form a limited company, Messrs Routledge & Co Ltd. (Cornett 1908: 163) By 1865 Routledge was importing 18,000 tons of Spanish esparto grass, and Bentley & Jackson of Bury in Lancashire had installed a new papermaking machine at Ford. (Maidwell 1987: 5) Routledge had also experimented with bargasse, jute, straw and various woods, but particularly with bamboo canes as a raw material, and published papers in 1875 and 1879 about producing paper from a bamboo cane furnish. (Chester 1976: 14)

Esparto grass was first mentioned in Excise returns for Newcastle upon Tyne in 1860, (Walker 1984: 52) import tonnage there reflecting the rapidly expanding production using this furnish, from 1224 tons in 1860 to 9534 tons by 1862. (Chester 1976: 5) The need was such that the River Wear Commissioners built a warehouse at South Dock in 1867 especially for the storage of esparto grass.[108] By the 1870s Routledge's Patent Paper Stock, (prepared esparto fibre) was being sent in bales to the American market.[109]

Unfortunately there were hazards attached to using chemicals to break down the esparto grass fibre. In June 1871, for example, there was a particularly serious accident that resulted in a death. Thomas Carolin of South Hylton, who had been employed at the mill for the previous three years working in the chemical department, was attending tanks filled with boiling carbonate of soda when the accident occurred. Another employee, John Parish, working nearby suddenly heard tremendous shouting from Carolin. He rushed over and found him immersed to the neck in chemicals but managing to hold on to the horizontal bar that crossed the tank. Carolin was pulled out by Parish and several others, but the Doctor 'pronounced the case hopeless'. Inevitably Carolin died soon afterwards.[110]

Intermittent Water Supply

Unfortunately the site at Ford Mill was often lacking in a sufficient supply of water, essential for washing, mixing and power and that caused delays in production. In 1866, because the spring had proved inadequate, a large well was sunk and borings made, with little result. Water was pumped from the river to feed the steam boilers and reservoirs were being built to provide high-level storage of water, but the river water had to be clarified. The expectation was then of an average output of 100-120 tons of paper a week. Both problems of supply and quality were aired in the Directors Report of 1866. (Chester 1976: 7, 19) The inadequate water supply was to become a recurrent problem.

By 1866 Routledge, with Mr Frederick Norton Miller as Manager, (Chester 1976: 5) had been producing half stuff and paper stock as well as printings, news and cartridges from esparto stuff, and later added common writings. In that year the company became the Ford Works Co Ltd with Thomas Routledge as Managing Director, supported by J. P. Cornett who was later to become Manager. A 74 inch machine had been installed by 1871 to help extend the range of papers offered to customers, and this would include engine-sized writings by 1876. These details were noted in trade directories between 1866 and 1887.

Growth and Extensions and Additions

Growth was indicated in correspondence of 26 May 1868 between the Bank of England and Thomas Routledge. The manager of the Newcastle Branch noted that the plant showed 21 per cent profit on capital, offering only a dividend of 7½ per cent because the rest of the surplus was used for innovations including equipment to recycle the bulk of chemicals employed and so reduce production costs. (McCord 1979: 142) A description from Walker (1984: 56) cites the whole chemical digestive processing of esparto grass being carried out at Ford in the chemical plant built at the east end of the works, with a huge rotary boiler and extensive settling tanks, with a recovery plant.[111]

Milburn & Miller (1988: 29) record that in 1872 Works Manager, Frederick Miller, left to become Managing Director of Hendon Paper Mill. He was replaced by Joseph Augustus London, a stepson of Routledge, until 1883 when Mr J. P. Cornett became Works Manager for the next 35 years. James Porteous Cornett had joined the company in January 1869 to work with Routledge, and had had 11 years commercial experience and 12 years practical papermaking experience by 1887 when he was appointed Manager of Ford Mill, the mill that 'contains every modern appliance for the successful working of esparto'. A member of the Paper Makers Association and of the Paper-Makers Club, he was 'enthusiastically fond of paper-making, and absolutely revels in the details of the manufacture'.[112]

A new fibre warehouse of 1872 was probably an extension to the 1868 building. Here esparto bales were tipped from wagons on the North Eastern Railway line down the bank using chutes, directly in to the warehouse. (Chester 1976: 8) By 1875 it was reported that 'All the work of the establishment is done on the premises ... there is a small gasworks which supply the whole place with gas. The chemicals are also made on the premises with an exception'.[113] G. & W. Bertram installed a 60 inch papermaking machine in 1876 at an invoiced price of £3250, but with installation costs Routledge recorded in his diary a final payment of £4447 10s 3d. (Maidwell 1987: 5) By 1878 two Sinclair high pressure (50 psi) vomiting boilers had been installed, probably in parallel with some atmospheric digesters initially. More were gradually added and all the machinery at the mill was driven by steam engines of all sizes, from fractional horsepower for pumps to larger engines for papermaking machines and beaters. (Chester 1976: 15) In 1880 the Directors recorded that 'we have at considerable outlay increased our spring water supply'. (Walker 1984: 64)

Fire and Routledge's Demise

Much of the extensive additions and installations, the continual completed repair work, were mostly lost in a disastrous fire on 4 April 1887 that gutted the digesting and preparation plant. It began at 7 o'clock, the flames spread rapidly and the fire burned for some hours causing considerable damage. Local people were especially distressed as the majority in the district were dependent on the mill for their living.[114] Census returns reflect the importance of jobs at Ford Mill. In 1871 Routledge had been employing 96 men, 27 boys, 136 women and 12 girls; by 1881 the total had almost doubled, male employees then numbering 182.[115] This fire occurred only a few months before Routledge died on 17 September. (Chester 1976: 14)

'At this time [1887] all the machines were driven by steam engines of various sizes, from fractional horsepower for pumps to larger ones for paper machines etc.. The mill was partly rebuilt and a 104 inch (90 inch deckle) machine, the third Fourdrinier, was installed at right angles to the existing machines'. (Chester 1976: 14) The mill was restarted in January 1888, (Cornett 1908: 164) and the company reconstructed as Ford Paper Works Ltd; James Porteous Cornett continued as Works Manager with a Dickinson-oriented Board: Sir John Evans, A. H. Longman, F. B. Barlow, George Chater, and T. B. Barker. (Chester 1976: 15) Evans, (1955: 139) in her history of the John Dickinson Co., considers the fire to have ended the corporate interest of that company in the Ford Mill, but the composition of the Board suggests otherwise. In 1909 Sir John Evans died and was succeeded as Chairman by his son, Lewis Evans. (Chester 1976: 15)

Development and Extensive Installations

During 1888 paper production increased again, 'nearly double what it was before the fire', and this required an increased supply of spring water, 'an absolute necessity'. (Walker 1984: 64) It was decided to extend further the 250 yard drift from the well. Directors Reports between 1888 and 1992 (Chester 1976: 20) show that in 1889 they were particularly concerned with the high cost of paying water rates at £1000 a year, but they assured shareholders that a further drift extension had made them practically independent of any water company. Three years later the problem was sufficiently acute in terms of inadequacy of water and charges by the water company, to have to arrange with the landlord to divert water from two surface streams nearby in to a large reservoir then being built, as well as try to find some ways to economise on water usage.

In 1892 the company's financial situation can be partly gauged by its registration with capital of £100,000 in 600 Ordinary £100 shares, 10,000 Redeemable £1 shares and 30,000 Redeemable Preference £1 shares for Ford Paper Works Ltd, in order to acquire the firm of Ford Works Co Ltd and to carry on the business as paper and paper pulp manufacturers, as stationers, and also as manufacturers of envelopes, account books and cardboard. The qualification for becoming a Director was to be able to invest £1,000; they were to receive a remuneration, to be divided as agreed between them, of 200 guineas a year. Six directors were appointed: [Sir] John Evans, G. Chater, T. B. Barker, A. H. Longman, F. P. Barlow, and G. Chater jnr.[120] When Mr Barker died in 1905 he was replaced by Sir John Evan's son, Lewis. He eventually became Chairman, with Lionel G. Chater as a new Director, when his father and Mr Longman both died in 1909. (Walker 1984: 59)

A paper makers directory of 1894 notes three papermaking machines of 60 inch, 75 inch, and 90 inch width, producing fine printings, news, music, cartridges and ES Writings. A further machine, 100" deckle, was installed parallel to the 1887 machine in 1920. (Maidwell 1987: 5) The installation of a Triple Effect Yaryan evaporator by Mather & Platt in 1889 for the concentration of spent caustic liquor prior to burning off the liquid matter was one of the improvements. Others included a Pollitt & Wignell Corliss Compound Engine (600 hp) installed in 1898 at the east end of the beater house to drive beaters, potchers and various pumps from counter-shafting. A similar engine (400 hp) was installed at the west end of the beater house two years later; electric light was introduced with a small steam-driven generator and switchboard alongside this engine house. Gas engines drove a small generator for weekend lighting, the fitting shop line-shafting and the joiner's shop. 'In 1910 the Presse Pate was scrapped in favour of bleaching towers'; it is said that on one occasion a governor failure on the steam engine driving it resulted in a flywheel bursting, partly through the roof. (Chester 1976: 15) By 1913 an electrification scheme that included electric runways had been completed and a new chemical plant installed at Ford Mill.[121]

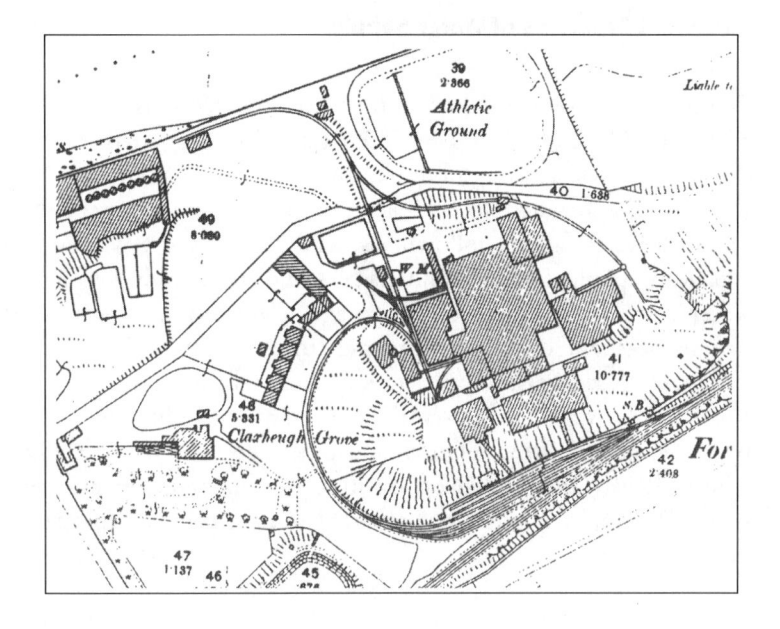

Plan of Ford Paper Mill 1896

Situated at Claxheugh nr. Sunderland, on the River Wear in County Durham, it was here Thomas Routledge developed the use of esparto grass as a furnish for papermaking from 1860 until his death in 1887. Esparto was processed in the mill's own chemical plant at the east end of the works. Despite a major fire in 1887 the mill continued to make paper from esparto until 1939.

Persistent Problems of Water Supply

The pressing matter of water supply that had 'lamentably diminished' by 1896 resulted in further drift extensions at a cost of £700 in 1897 and £1,500 in 1898, returning 'a good percentage on the outlay', although the supply was still inadequate. The Directors Reports of 1896-1900 (Chester 1976: 21) reflect their fear of a water famine following several relatively dry winters, an expanding population in Sunderland and water already low in the water company's underground storage system. A sum of £1,200 had to be spent on water purchase from the Sunderland Water Company. New measures were needed so a well was sunk at Hylton Road a mile away, Cornish-type Beam Pumps were installed driven by a Marine-type steam engine, and pipes laid at a cost of £5,000. The well was 245 feet deep by nine feet in diameter and this particular supply of water was reported to have helped improve the quality of paper.

The ample supply of water reported in 1903, because of a new well in which a new drift and borehole had been made, had become inadequate through lack of sufficient rainfall by 1905; the Directors procrastinated and deliberated over a further drift extension for five years until it became imperative to sink another well even further from the mill site at a cost of £5,000. This well at Chester Road was 336 feet deep, 11 feet in diameter, capable of producing 30,000 gallons of water each hour. (Chester 1976: 22) In1913 electric runways and other electrical equipment were installed as part of an electrification scheme, as well as a new chemical plant.[122] After a fire there in 1922 the well was re-equipped and served the mill until its closure in 1971. (Walker 1984: 66)

Labour Disputes

The 1892 Annual Report of the National Union of Paper Mill Workers referred to a dispute with the management in that year, without any suggestion of a strike being mooted, but neither the reason nor the resolution was mentioned. The only strike here ever recorded took place in 1913, the employees urging a Monday morning start-up time instead of the traditional Sunday night. Day workers hours were 6am until 5pm; those on shift worked 6am until 6pm or 6pm until 6am. (Chester 1976: 15) A local newspaper reported that:

> the employees have made a demand for a 10 per cent increase in wages and a reduction of hours. As the firm would not concede this 100 men and boys and 70 girls ceased work at six o'clock last night [Wednesday 18th June, 1913] and are absent from the establishment to-day. They are members of the National Union of Paper Workers.[123]

There may have been either a 'stalemate' position or a 'stand off' situation during the next three weeks for no further mention is made until:

> The strike which has been operating at the Ford Paper Works for nearly a month has been settled and the works will resume activities on Monday. It seems that during the past few days several interviews have been arranged between the employers and representatives of the work people, and as a result the masters have agreed to concede a 10 per cent advance to several of the departments and also to reduce the working hours.[124]

However, not until the 1920s were eight-hour shifts eventually introduced. A widespread strike by miners in 1921 affected many mills reliant on coal for power. Old colliery embankments were bought and the coal extracted mixed with tar to keep the steam boilers working at Ford. (Chester 1976: 15, 16)

Reconstruction and Changing Ownership

Further reconstruction took place in 1923 when Ford Paper Works (1923) Ltd was acquired by Ford Paper Mills Ltd, later Ford Paper Mills Holdings Ltd, and registered on the Stock Exchange. This was under the management of Mr J. Markham. (Walker 1984: 60) Opening a London sales office provided a further outlet for the now extensive range of papers, all listed in paper trade directories from 1922 to 1924: pastings, off-set papers, litho; typewriting paper, drawings, account books, cover envelope paper; white and tinted esparto boards, pulp boards, parchments, plain linear, white and coloured. However, by 1926 the company could not manage its affairs adequately so went in to liquidation, operating under the Official Receiver for the next two years. (Chester 1976: 16) In 1932, the general economic depression and slack demand for paper caused the company to be struck off the Stock Exchange Register.[125]

The mill was bought in 1937 by Wiggins Teape Group (Chester 1976: 16) with whom its fortunes then lay. The original machine was shut down and a cleverly rebuilt 66 inch machine built alongside the 1887 and 1920 machines. The no. 1 machine, a 70 inch deckle with only one drying cylinder, much improved since 1838, had finally been dismantled in 1934; it is said to have produced the best paper ever to have come from Ford Mill. (Maidwell 1987: 5) The mill was extensively modernised and a new power plant built. The old mill cottages were destroyed and new ones built. During the 1939-1945 war years, wheat straw became the principal fibrous raw material, digested by the esparto process; post-war this was gradually changed to wood pulp. (Walker 1984: 49, 60)

In 1947 the mill was transferred to an associate company, that of Alex Pirie & Sons Ltd of Hylton.[126] By 1954 there were 370 people employed at the mill and three papermaking machines were working.[127] Paper makers directories in 1951 and 1961 refer to Ford Mill as Hylton Mill of Alex Pirie & Sons Ltd, working two machines by electric and steam power, producing 100 tons a week. The state of production recorded in the 7 June 1956 issue of *Gateway* noted that the no.4 machine was producing 23.9 tons of paper in 24 hours and making pulp boards. In a subsequent issue of 31 August, no 3. machine was reported as having an average production of 272 feet per minute over 24 hours on offset cartridge paper, and the maximum ever achieved as 280 feet per minute. The firm successfully made tabulating card for machine accounting systems, also photographic wrapping paper for X-ray films, cigarette filters, litho printing board and airmail papers. However, crepe papermaking was a failure. During the mill's final period of commercial activity a variety of special papers were also produced, and some rag paper was again made there. (Walker 1984: 49, 61)

Wiggins Teape had announced the impending closure of Hylton Mill by the end of June 1971 because of increasing competition from imports and because of highly inflated costs. Three machines had been making white and tinted board and cartridge paper and some airmail paper to the extent of more than 10,000 tons a week. The firm employed 333 men and 86 women and redundancy terms were to be agreed with trade union representatives.[128] The mill closed in 1971 when it became apparent that there was a severe problem of financial liquidity. (Millburn & Miller 1988: 29) Ford Mill had been 'an efficient mill … in the forefront of technical innovation. It was the first to establish a 24-hour quality control system and pioneered the automatic control of the moisture content of paper, and of basis weight correction'. (Walker 1984: 61) A proportion of the machinery was transferred to other mills in the group; some sold to scrap merchants, as Chester (1976: 19) records. The mill was finally demolished in the winter of 1974/1975.[129]

Chapter 5

Paper Mills Established 1841 to 1891

Those who established paper mills during this period were clearly aware of the need for secure financial backing, scale and modern machinery. Although one mill closed after nearly fifty years in business, the other five continued for many years, four of them working at least in to the 1960s. One, still working in 1980, became the largest paper mill in the north of England.

Springwell Mills[1]

Springwell Mills were situated five sixths of a mile south west of St Paul's Church in Jarrow on Tyne, near the confluence with the Monkton Burn.[2] Locally the first mill became known as Jarrow Paper Mill. A decision of 1928 concerning the diversion of Paper Mill Path, Monkton, reflects on the location of the site:

> Ordered that a portion of a certain public footpath called Paper Mill Path within the parish of Monkton, commencing at the wooden footbridge across the Paper Mill Stream at a point where the said footbridge intersects the boundary of the Borough of Jarrow and the said Rural District ... to be diverted and the new road to be called Springwell Road.[3]

Lewis (1949: II, 632) is more specific:

> On the Don, which empties itself in to the Tyne, an extensive paper-mill was established in 1841; the machinery is on the best

and newest principle, and one of the engines, which is upwards of 100-horse-power, is the largest standing-engine for driving paper machinery in England.

Building the First Mill

The first mill began to be built on the 28 November in 1839 by Thomas Bell to make white paper. (Cornett 1908: 164) At the opening day two years later, on 10 November 1841, the proprietors, J. Hargrave, R. H. Bell, E. Bell, & R. Hastings invited manufacturers from neighbouring paper mills to attend and see the first paper being made at the mill by Thomas Bell. The visitors included John Fletcher, W. H. Hargrave and Mr & Mrs Gallon. (Maidwell 1987: 8)

In correspondence with Excise authorities later that month (30 November 1841) Hastings was not mentioned, although an R. Hastings was a proprietor. The mills were listed in some directories and, more specifically, in Excise correspondence, as under the proprietorship of Joseph Hargraves with Hargraves as the occupier, at mill no. 89. (Wallis 1981: 4) Trading as Jarrow Paper Mill Co this partnership of J. Hargrave, R. H. Bell, E. Bell, and R. Hastings was dissolved a few years later in 1848.[4] By 1851 the mill was referred to as Jarrow Mill, and, apparently, business was good, for ten beating engines were recorded as working here, with only one beating engine silent and not in use.[5]

Jarrow Mill now Monkton Mills

By 1851 a second mill had been built but the fortunes of the Bell family were soon to change. Noted by Simmons (nd) as Bell & Co., paper manufacturers of Monkton, South Shields, (presumably this is at Springwell Mills), Richard Hansell Bell and Errington Bell were listed in the *London Gazette* in 1852 as having been examined by the District Court of Bankruptcy, Newcastle upon Tyne. Further official mentions note a certificate for R. H. Bell, and dividends payable on his estate, including dividends of quite small proportions of debt. In January of the following year a petition for adjudication of Bankruptcy was filed against R. H. Bell and E. Bell in January; dividends were declared on 'new proofs' in February. Errington Bell had died by the 19 July 1853. In the same year Joseph Hargrave, late of Monkton paper manufacturer, now of Newcastle upon Tyne, banker was declared bankrupt.[6]

In view of these financial difficulties, Monkton Mills, lately in the occupation of Messrs R. H. & E. Bell, had already been submitted to be sold at auction with machinery; they were described as, 'recently erected and extensive paper mills known as the Monkton Paper Mills'.[7] It is not known if the mills were then sold, but five years later when the Jarrow Hall Estate was offered for sale, a paper mill was included with the property.[8] It seems reasonable to assume that the mills were sold or sub-let, at least for a period, as Fordyce, (1857: II, 747) recorded Messrs Blackbird & Co at Monkton Mill in 1857, and a paper makers directory of 1860 noted the company as F. Blackbird & Co; there were no further mentions of Blackbird & Co after this date.

The Richardsons and Reorganisation

The eventual purchasers were the Richardson family and the mills became known in due course as Springwell Mills and were allocated Excise number 91 from c1860. There is a reference in a newspaper article to the Richardsons having taken over the mill in 1861.[9] They used esparto grass as the furnish and operated two widths of machines, 60 inch and 70 inch. On this basis the Richardsons were able to produce esparto printings and writings, litho, and SC papers, antiques, white and tinted boards, colourings and gummings. By the 1860s the Richardsons, William Henry and Albert, were making printings, small hands, news and long elephants at Springwell Mills, (Shorter 1971: 142) and were listed in a directory of 1864.[10]

After 1861 the 'irregular supply and occasional defect in the quality of the water were overcome by the construction of a system of filtre and reserve ponds', by the Richardsons. In 1869 they had gutted the mill and 'machines of the most approved construction' had been erected. Five years later (1874) the mill had been closed for the whole of June, July and most of August for refurbishment and, while Messrs Turnbull, Jack & Grant of Glasgow installed a powerful new engine house, the boilers had been repaired and a new compound horizontal condensing engine of 260hp had also been installed. This temporary 'lay off' during refurbishment resulted in 'many of the grass hands being in a state of destitution' and eagerly awaiting their return to work. Unfortunately their hopes of immediate re-employment were to be destroyed. [11]

Conflagration

Just before the mill was to be reopened for making paper again, a disastrous fire at the mill on Saturday the 22 August 1874 caused inevitable disruption at the mill and further delay in returning to papermaking.[12] Earlier that year *The* [Jarrow] *Guardian* of 29 April referred to work having just restarted and the grass loft had just been fully stocked with esparto, statements somewhat in contradiction to the newspaper reports of August 1874. No other record of work having been discontinued during April has been found.

When the fire broke out on that Saturday in the large machine house, the manager, Mr Fleming, was fetched. He 'despatched his son for the Local Board hose and reel ... giving orders to fix the hose belonging to the mill and set the donkey engine a-going, [to pump water from the River Don] likewise to ring the fire bell'. Mr Fleming was soon joined by the Chief Engineer, John King. It was an almost impossible task for the wind was westerly and very soon the 'flames had broken out through the roof of a grass loft, and was shedding a lurid gleam over the mill'. The fire had burst through in 'dense volumes'. Within an hour or so the roof of the finishing house fell in and fire engulfed the mill.[13]

> The fire had extended to the finishing room where two or three valuable machines and a large quantity of paper packed up ready for the markets amounting to about £4,000 presented the appearance of a large volcano, the greater part of the paper being reduced to ashes.

A wooden store shed containing chemicals was lost in the fire. With help from fire engines of two local chemical works, they 'succeeded in quenching the fire within the beating machine room, thereby saving the most part of the valuable machinery'. The overall cost of damage was estimated at £25,000 and 250 men and women were out of work. A row of workman's cottages in the immediate vicinity was spared.[14]

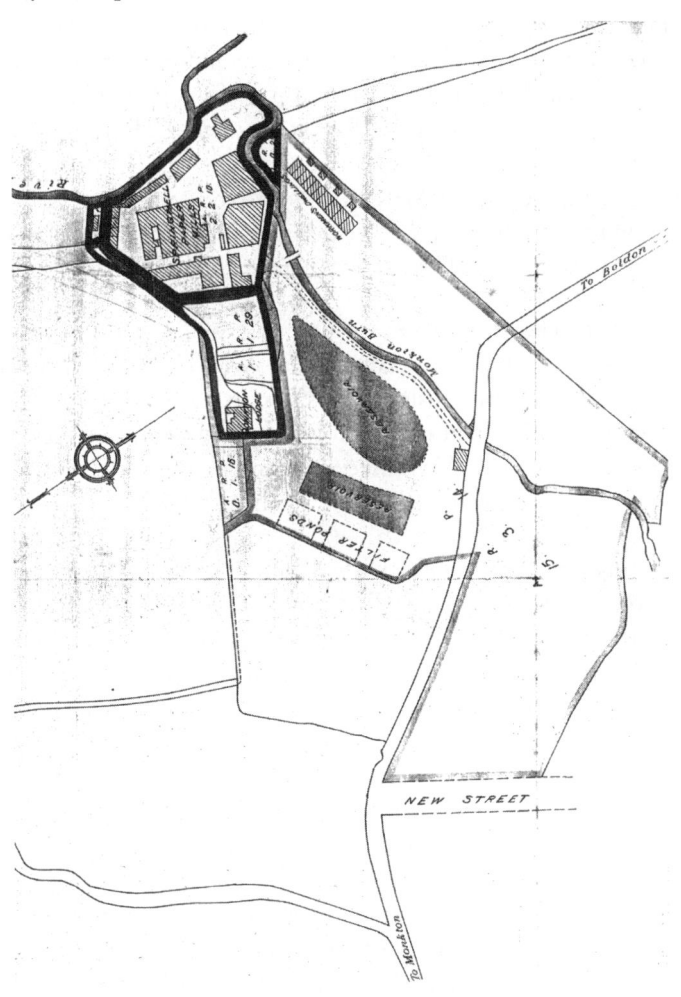

Plan of Springwell Mills c. 1900

Papermaking Continues

Despite the inevitable disruption from the fire in 1874, two years later the firm of Wm H. & A. Richardson was listed in trade directories and shown to be producing printings as earlier, but having extended their range of sorts of paper on offer: Writings, White, toned and lemon printings, engine and tub-sized writings, and envelopes. One of their two papermaking machines had been upgraded to 74 inch width by 1885.[15] The range of paper produced had been extended further by 1894 to include fine printings and Super calendared paper. This same firm of Richardsons was located here in 1896,[16] although W. H. Richardson had died in June 1895.[17] Near the beginning of the twentieth century the Richardsons had moved in to the export market, their advertisements particularly featuring litho in sheets and reels, although by 1905 super calendared paper was also being offered for export.[18]

Another major fire in 1898 caused £25,000 worth of damage,[19] and, towards the end of the century, there were clearly some financial difficulties within the business, perhaps as a result of that fire, or because the concern had expanded too quickly or extended its range of papers too widely. Various extensions to the mill reported in 1913 may have exacerbated the difficulties.[20]

During the early 1900s, with Mr E. Richardson as Managing Director,[21] (the manager, Mr Dickson, had died in June 1906 aged 56),[22] the firm continued to produce paper at Springwell Mills using esparto grass as the main furnish. Their business had expanded to the extent that they used marketing agents in Glasgow, Manchester, London and Dublin. An extensive range of papers was being offered in reels or sheets for export in 1906 including white and tinted boards, and antiques paper sorts; cartridges had been added to the range by 1911. There is some suggestion, but no actual evidence, that the firm of Samuel Jones (Ltd) was in some way connected with these mills by 1922, probably in relation to the gummed paper produced. A paper trade directory of 1922 notes that the mill produced paper at 68 inch and 74 inch widths, offered fine printings, engine-sized writings, envelope and gummed papers in reels or sheets, as well as an export packaging service.[23]

Uncertain Ending

It is generally believed that a creditor, Isaak Hassan, an importer of esparto grass and fine feathers, took control of the business in 1899, but had failed around 1914. (Maidwell 1987: 9) As the firm, in the name of W. H. & A. Richardson at Borough Road, was listed in directories of 1921 and 1922,[24] but was eventually sold by W. Richardson in 1924, it is difficult to be sure about the exact situation between the Richardsons and Mr Hassan. Perhaps he had shares in the company or was on the Board of Directors, as so often happened at this period between paper manufacturers and men of related trades. Richardsons had always produced good quality paper, but now sold to a manufacturer that continued to make paper at Springwell Mills until 1948, but paper of a lesser quality.[25] It is possible that the original mill may have been resurrected at some later date as it was listed as Jarrow Mill again in 1961.[26]

Still in 1987 good traces of the mills could be found, although a furniture factory occupied the site of the Salle and stock rooms. It is not known if the well-built houses that the Richardsons provided for their workers are still in existence. (Maidwell 1987: 9)

Team Valley Mills[27]

The paper mills were situated at Low Team, at the bridge on the Dunston-Gateshead Road; Clavering considers that the proximity of tidal water confirms the paper mill's location.[28] A local newspaper of 1900 describes the mill's location as 'close to the borough boundary where the tramway line terminates'.[29] Once a mediaeval corn mill on land owned by St Bartholomew's Convent, it was noted in 1528 when let.[30] With 'a dam and a short leat where the river begins to meander, it is likely' to have been used as a coal mill for Bensham Colliery to supplement existing facilities sometime before 'invading Scots wrecked the colliery' in 1640 and the mill reverted to grinding corn.[31]

Papers from the Clayton & Gibson Collection refer to Low Team Mill, with High Team Mill, as Law Mill, both water corn mills, in 1673. Later, in 1718, the mill is noted as Team Bridge Low Mill. [32] On an estate plan of 1810 the mill appears as Low Team Forge,[33] but is not titled on a 6 inch Ordnance Survey map of 1850s, so may have fallen in to disuse. It was also referred to as Teams. (Cornett 1908: 164)

Paper Mill Established

In 1868 a Mr William W. Burdon established a paper mill at Dunston, near Gateshead, called Team Valley, with one Fourdrinier papermaking machine producing white papers from rags. (Maidwell 1987: 17) Excise authorities listed the mill as no. 16. Three years after Team Valley Mill had been established the concern was under the management of Edward Richardson from 1871 until 1875, the business then entitled Edward Richardson & Son.[34] The business continued under that title for some years, changing only to include Sons rather than Son from 1883; the concern became a limited company and had changed its title to E. Richardson & Sons Ltd in 1892.[35] A second Fourdrinier machine was installed in 1890 and production widened to include wrappings and caps. The firm also developed the production of special felting. (Maidwell 1987: 10)

Maidwell (1987: 9-10) suggests that the Papyrus Fibre Company, established in the 1880s at Claypath Lane, South Shields to produce papermaking half stuff, using chemicals piped across the road from Westoe Soda Works, was taken over by Team Valley Mills in 1890. He noted that the Papyrus Fibre Company also installed papermaking machinery and was shown in local trade directories as manufacturing paper under the title South Shields Fibre Company, a concern that had also tried to make carpet felts. It seems probable that the Fourdrinier machine installed at Team Valley Paper Mill in 1890 had been transferred from the South Shields Fibre Co Ltd.

Paper makers directories, for example in 1892, list E. Richardson & Sons Ltd making rope and other browns for paper bags and wrappers in reels and reams, mill wrappers, duplex wrappers, coarse papers generally, (until 1894) and carpet felts on two machines of 60 inch and 72 inch width. An advertisement in a directory of 1894 offers particularly pure rope papers, hand-sized, and guaranteed not to rust steel goods. By this date a London agent had been appointed to further sales of Team Valley's products.[36] An indenture of 27 January 1898 shows that, while making paper at Team Valley Paper Mills, E. Richardson & Sons with the Richardson Printing Ink Co Ltd also leased an ink works and premises at The Teams, Gateshead.[37]

Conflagration and Damage

Early on a Saturday morning in April 1900 fire broke out at the paper mill and 'the Fire Brigade of Teams and Gateshead were apprised [of the fire] by messengers. The steam fire engine and tender' arrived quickly but 'found that the building was enveloped in flames'. The men 'displayed great vigour in endeavouring to quench the flames and prevent the possibility of them spreading'. They drew water from the pond inside the yard. The origins of the fire remain a mystery.[38]

The fire was thought to have broken out in the engine house that was located in the centre of the buildings that were three storeys high. 'On the ground floor are the main engines which drive the mills, which have through the conflagration, suffered considerable damage. The top floor contained the tanks and hoists, etc. all of which have been totally destroyed'. On the middle floor raw materials were pulped and there was much valuable machinery, but this floor was also totally destroyed. Near dawn there was a 'thunderous crash' as the roof fell in; a fireman and two employees, Tom Hood and John Parker, were 'precipitated on to the ground among the debris' as a result but had a miraculous escape.[39]

Maidwell (1987: 10) refers to a disastrous fire in 1900 that destroyed the rag lofts and much of the plant, and a comment that the mill had been 'badly damaged by fire' appeared in a trade journal.[40] In contrast a report of 21 April 1900 in the firm's letter book[41] indicated some damage to the beating and boiling departments with those roofs destroyed, but only some relatively minor damage to machinery. During repairs papermaking was carried on at Fellingshore Mill.[42]

This mill was considered to have been one of the largest brown mills in the north of England employing some 60 hands. Paper was being produced at the rate of 40 tons a week on two modern papermaking machines and a new steam boiler plant had recently been installed. These machines and the boiler plant were saved from the fire. Mention was made of a fire here twelve years before in the newspaper report, but no other reference has been found.[43]

Water and Financial Shortage

From the mill's letter book we learn that by 1900 the concern was running at a loss and the directors were considering becoming a limited company; there was also a problem with the supply of water. Mr Edmund Richardson, reporting on the situation on 12 December, 1900 stated:

> The River Team flows past, is diverted by the Dam and laid leading in to large settling and storage reservoirs, the surplus escaping by by-pass or overflow channel of ample dimensions. The supply is sufficient at all times but of poor quality, being polluted above the mills, but sufficiently clean for brown papers. The company has the water rights and access to the bank and the Dam. The tide rises within a few yards of the mill boundary and therefore gives free delivery for mill drainage and polluted waters in to the stream below the property, so drainage is effective.
>
> Power is provided by 12 h.p. turbine that pumps all the water required, but could be more effective. Deposits of ashes and rubbish and old brick pits deposits are of importance to the mill. Coal for the steam boilers is supplied from three collieries within ½ mile. There is no rail link to the mill so goods are carted to the railway or direct to the Steamer; materials are brought alongside Cail's wharf on the River Team below the mills.

Cartage costs:

> 4/6d per ton to and from steamer
> 2/6d per ton by rail
> 6d per ton via Cail's wharf.

On the basis of this information, not surprisingly, Richardson recommended using Cail's wharf to a greater extent:

> The buildings are mainly of sound construction and in good repair. Some departments are not very accessible to each other but could be by conveyors, tramlines etc.. There is an ample warehouse; Beating House; boiling department; machine house; finishing house; cutting department and other departments.
>
> There is a large papermaking machine of modern design, well-maintained, and a small papermaking machine that is out of date. There is a sub-lease of a building to Tenant's Ink Works well away from the paper mill. The lease of the paper mill property expires in 1915 but an extension is expected. The rent is £275 per annum but does not include the workmen's cottages.[44]

A further letter written by Richardson a few days later on the 19 December to Mr H. W. Lewer and to C. L. Stevens of Tovil Mill, Maidstone in Kent, implies that the report was required in connection with a possible sale of the mill.[45]

Evaluation and Revitalisation

In 1901 letters of 1 March examined the cost of making paper in considerable detail, and noted a discussion concerned with restarting the mill after liquidation, that included a complete overhaul of everything and the purchase of various items:

> Fuel economisers from Messrs. E. Green & Sons of Wakefield;
>
> Water softeners and a filter from Messrs. Babcock & Wilcox of London;
>
> Lathe and other tools for the repair shop;
>
> Fullner Patent Fibre Saving Apparatus from Jas. Bartram & Sons.

A renewal to the main engine of tandem Horizontal Condensing is mentioned on 11 March in that year.[46]

Messrs E. Richardson & Son Ltd went in to liquidation later in 1901 and the leasehold of the mill and premises was assigned to that company reformed and registered as the Team Valley Paper Mills Ltd on 16 March 1901. It was so listed in directories from 1902 until 1915. The Directors included H. W. Lewer, Chairman, also London paper merchants Stanley and Percy Galpin, with E. R. Richardson of Springwell Mills at Jarrow as Managing Director.[47] Under Richardson's direction, and with Mr Turner Crankshaw, of Radcliff, paper manufacturer, (previously paper maker with Yates Duxbury or East Lancashire Paper Mill) as Manager from 23 February 1907, the business continued.[48]

Initially production began on common browns, rope browns, carpet and hat felts running on no.1 and no.2 machines,[49] but later ran three machines of 60 inch, 72 inch, and 74 inch width until 1967. (Maidwell 1987: 11) By 1902 the company had become the sole proprietors of Feltine, a particular type of felt material. Agents were gradually appointed in Glasgow, Dublin, Birmingham, Manchester and London during the next four years to help increase demand.[50] Early in 1905, although trade, and therefore finance, was somewhat precarious, it was decided to change gradually to white paper production, a change that caused a rebuild of no.2 machine to enable the making of MF white printings, and the purchase of a supercalender for making sc papers.[51]

Some loss by flood in 1903 caused concern but, even more worrying by 1906, was the extent of the company's overdraft, accentuated by the terms of the lease and the reason for the appointment of sureties. A lease of 7 July 1906 gives Edmund Rich Richardson paper manufacturer, (with Sureties, London Paper Merchants, Henry William Lewer, Percy Herbert Galpin, and Stanley Ingram Galpin), as lessee of the mills from Augustus Edward Burdon of Cramlington, Northumberland for 21 years at a rent of £320 per annum, payable half yearly.[52] However, the company overcame these difficulties and survived.

Improving Business

A considerable improvement in the fortunes of the business was reflected in the level of employment: 36 hands had been employed by the company in December 1903 but, by 1908, the number employed had risen to 84. (Manders 1973: 84) Papers made ranged from common and CS Printings, both white and coloured, news and caps in sheets and reels in 1906. A second supercalender was purchased in June 1909, but advertisements in trade directories from 1908 already included MF and SC printings, pastings, colourings and foil papers.[53] Later directories note one 64 inch machine and two machines of 74 inch, both finished paper width, in 1912; one machine had been replaced by a 76 inch version by the following year.[54] This new papermaking machine was installed with auxiliary plant, including two drying cylinders, in 1913.[55] The no.2 machine, that had already been lengthened in 1905, was again improved by the addition of two new drying cylinders in March 1913.[56]

The company improved its position in the market, despite restrictions on output during the first world war, and was in a sufficiently strong position to acquire the freehold of the premises in February 1919. That year the cutter house was extended and a new finishing house built, and in 1952 a new duplex cutter and two Vickery's laying machines were installed. Nominal capital increased from £10,000 to £50,000.[57]

Changes in the range of papers produced can be found in subsequent directories. In 1922 the concern was also offering wood pulp boards, cartridges, tea lappings, and colbrings. By 1934 the list of papers was somewhat different from those being produced around the turn of the century. Papers made included mechanical and wood free, creams and azure laid, foil body in sheets and reels, imitation Krafts, cheque book papers, antique book, glued and unglued imitation parchment, and chocolate papers; white and tinted banks had become part of the standard range.[58]

The founder and managing director, Mr E. R. Richardson, died in June 1935 but was succeeded by Mr O. B. Richardson who continued the family name within Team Valley Paper Mills, at least until 1951. A long-standing member of the Board, Mr Turner Crankshaw died in 1937, but his family name was also continued through Mr C. T. Crankshaw who had completed thirty five years service at his retirement in 1947; his son A. E. Crankshaw then became Works Manager.[59]

Team Valley Paper Mills Ltd continued to be listed in paper makers' trade directories during the 1950s. Both electric and steam power was used, and the firm was able to produce MF and SC white and tinted printings and bonds, some 140 tons of paper a week, on their three machines of 60 inch, 72 inch and 74 inch widths. However, during the 1960s production ceased as the company could no longer compete with its rivals, mainly large groups of mills, (Shorter 1971: 176) and then the mill site was purchased compulsorily in 1967 for road widening. (Maidwell 1987: 11)

Hendon Mill[60]

A mill, thought to have been for grinding corn, at Hendon Grange with a house and farm was advertised for sale in 1825. (Maidwell 1987: 5) This was possibly the site of Hendon paper mill, Sunderland, on the River Wear. Shorter (1971: 151) commented that the water here was very hard but the supply adequate, and presumably reliable. He considered that the advantage of the proximity of docks for easy importation of raw materials and export of finished goods, the labour supply in Sunderland, an adjacent railway, the North Eastern, and nearby collieries as a source of coal for fuel, with the sea conveniently close for the disposal of effluent, together outweighed the disadvantages of hard water.

A Speculative Mill

The buildings here had been used for a short period by the Patent Fuel Company until it ceased to trade in 1862, then the site remained idle until 1872. It is possible that this mill, converted to papermaking by the new owner Mr F. N. Miller, was a speculative venture for it appears to have been put up for sale almost immediately after conversion rather than worked.[61] The Hendon Paper Works Co Ltd was set up under a Memorandum & Articles of Association dated 30 July 1872, and this concern then purchased from Mr Miller 'all his interest in the freehold lands, buildings and premises situated at Hendon, near Hendon Grange, containing seven acres, three roods, twenty nine perches, and the erection thereon of a paper works'. Incorporated on 31 August that year, the Board was appointed: MrHenry Bell, ironfounder of Tynemouth, became Chairman and Frederick Norton Miller, paper manufacturer from Ford Paper Mill nearby, the Managing Director. He lived at The Rock, Claxheugh, Hylton, previously the home of his deceased stepfather, Thomas Routledge, the man who had developed paper made from a furnish of esparto grass. (Linforth/Maidwell 1987: 5, 8)

Situated on the southern side of Sunderland and working under Excise no.8 making white paper, (Cornett 1908: 164) Hendon was to become the largest paper mill in the north of England. (Millburn & Miller 1988: 29) The particular advantages of this mill were its situation on level ground with 'buildings laid out to the best advantage with a view to economising time and labour, and avoiding dust and dirt. The machinery too is of the most approved construction, and all the latest improvements have been added. About 25 tons of paper are turned out weekly, some of it being of very high quality. ... Every precaution seems to have been taken as well for the comfort and health of the work people as for the efficient conduct of business'.[62]

The paper mill was described in some detail in a local newspaper, and was expected to 'bring increased prosperity to the port'. It was 'admirably supplied with a magnificent well of pure water [but] the most striking feature ... is that the manufacturing process is carried on in a continuous and progressive line of buildings, the locomotive taking in the raw material at one end, and the finished article being taken out at the other'. The subsidiary processes were separated from the initial papermaking to obviate the risk of contamination by coal dust and other foreign bodies, also to guard against fire. Chemicals were mixed on the opposite side of the road to minimise accompanying risks. Three Galloway boilers, 28 feet long and 7 feet 6 inches in diameter were coupled with horizontal high pressure and condensing regulating tubes, supplied by Umpherston Lawn, that had been fitted with patent self-acting expansion gear, working on 70-80lbs pressure so giving 'the highest degree of economy'. The engine was noted as capable of 200/250 hp and was made by G. & W. Bertram of Edinburgh.[63]

The firm's premises were situated in Commercial Road, New Hendon, Bishopwearmouth and listed as such in Kelly's trade directory of 1890. Once steam boilers had been brought in and were working, and G. & W. Bertram had installed a Fourdrinier papermaking machine in 1873, production began on paper made from esparto grass and straw, producing initially about twenty-five tons each week. Mr Miller continued as Managing Director for twelve years until he resigned in 1884. Thomas Goodall was then appointed as both Manager and Company Secretary. (Linforth/Maidwell 1987: 18)

Unabated Nuisances

Despite the modern equipment installed in the mill, the processes necessary for papermaking caused both effluent and smoke nuisances that brought the company to court.

A Mr Ritson lodged a complaint under the Public Health Act 1873 against Hendon Paper Works Co Ltd on the grounds that the paper mill chimney 'sent forth, on the 28 October, 1875, black smoke in such quantity as to be a nuisance, [with] very great injury to the trees and shrubs in his garden'. It was alleged that fireplaces and furnaces were not being carefully attended. The complaint was upheld at the Borough Police Court and the company firmly ordered to abate the nuisance. This complaint had been raised before and, it was stated that numerous promises to deal with the problem of smoke had not been fulfilled, despite the court order.[64]

That summer attempts by the company to reduce the smoke were detailed in court in the firm's defence. It was explained that the smoke emanated from two furnaces, one generating steam, the other a soda furnace. A new boiler had been purchased and another ordered, although neither was needed for processing, fitted with a special stoking device attached to reduce smoke emissions to one tenth and good fuel had been used. Various experiments and other apparatus had been tried to deal with the problem. Four firemen had been dismissed and four better qualified men employed to ensure more competent workmanship as this may have been part of the problem. The directors said they had tried everything possible to deal with the nuisance. With the complaint upheld, Hendon Paper Works Co Ltd was fined 10/- and ordered to pay costs, but clearly the court was not entirely satisfied for the matter was adjourned for later consideration.[65]

A different complaint in 1876, this time of the nuisance 'arising from the flow of offensive water from the Paper Mill over the beach at Hendon', was accepted and the directors of the firm ordered to abate the nuisance.[66] It is clear from a reader's letter to a local newspaper three weeks later that nothing had been done to deal with the problem as 'offensive, obnoxious and disgusting water' continued to flow on to the beach and the officials concerned were urged to stop this happening.[67]

Rapid Expansion

Expansion in the next fifteen years was rapid and considerable. In 1882 the concern was making paper on one 90 inch machine and offering music papers, ruled cartridges, fine printings, news, and engine-sized writings as advertised in a trade directory.[68] To produce the better quality papers it was unlikely to have used straw in that furnish. A second machine installed in 1886 helped increase output to 65 and 70 tons a week; introducing a third machine in the next year enabled the company to produce 120 tons a week. By 1887, with three machines now working, the firm diversified by including wood pulp in the furnish with esparto grass and straw, raising the output to 150 tons a week following the installation of a fourth machine in 1891. (Linforth/Maidwell 1987: 5, 18-19)

By 1919 Hendon Paper Works was employing some 430 hands and 'every description of paper is manufactured', serving United Kingdom and overseas customers. Approximately 18,000 tons of the principal raw material, esparto grass, was being imported annually to produce 200 tons of fine writing and printing paper weekly. The mill had its 'own electric lighting installation and the motive power for the machinery throughout [was] steam'. (Mitchell 1919: 157-158)

The range of papers offered by 1895 included envelope, fine and superfine printings, superfine, calendered, friction glazed & surfaced, still music and cartridge papers, but also ES & TS cream laids, coated, litho, enamellings, gummings and duplicator papers. Hendon Paper Works Ltd had its own railway siding and agents were working on the firm's behalf in London and Manchester. The range was widened still further by introducing tinted papers and offering news in reels or sheets; as a service to customers goods would be packed ready for export. Two years later map papers and antiques deckle edged and plain had been added to the production range, made on an 84 inch, a 92 inch and two 90 inch Fourdrinier papermaking machines, with concentration still on esparto grass as the main furnish.[69] Output had reached 190 tons a week by 1900. (Linforth/Maidwell 1987: 19) By 1902 friction glazed and coated papers were no longer being produced. The labour force at this period was of the order of 430 people. (Mitchell 1919: 157-158)

Serious Labour Problems

The business seemed to be developing successfully but by August 1899 and in to 1900 there were serious labour troubles within the company. (Linforth/Maidwell 1987: 19) On 24 August 1899 Hendon Paper Works was brought to a standstill because two men, bleach mixers, had had their bonuses reduced and refused to work; other employees refused to stand in and cover the bleachers work so were discharged. Then 140 men were dismissed, and 100 women were expected to be 'laid off' soon after.[70] Headlines in a local newspaper: 'The dispute comes to a head' and 'All the men idle', alerted the general public to the situation. In the report it was noted that this alteration in pay was said by the men to be the equivalent of a reduction of 10s a week in their wages. A meeting was called and the employees declared that they would 'not return to work until affairs had been satisfactorily settled'. It was reported that the 'managers have failed to find satisfactory substitutes as, one after the other, the men who took over the work have thrown it up from some cause or other'.[71]

Meanwhile, as a result of the 'shut down', the mill manager, Mr T. Goodall, had been forced to write to Team Valley Mills giving that concern an open order for their wrappers to fulfil Hendon's orders. (Maidwell 1987: 22) A deputation, led by Mr H. Lynas, Secretary of the Gasworkers & General Labourers Union, eventually met the mill manager and the dispute was finally settled. Mr Goodall agreed to reinstate all the men discharged and to pay the two bleach mixers 33s per week; the men had asked for 35s but accepted the compromise.[72]

Shortage of Raw Material

Following these difficulties Mr T.Goodall was asked to resign after sixteen years as manager; it is not clear whether this was as a direct result of his handling of the strike. Mr Wm. R. Aitkin was appointed in his place and remained there until his death in 1917. Mr John Pattinson of Newcastle became Chairman in 1908. (Cornett 1908: 164) Additional machinery was installed in 1913,[73] but problems of supplies of raw material was to become a major issue during the war years, 1914-1918, when there was a shortage of esparto grass; it was impossible to import from north Africa so an increasing amount of straw had to be used as a substitute in the furnish. (Linforth/Maidwell 1987: 19) A photograph taken at Hendon Mill in 1912 shows a group of 'grass loft men sitting on bales of flax'; perhaps there was already a shortage pre-war and flax was a partial substitute.[74]

Post 1914-1918 War Changes

After the war Mr R. A. Sandilands became Resident Manager and Company Secretary, but his employment was terminated in 1921 and the next Chairman, R. W. Armstrong, was appointed to replace him. In the following year Mr Percy Davidson from Fourstones Mill, Northumberland, was appointed resident manager and Company Secretary; two years later he became Managing Director. (Linforth/Maidwell 1987: 19)

Between 1923 and 1939 the mill was completely rebuilt, electrified and modernised. Tinted boards had been added to the range of papers and by 1930 output had reached 250 tons a week, paper being made on an average of 300 feet per minute. An advertisement in a trade journal of 1931 offered specifically litho printings, offset cartridges, laids and woves, and superfine tinted writings.[75] Pulp boards and parchments appeared in advertisements in trade magazines in 1934, while superfine tinted papers were again offered. A 137 inch twin wire machine was erected in 1936 to replace the no.4 machine that had been sold, and the twin wire converted to a single wire a few years later. (Linforth/Maidwell 1987: 19)

Post 1939-1945 War

After the second world war, in 1947, a new causticising plant and roasters were installed and a large, new grass shed erected. Mr Ian Davidson replaced his father, Percy, as Managing Director in 1948. Post-war output reached 200 tons of paper a week and, by 1950, the no.1 machine had been scrapped and an additional 124 inch wire machine installed in 1952. Noted as Hendon Paper Works Co Ltd, this concern was making 200 tons of esparto printings a week on three machines of 86 inch, 90 inch and 125 inch widths in 1951 and 1961.[76] Howard Smith Paper Co. bought the business in 1965 and Mr Ian Davidson went to Canada, but returned in 1971 to manage Howard Smith's Cornwall Plant. From this time the mill produced bond, duplicator and all-purpose wove papers. (Maidwell 1987: 6)

Hendon, the only paper mill in County Durham to be still working in 1980 closed that year, but was reopened a year later by Edward Thompson to make low grade paper for Bingo tickets. (Millburn & Miller 1988: 29)

Swalwell Mill[77]

'The Damhead dam on the River Derwent and a mill race 1,200 yards long', originally powered the manorial corn mill at Swalwell that belonged to the Bishops of Durham; it was leased by 'a consortium of coal owners, who used it to drive their pumps, and built their staiths on its river frontage' but the foundry ceased before the Civil War to be later acquired by Sir James Clavering as a 'working water corn mill', but probably used for his mines. By 1700 and in to the nineteenth century Swalwell Ironworks became famous under the Midlands ironmaster, Ambrose Crowley,[78] and a detailed plan of 1720 depicts the layout of the works.[79] A 25 inch Ordnance Survey map of 1897 shows the paper works on the north side of the pond. Clavering considers the purpose of the Mill Race to have been 'to bring the abundant waters of the River Derwent, less polluted than those of the Team',[80] and, it is indicated that the Damhead dam on the River Derwent in that area was fed by a leat. (Clavering & Rounding 1995: 255-256)

William Grace & Co at Swalwell

It is known that William Grace & Co of Northumberland Paper Mills transferred that business from Scotswood Mill, Excise number 245, to Swalwell-on-Tyne, a mill west of Gateshead. Before 1886 William Grace & Co had been operating at Scotswood Mill in Northumberland, and entries in Paper Makers Directories suggest that the company worked Swalwell between 1887and 1908; there are no earlier entries.[81] A directory of 1894 lists the paper made there, a description that is typical of other years: manillas, rope and other browns, glazed and unglazed, casings and tips on one 100 inch machine, with transportation from its own goods railway siding; colours had been added by 1904.[82]

By 1902 the London agent had been joined by an agent in Manchester, and another in Glasgow by 1906, giving every indication that the concern was prospering. However, despite the agents efforts and of those within the firm, the business failed and Swalwell Mill was listed as standing idle by 1909.[83]

Marsden Mills[84]

Originally a chemical works at Marsden near South Shields, Marsden Paper Mills were situated near the cliff edge between Whitburn colliery (usually referred to as The Pit) and the army rifle range. (Mitchell 1981: 1) Even in the early 1900s local people still referred to the mill as the chemical works. A 1902 ordnance survey map of Whitburn parish locates the mills at the end of a lane from the main Marsden Road, between the road and the coast, about one mile north, north east of the church. This position near the coast with a railway line only one hundred yards from the mill, possibly a private line from South Shields, made it easy to import raw materials and transport finished goods. Easy access to the sea was necessary for a drainage outlet from the mill. The mills had been built with bricks from Birtley, iron girders from Gateshead and completed with local slate. They later became the North Eastern Paper Mills.

Pulp and Newsprint

By 1870 the chemical works had been converted to a pulp mill using ground wood as a furnish, pulp that was brought from Tyne Dock despite high handling charges, with water provided from a private well, but papermaking was not established here until 1889. Maidwell (1987: 9) refers to a second-hand Fourdrinier papermaking machine, purchased from the *Sun* or *Star* in Blackburn, Lancashire that was adapted for running newsprint paper by lengthening the machine, adding more cylinders and making adjustments needed because of those changes. Mitchell (1981: 1) echos notes found at the Tyne & Wear Archive Service office that suggest the largest shareholders, including Sir A. Wood the largest shareholder of all, bought out the smaller shareholders of mainly shopkeepers and tradesmen from Sunderland and the pulp mill, then began to make newsprint that was to supply the *Sunderland Echo*, *Newcastle Chronicle*, *Northern Echo*, and the *Shields Gazette*.

The new company was entitled the North Eastern Paper Mills, registered with £70,000 capital in £1 shares to acquire the works, property, plant and undertaking generally of the Marsden Chemical Company Ltd, and to manufacture and deal in paper, paper pulp and any substance, chemical or otherwise, used in the manufacture of paper. In September it was recorded that the capital had been raised as £15,000 in £1 Preference shares and £45,000 in £1 Ordinary shares, in order to buy the Marsden Chemical Company for £35,000.[85]

Trade directories noted that the mill's output was 60 tons of newsprint a week in 1894, but also in white papers by 1895. The mill machinery was powered by using coal from nearby Whitburn Colliery; it was said that, by 1901, to make one ton of paper it was necessary to use one ton of coal. Production increased, as advertisements in the paper trade magazines demonstrated, increasing to 75 tons a week by 1904.

Electricity, New Installations and Reorganisation

By 1905 electric power had been introduced to run the beating plant, two new water-tube replacement boilers had been installed and extra cylinders added, so the mill output reached 86 tons per week. Only mechanical and sulphite pulp from Norway and Sweden was used for newsprint, but Canadian wood pulp provided the furnish for the best quality paper that was transported from South Shields docks by a steam engine dubbed the 'Marsden Rattler'. The finished reels of newsprint were delivered locally using chocolate-coloured Foden steam wagons. By the end of the year the number one machine had an output of 179 tons a week. During that year Sir Lindsay Wood, Bart, the Managing Director, was succeeded by (Sir)Arthur Wood.

A complete reorganisation took place in 1910 when the mill was rebuilt. The bills for the extension included tie rods for strengthening the beater house roof and a sliding door for a new lift at the south west corner of north bay, work that was carried out by the Cleveland Bridge & Engineering Co Ltd. Work required in the construction of new machines and other shops at Marsden was put out to tender and two new, 'fast and up to date' modern machines were installed by Walmsley & Co. of Bury, Lancashire in 1911; they were given four months to complete the work that cost the company £13,836 2s 10d.[86]

In 1910 number two machine had produced 130 tons of paper a week, but the fast and up-to-date machines installed here to revolutionise production in 1911 had become antique by 1932. Early in the twentieth century the new machines installed to revolutionise production were running at 260 feet per minute, producing 80 tons of newsprint a week. Such an expansion required an extension to the premises, for which there are records of estimates and drawings produced between May and August 1911.[87] The concern employed about forty five people on 11 hour day shifts and 13 hour night shifts, a 144 hour week; shifts were worked from Monday morning to Sunday morning,[88] making paper for the *Sunderland Echo*. (Mitchell 1981: 1) This system continued until 1919, after which a three-shift system covered the period from 6am on Mondays until 2pm on Saturdays.

By installing one of largest machines in the country, 160 inch wide, trimming to 148 inch, the firm was able to produce newsprint at 600 feet per minute in 1912, (Shorter 1971: 176-177) although it generally ran at 480 - 500 feet a minute, making 20 tons per week. The installation of this particular papermaking machine was mentioned in *The Times*; at the same time an electric crane, hoists and other auxiliary equipment were introduced to complement the new papermaking machine.[89] Subsequently, a new beating plant and boilers were installed in 1914, also a number two machine, 120 inch wide, trimming to 112 inch that was remarkable for full running after only two hours trial. Its output was 150 tons in the first week, just one week before the first World War began. The company had a good stock of pulp in hand so could supply paper more easily than some competitors.

Fire and Recovery

A disastrous fire broke out in 1921, so extensive that it burned for a week. Despite this the company recovered during the 1920s, developing a good export trade to the continent of Europe. Local gossip promoted the idea that the firm had bought out a German company to eliminate some competition. The mill employed 200 people during this period. Key workers were housed in mill-owned houses in Arthur Terrace but the majority lived elsewhere in South Shields, Whitburn and Sunderland. (Mitchell 1981:3, 5)

A paper makers directory of 1922 confirmed that a wider range of paper was being produced than newsprint, a range that included banks, cartridges and casings, grease proof, MF & SC printings as well as fine news. By then the company had agents in London, Birmingham, Dublin and South Shields. Larger papermaking machines were installed to produce paper finished at 146 inch width. Mitchell (1981: 1) recalled that good quality paper was being produced here in the early twentieth century which seems to confirm this extended range. Overall it is suggested that some 300 tons of paper was being produced at these mills in Whitburn parish at this period.

Among other recollections Mitchell (1981: 2, 3) mentions wood pulp being imported from Canada in large bales, brought from the docks in the 'Marsden Rattler', an old steam engine that visited the paper mill and the local coal pit. Eight-wheeled Leyland lorries loaded with enormous rolls of paper, destined for the *Sunderland Echo* at Bridge Street in Sunderland, left the mill regularly.

Economic Depression and Closure

Eventually general economic depression in the 1930s and overwhelming competition among large, post-war combines of newsprint producers caused the mill to be closed in May 1933. Attempts at wallpaper manufacture found similar competition so closure could no longer be forestalled. The machines were dismantled and sold, the smaller machines being taken to Kilbargie in Scotland. (Shorter 1971: 175) In 1981 the only building remaining from the paper mill site was being used by the National Coal Board as a store.

Hartlepool Mill[90]

Compared with many other mills, that at Hartlepool was more sophisticated with its up-to-date machinery, level of financing, and corporate status; its proximity to chemical works, access to coal for fuel, and its location at the coast for importing materials and transporting the paper to buyers were vital to its success. Despite trade difficulties during the general depression of the 1920s and early 1930s, paper was produced here under the aegis of various proprietors until 1965.

In 1891 the Hartlepool Paper Co Ltd established a pulp works at Moreland Street in West Hartlepool, (Maidwell 1987: 14) with a view to making white paper. (Cornett 1908: 164) It was registered on the Stock Exchange in that year as the Hartlepools Pulp & Paper Co Ltd.[91] The position of this mill enabled it to take full advantage of the port on the coast to import materials needed for papermaking and for transporting coal for fuelling the power source, as well as sending finished paper to customers; (Shorter 1971: 151) it also boasted a railway link to its own sidings.[92]

Paper Production

Soon after it had been established the mill was able to make a wide range of paper qualities from its own and from imported pulps, including white and SC printings, cartridges, imitation parchments, MG skips, caps and envelope papers, using two Fourdrinier papermaking machines that could produce 86 inch and 96 inch width finished paper, and a 74 inch cylinder. (Maidwell 1957: 24; 1987: 15)

Under Excise no.256, the company advertised in paper makers trade directories offering white and toned printings, machine finished and super calendared papers, ES writings and cartridges, both glazed and unglazed. The smaller machine was soon upgraded to match the larger machine and also produce 96 inch width finished paper; this was recorded in tpaper makers directories of 1894 and 1896. In 1899, Walter Andrew, a senior member of this company, joined other British paper makers to visit some Scandinavian paper mills to compare methods and processes.[93] By 1901 a London agent had been appointed; four years later the company also offered bleached and unbleached paper, and declared an additional machine producing 74 inch width finished paper. In 1913 business was flourishing sufficiently for various extensions to be made to the mill.[94]

Alleged Infringement of Patent

An alleged infringement of patent caused the company some problems. Edward Partington and the Kellner & Partington Paper Pulp Co decided to sue the Hartlepools Pulp & Paper Co Ltd in 1895, a case that was heard in the Chancery Division of the High Court. Partington alleged that an infringement of a patent of August 1894 had occurred when Hartlepools Pulp & Paper Co Ltd had dealt with a problem of accumulating residue by using a method for which Kellner & Partington Paper Pulp Co had exclusive rights by virtue of a patent.[95]

The Hartlepool firm faced the problem that when boiling wood with bisulphate of lime a considerable quantity of amorphous resinous matter was left in the pulp. This problem was resolved by using paraffin in connection with sulphite pulp in order to avoid resin specks on the paper, as well as deposits on the Hollander beater and strainers, equipment that had then required constant cleaning. Hartlepools Pulp & Paper Co Ltd had been using a similar method since January 1894. Mr Makin, the manager knew that paraffin had been used in 1888, and had used it himself at the Union Works in Rochdale between 1889 and 1890; it had also been used at the Hull Pulp Co since December 1892. John Hamilton, Foreman at

Hartlepools Pulp & Paper Co, confirmed that it had been used there before 1894 'for making the stuff travel in the engine and for killing froth'. After considerable technical discussion it was adjudged that paraffin had been in use well before the patent, although for different advantages, so the 'patent clearly failed and the action with it, which was dismissed with costs'.[96]

Relations with Trade Unions

Several of the skilled employees belonged to the Amalgamated Society of Papermakers, the lesser skilled to their own trade union, the National Union of Paper Mill Workers (NUPMW). In April 1906 Mr W. Dyson, secretary of the NUPMW, wrote to Mr J. Makin, manager of the Hartlepools Pulp & Paper Co, to emphasise the high tension under which the men were working, and that he considered it essential to relieve the stress of the 'long drag' as the men dubbed it. He asked that the manager consider a shut down from Saturday lunch time until Monday morning to remove the need for Saturday afternoon and Sunday working; despite his persuasion this took several years to achieve. (Bundock 1959: 393-394)

During the following month another trade union tried to recruit new members. 'With the object of organising the paper mill workers of West Hartlepool, a well-attended meeting was held on Saturday evening under the auspices of the Dock, Wharf, Riverside & General Workers' Union'. The District Secretary pointed out the advantages of membership, and reminded the audience that the union had already secured improved conditions and wages for its members. 'At the close of the meeting those present joined the union, and other names were handed in of those unable to attend'.[97] It is not known whether there was any connection with the dispute over working hours or whether the recruitment drive by the Dock, Wharf, Riverside & General Workers Union was coincidental.

Success and the Depression

Business was good and a new chemical plant and pulp stores were added.[98] This apparent success lasted for some years until general economic depression and poor trade, the fall in demand for both the raw material and for paper, forced the company in to voluntary liquidation in 1920. In October that year the company capitalised its reserves: the accounts in brief showed the loss between 1 February and 21 April in 1920 to have been £24,486; sundry creditors owed £178,929; assets were shown as preliminary expenses £14,997, cash in hand £53, and debtors £46,853.[99]

The mill was then sold to the newly established Hartlepools Paper Mill Co Ltd and registered on the Stock Exchange.[100] It was stated in a paper maker's trade directory that in 1923 a papermaking machine of 110 inch width was added, presumably to extend the scope of paper that could be offered for sale. The state of trade did not favour the company and the business was subsequently acquired by Durham Paper Mills Ltd in 1926.[101] Production concentrated on specialist Kraft paper, glazed and unglazed, made on a 108 inch Fourdrinier machine and on two 120 inch MG machines, (Maidwell 1987: 15) but four machines were mentioned in a trade directory of 1926. Three years later in 1929, with the country in deep economic recession and papermaking concerns generally in some difficulty, the company failed to qualify any longer for the Stock Exchange Register and was struck off.[102]

Papermaking Ceases at Hartlepool

Durham Paper Mills Ltd continued in business despite uncertain trade, and to be listed in trade directories. The entry for 1934 is typical: the firm advertised unglazed Kraft and coloured, unglazed sulphites and coloured, MG sulphites, and MG Krafts, plain, ribbed or striped. In 1951 and 1961 the mill still produced Krafts on three machines, a 108 inch Fourdrinier and two 120 inch MGs. The concern was eventually taken over by the Inveresk Group via Olive & Partington Ltd. (Maidwell 1987: 15) Earlier in 1965 the company had 'stopped making Kraft and turned over to the manufacture of paper towelling', but finally ceased all production of all papers on 28 August 1965.[103]

Chapter 6
Review of Trends and Changes in County Durham Papermaking

During some two hundred years of making paper in County Durham it was the enterprise of prospective paper manufacturers investing in mills and risking the change from making paper by hand at a vat to virtually untried making by machine, facing possible vagaries of fire, flood, drought, escalating costs and a changing market, that drove the industry forward to achieve an importance for the county that has been previously and seriously underestimated. In many ways, but not all, its development mirrored that of the English papermaking industry generally.

The Market
In the early period the market for paper in England was usually supplied locally and this was the case in County Durham. The demand initially came mainly from the complex legal and administrative structures attached to the cathedral and palatine bishopric or from local industry. The rapid development of the coal trade in the eighteenth century on both Tyne and Wearside widened commercial markets that also created demands for newsprint and social stationery. Even before the railway development of the second and third decades of the nineteenth century, many manufacturers in County Durham were adapting to making paper by machine to meet the demands of the changing economy.

Raw Material

The increased production resulting from mechanisation to meet demand placed a strain on the traditional sources of raw materials: rags for better quality paper, canvas and cordage for brown paper. Advertisements encouraged 'genteel women' to save scraps of material from their sewing, and substantial rewards were offered for alternative sources of raw material. When in the 1860s Thomas Routledge of Ford Mill found a way to treat esparto grass from North Africa and Spain so that it could be used as a furnish for good quality white paper as well as for brown paper, he saved his own mill and others in the county, but also benefited English papermaking generally. Esparto was available in quantity and cheaper than rags so it became the best substitute raw material; also soda ash and bleaching powder used in its treatment were readily to hand in the north east. (Linsley 1994: 8)

From the late 1880s, although esparto grass continued to be used in some mills until the 1960s, import figures show it being supplanted by wood pulp, another material brought in through the ports of Newcastle, Sunderland and Hartlepool.[1]

Water

Water was essential to papermaking and mills with a regular supply of good, clear water were fortunate. In County Durham many mills had a reliable supply of water, but not all. Ford Mill in particular suffered an erratic water supply but counteracted it by repeatedly sinking boreholes, digging wells, creating drifts, and building reservoirs. Similarly manufacturers at Springwell Mill solved this problem by developing a system of filtre and reserve ponds. Every concern had to contend with the problem of treating and disposing of effluent after using the water, Hendon in particular.

Skilled Workforce

Evidence of the specific role played by the trade union, The Original Society of Papermakers (OSP), in the County Durham mills is rare before 1850 but, at that period, there were OSP members in seven of the seventeen mills working; by 1870 in five mills of eighteen and, after 1876, only in one mill, Wearmouth, until 1901. (See Appendix III) This is hardly surprising considering the rapid spread of mechanisation in the county but it meant that few employers were under pressure from that union.

There was only one serious strike among OSP controlled mills in the north of England, that in 1845/ 1846 because employers were diverging from long-established customs usually mutually accepted by employer and employees. It is believed that this led to Wearmouth Mill being set on fire in 1846, and the instigator being dismissed from membership by the OSP. (Maidwell 1987: 7) Otherwise strikes did not seem to occur until the unionisation of skilled machine men in the 1860s and unskilled workers in the 1880s and 1890s, then usually for fewer hours and higher wage rates.

Finance

Until its abolition in 1861 all manufacturers were affected by the Excise Duty on paper. From the time of the Napoleonic wars there was a steady rise in the costs of raw materials, wage bills, and outlay on machinery as well as for repairs and renewals. The Durham manufacturers participated in the attempts by the Master Paper Makers nationally to control the price of raw material by boycotting rag merchants, but this failed through lack of solidarity.

Wage costs were another burden as the vat-trained craftsmen were paid at almost the same level as the most highly paid skilled artisans, the mechanics. Opportunities for work in vat mills diminished and many vat-trained paper makers transferred to machine papermaking. They remained members of the OSP, their craftsmanship still recognised, and so these members were paid at or near the wage rates agreed for OSP hand paper makers. However, northern wages in this industry were generally appreciably lower than those paid in the south of England. Coleman (1958: 297-307) gives some detailed comparisons.

The cost of repairs and renewal of equipment, with other unanticipated payments, added to financial worries. With wood, paper and raw material in every mill, all inflammable, insurance was essential and premiums were high. County Durham mills were not exempt from such hazards. Records located so far show that in sixteen mills extensive fires broke out. Those situated on the rivers Team, Tyne and Derwent were particularly prone to being flooded, Butterby Mill was blown down in a gale, and boiler explosions at Fellingshore and Ford mills caused considerable damage and loss of life.

In common with manufacturers in other industries who mechanised and adopted steam for power, the paper manufacturers had to entice others, financiers and men from integrated businesses, in to their concerns to spread the financial risk. For example, Team Valley offered directorships to paper merchants and at Ford Mill directors were appointed from the major papermaking firm and stationers, John Dickinson. Shares were offered in Marsden and Ford mills to attract financial investment.

Output and Expansion

From a slow but steady development in the eighteenth century, growth in the paper industry accelerated during the last quarter to meet increasing demand from expanding industrial enterprise, helped by a number of technical innovations in papermaking. This expansion was reflected in the rapidly rising number of licences for papermaking issued by the Excise authorities between 1785 and 1800 to businesses in England. According to Shorter (1957: 72) this was an increase of just under 10 per cent nationally compared with a 55 per cent increase in County Durham in the same period. (See Appendix I and Appendix II)

The scale and pattern of the industry in England changed from that of mainly small one or two vat mills in relatively rural places to larger mills, amalgamated businesses or conglomerates, that established their firms in industrial areas, nearer to major rivers, ports, and, once the system had been developed, to railways. This was mirrored in County Durham, but with more alacrity, mainly because some two thirds of the work here was in brown paper and then also newsprint. Thirteen mills closed in the 1830s, six of which had been among the earliest established, including Croxdale, the oldest recorded; seven had only been established within the previous thirty to forty years.

County Durham was among the busiest counties; output increased from 4,000 tons of paper in 1838 to 8,000 tons in 1864, half the total United Kingdom production as noted by Linsley (1994: 7). This expansion, Coleman (1958: 129) comments, was paralleled by a marked increase in the numbers employed in papermaking in leading counties. In Dye's work (2000: 11) abstracts from census returns for County Durham show that 118 paper makers [the craftsmen] were recorded in 1831, 192 in 1841, 245 in 1851, and only four fewer by 1861. Lancashire was the only other county to record such a major increase in that period.

Paper manufacture became dependent on the proximity of coal for power, good rail links to Tyneside and coastal ports, and the supporting structure was provided by the proximity of other industries such as the chemical industry, particularly as, Linsley (1994: 9) states, the industry became more dependent on bleaching materials, chemicals to treat esparto grass, barites as a filler in the furnish and Hypo derived from waste products. These provided the supporting structure needed to serve the paper manufacturers. Another characteristic was a degree of integration between related activities. Marsden Mill is a good example, combining pulp and papermaking with chemical production and preparation of other substances used in the processes. By the end of the 1870s only five mills remained that had been established more than a hundred years earlier. By 1900, apart from Lintzford Mill and two at Shotley Grove on the River Derwent, the remaining thirteen mills were in the Tyne and eastern port areas.

The Decline of Papermaking in the County

The trend to become mainly larger scale and more specialist continued in England during the first half of the twentieth century. In County Durham several smaller mills closed, some larger mills could not compete and others, such as Langley, were sold because their sites offered more lucrative coal or mineral rights, or were premium locations for other businesses such as shipbuilders as at Wearmouth Mill wharfside. Only one new mill opened during the first quarter of the century, Pembertons of Gateshead in 1922 which became a waste paper business in conjunction with making brown paper products. Demand was boosted during the first world war, deflated during the depression, then partly revived by the needs of the second world war. Of the 45 mills located in the county, of which 18 were in pairs, only five were still working in the period after the second world war and only one by 1971. Hendon was the last mill to close in 1980.

Analysis of the Number of Mills at Different Periods

An analysis of the number of paper mills functioning at particular periods shows the rise and decline of papermaking in the county over some two hundred years. (See Appendix I and Appendix II) Three mills began to produce paper here in the seventeenth century: Croxdale in the 1670s, then Lintzford in 1695, followed by Chopwell in 1697. There was a gradual increase in the number of mills during the eighteenth century; the most new mills in one decade was eight in the 1790s. The most active period of papermaking was between 1770 and 1870 when eighteen or more mills were working, at least twenty five or more from 1780 until 1830 and, in the peak decade the 1830s, thirty three mills produced paper. No new mills have been included after 1900 so the decline from sixteen mills working in 1900 to one in 1980 is not an entirely true picture, but is indicative of the decline of papermaking in the county.

The duration of papermaking at the paper mills, estimated in decades as some opening and closing dates are a little uncertain, is in the range of two to seventeen decades, with the exception of

Lintzford Mill that operated for nearly twenty four decades. The average duration is eleven decades, but more mills produced paper for nine decades than for any other length of time. The length of the production period does not seem to correlate particularly with the age of the mills.

An Important Industry in County Durham's History

In a number of ways the nature and timing of papermaking development in County Durham can be seen to reflect the history of this industry in England generally. The story of each paper mill mirrors at least some aspect of this history, whether scientific, industrial, economic or human, and the reliance on the elements essential to papermaking. Considering the 'life stories' of the mills also points up the degree of integration with other industries at different stages and the importance of local context.

Perhaps the place of papermaking in County Durham's history may best be summarised in the remarks made by Atkinson (1974: II, 272) when referring to the few paper mills ruins that could still be detected; he considered them '… the slight remains of what was once an important industry'.

Appendix I

Duration of Mill Production 1670-1980

	1670	1700	1800	1900	1980

Croxdale
Lintzford
Chopwell
Egglestone
Blackhall
Gibside
Fellingshore
Lamesley
Lendings
Relly
Shotley G.
Langley
Hett
Tudhoe
Urpeth
Cornforth
Butterby
Ewhurst
Moorsley
Stonebridge
Snowdon
Thinford
Washington
Aycliffe
Blackwall
Whitehill
Tyne
Wearmouth
Egglescliffe
Ford
Springwell
Team
Hendon
Swalwell
Marsden
Hartlepool

Appendix II

Number of Mills Working Per Decade 1670-1980

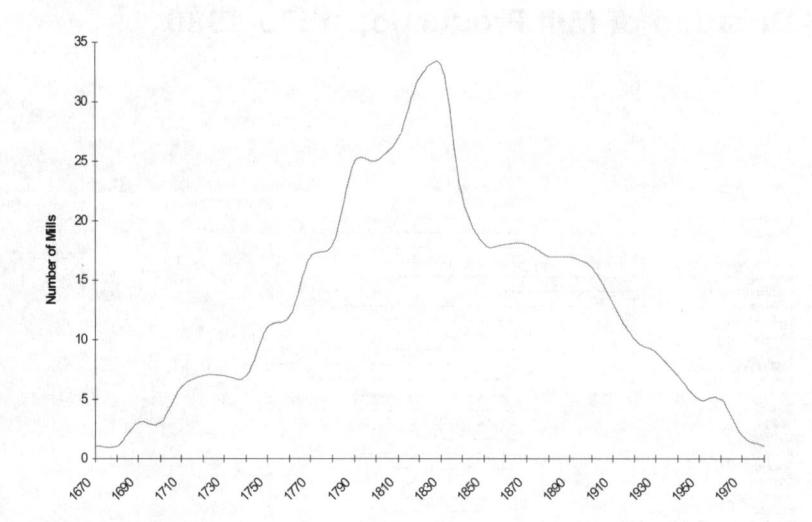

Appendix III

Number of Paper Makers (Craftsmen) Employed who were Members of a Trade Union

Paper Mill	Dates: no. members employed	Trade Union
Fellingshore Mill	1867-1876 3 men	OSP
Ford Mill	1847-1867 4-8 men	OSP
	1891 – 76 men	NUPMW
	1892 – 40 men	
	1893 – 60 men	
Hartlepool Mill	1892 – 40 men	NUPMW
	1893 – 30 men	
	1896 – 1 man	ASPM
Hendon Mill	1891 – 120 men	NUPMW
	1892 – 52 men	
	1893 – 120 men, 11 boys	
	1896-1899 1 man	ASPM
Hett Mill	1847 – 1man	OSP
Langley Mill	1847-1874 11 men – 3 men	OSP
Lintzford Mill	1847-1871 1 man	OSP
	1891-1893 13-11 men	NUPMW
Moorsley Mill	1847-1875 3 men	OSP
	1877 – 2 men	UBPM
Shotley Bridge Mill	1877 – 2 men	UBPM
	1891 – 28 men, 8 boys	NUPMW
	1892 – 13 men, 3 boys	
	1893 – 13 men	
	1896 – 2 men	ASPM
	1897 – 1 man	
Springwell Mill	1847-1854 14 men	OSP
	1891 – 35 men, 32 boys	NUPMW
	1892 – 37 men	
	1893 – 7 men, 11 boys	
Teams (Low) Mill	1868 – 3 men	OSP
	1896 – 1 man	ASPM
Tyne Mill	1848 – 1 man	OSP
	1891 – 38 men, 15 boys	NUPMW
	1892 – 29 men, 12 boys	
	1893 – 30 men, 5 boys	
Urpeth Mill	1862-1863 2 men	OSP
Wearmouth Mill	1852-1901 3 men	OSP
Whitehill Mill	1857-1858 2 men	OSP

Bibliography

Anderson, R. ed. (1975), *A History of Blaydon,* Winlaton & District Local History Society.

Armstrong, D. (1864) *The Industrial Resources of the District of the Three Northern Rivers, the Tyne, Wear & Tees, Including the Reports of the Local Manufacturers,* Paper read before The British Association in 1863.

Atkinson, F. (1974), *The Industrial Archaeology of North East England: The Counties of Northumberland & Durham & the Cleveland District of Yorkshire,* David & Charles.

Ayris, I., & Linsley, S.M. (1994), *A Guide to the Industrial Archaeology of Tyne & Wear,* Newcastle City Council.

Bailey, M. R. (March 1990), *Robert Stephenson & Co. & the Paper-Drying Machine in the 1820s,* History of the Book Trade in the North.

Beamish, H. (2001), The Gibside Paper Mill in *Northumbrian Mills* no.17, Jan 2001, pp.5-10.

Bennett, G. Clavering, F. & Rounding, A. (1990), *A Fighting Trade: Rail Transport in Tyne Coal 1600-1800,* Portcullis Press.

Bourn, W. (1896), *The History of the Parish of Ryton.*

Bower, P. (1993), *Egglestone Abbey Paper Mill: Engraving from a Sketch by Turner,* History of the Book Trade in the North.

Bower, P. (1994), British Paper Mills: Egglestone Abbey Paper Mill, Co. Durham, in *The Quarterly* no.13, Dec 1994, British Association of Paper Historians, pp.15-17.

Bundock, C. J. (1959), *The Story of The National Union of Printing, Bookbinding & Paper Workers*, OUP.

Chapman, V. (1977), *Rural Durham: Beside the Stream*, Durham County Council.

Chester, C. A. (1976), *History of Ford Paper Mill: The Introduction of Esparto Grass for Papermaking*, History of the Book Trade in the North.

Clavering, E. (1999), *Papermaking & the Coal Trade*.

Clavering, E. & Rounding, A. (1995), Early Tyne Industrialisation in *Archaeologia Aeliana* vol. XXIII, pp.249-268.

Coleman, D. C. (1958), *The British Paper Industry 1495-1860: A Study in Industrial Growth*, Clarendon Press.

Cornett, J. P. (1908), Local Paper Mills: Antiquities of Sunderland & Its Vicinity in *Sunderland Antiquarian Society*, IX (1908), pp.160-167.

Dingle, A. T. (1973), *Egglescliffe: A Short History of the Village*.

Dodd, J. J. (1899), *History of the Urban District of Spennymoor* (pub. Privately, Darlington).

Duncan, J. / Maidwell, C. F. (1952), Notes made by Duncan for Maidwell, in Maidwell (1987).

Dye, I. (2001), Census Abstracts as Indicators of Employment in Papermaking in the English Counties 1831-1861 in *Studies in British Paper History: The Exeter Papers* Vol.II, British Association of Paper Historians.

Evans, J. (1955), *The Endless Web: John Dickinson & Co. Ltd. 1804-1954*, Jonathan Cape.

Flinn, M. W. (1955), Industry & Technology in the Derwent Valley of Durham & Northumberland in the 18th Century in *Transactions of the Newcomen Society for the Study of the History of Engineering & Technology*, Vol. XXIX 9th June, 1955.

Fordyce, T. (1867), *Local Records; or, Historical Register of Remarkable Events Which Have Occurred in Northumberland & Durham, Newcastle upon Tyne & Berwick-upon-Tweed 1833-1866,* Newcastle upon Tyne.

Fordyce, T. (1876), *Local Records; or Historical Register of Remarkable Events Which Have Occurred in Northumberland & Durham, Newcastle upon Tyne & Berwick-upon-Tweed 1867-1875,* Newcastle upon Tyne.

Fordyce, W. (1855, 1857), *History & Antiquities of the County Palatine of Durham.*

Gooch, L. (1989), Papists & Profits: The Catholics of Durham & Industrial Development in *Bulletin,* Durham County Local History Society, no.42, May 1989, pp.49-56.

Hewitt, J. M. (nd), *The Township of Heworth,* Portcullis Press.

Hills, R. L. (1988), *Papermaking in Britain 1488-1988: A Short History,* The Athlone Press.

Hyslop, R. (1909), Notes on Bowater's Mill in *Antiquities of Sunderland* vol. X, Journal of the Sunderland Antiquities Society.

Kirby, D. A. (1968), 'The Economic Use of Water Resources in the Wear Basin & its Tributaries'. PhD Thesis, Durham University.

Lewis, S. (1833, 1840 & 1849 edns.), *Topographical Dictionary of England.*

Linforth, H. / Maidwell, C. F. (1987), Details from Company Archives extracted by Linforth for Maidwell.

Linsley, S. M. (1989), *Chronology Notes.*

Linsley, S. M. (1994), *Lecture Notes on Papermaking in the North East.*

Lister, G. (1946), *Consett & District, North-West Durham: A History from A.D. 1183 to 1945,* Pelaw on Tyne.

Lodge, M. (2004), *Paper Makers of the Parish: An Account of Papermaking in the Vicinity of Tudhoe Village*; Lecture to Tudhoe & Spennymoor Local History Society.

MacKenzie, E. & Ross, M. (1834), *History of Durham: An Historical, Topographical & Descriptive View of the County Palatine of Durham*, Vols. I & II.

McCord, N. (1979), *North East England: Economic & Social History*, Batsford.

Maidwell, C. F. (1957), *A Short History of Papermaking in the North East*, Newcastle.

Maidwell, C. F. (1987), *Some Notes on Papermaking in County Durham*, History of the Book Trade in the North.

Maidwell, C. F. (1990), *Some Notes on Papermaking in Yorkshire*, History of the Book Trade in the North.

Manders, F. W. D. (1973), *A History of Gateshead Corporation*.

Maughan, J. (1955), *A History of Blaydon District* serialised in *Blaydon Courier*.

Milburn, G. & Miller, S. eds. (1988), *Sunderland - River, Town & People*, Sunderland Borough Council.

Mitchell, G. (1981), *Potted Memories of a Whitburn Industry*, (ts. in TWAS).

Mitchell, W. C. (1919, reprint 1972), *History of Sunderland*.

Moore, T. (1988), *The Industrial Past of Shotley Bridge & Consett*, Derwentdale Local History Society.

Neasham, G. (1881), *The History & Biography of West Durham*.

Neasham, G. (1893), *North Country Sketches*.

Pevsner, N. (1953), *The Buildings of England: County Durham*.

Richardson, M. A. (1843), *Local Historian's Table Book*, London.

Richardson, R. M. (1908), The Hutton Family (Papermakers) in *Sunderland Antiquarian Society* 13th October, 1908, pp.168-179.

Richardson, W. H. (1864), On the Manufacture of Paper in *The Industrial Resources of the Tyne, Wear & Tees* by Armstrong, Sir W. G.

Richmond, T. (1968), *The Local Records of Stockton & Neighbourhood.*

Ridley, L. G. (nd), *Local History of the Derwent Valley.*

Shorter, A. H. (1957), *Paper Mills & Paper Makers in England 1495-1800,* The Paper Publications Society, vol.VI, Hilversum.

Shorter, A.H. (1960), Paper Mills in England in the 1690s in *The Paper Maker: Annual Review, pp.5-9.*

Shorter, A. H. (1971), *Paper Making in the British Isles: An Historical & Geographical Study,* David & Charles.

Simmons, H. E. (nd) compiler, Collection of records relating to British windmills and water mills, Co. Durham section, at Science Museum Library, London.

Stirk, J. V. (1999), Industrial Relations in a Trade Craft: The Original Society of Papermakers 1800-1948, PhD Thesis, London University.

Surtees, H. Conyers (1925), *The History of the Parish of Tudhoe &Sunnybrow in the County Palatine of Durham.*

Surtees, R. *History & Antiquities of the County Palatine of Durham,* Vol. I (1816) II (1820) III (1823) IV (1840).

Sykes, J. (1866), *Local Records; or, Historical Register of Remarkable Events, Which Have Occurred in Northumberland & Durham, Newcastle upon Tyne, & Berwick-upon-Tweed 1800-1832.*

Taylor, J. & Richardson, W. H. Proceedings of the British Association, Newcastle Meeting, Aug/Sept 1863.

Thomas, S. (1997), Thomas Berwick's Use of Papers in *Cherryburn Times,* The Newsletter of the Berwick Society Autumn 1997, vol. 3 no.4.

Tillmans, M. (1978), *Bridge Hall Mills: Three Centuries of Paper & Cellulose Manufacture,* (pub. privately).

Turnbull, L. (1978), *Chopwell's Story,* Gateshead MBC, Dept. of Education.

Tyne Industries – *The Tyneside, Newcastle and District: An Epitome of Results and Manual of Commerce* (1889) Historic Publishing Co.

Wade, F. J. (1968), *The Story of Tanfield & Beamish*.

Walker, C. B. (1984), Ford Paper Mill 1836-1971 in *Antiquities of Sunderland vol.29* pp46-73.

Wallis, P. J. (1981), *The Book Trade in Northumberland & Durham to 1860: A Supplement to C. J. Hunt's Biographical Dictionary*, History of the Book Trade in the North.

Wardell, J. W. (1957), *A History of Yarm*.

References

Introduction pages 1-16
1. This refers to the ancient county of Durham.
2. Material for the next two sections is from Shorter (1957) and Hills (1988).
3. Material for this section is from Shorter (1957), Coleman (1958), Shorter (1971), Hills (1988); examples are from the text of mill histories.
4. Clavering P/L 15 Feb 2000.
5. DUL: Will of James Cooke 1805.
6. CKS: Balston MSS: MPM & Minutes of meetings. For more details of OSP and the relationship with employers cf Stirk, 1999.
7. *The World's Pulp & Paper Industry* (2 Nov 1898) 186.
8. The earliest known name of a mill has been used as a title, but subsequent names occur in the text.

Chapter 1 pages 17-48
1. NZ 273373.
2. DCRO: D/Sa/E/634,635.
3. DCRO: D/Sa/E/28.
4. DCRO: D/Sa/E/634.
5. St Oswald, Durham City Parish Register 1678.
6. DCRO: D/Sa/D/387, 27 September 1682.
7. DCRO: D/Sa/E/460.
8. Durham Recusant Estates, *Surtees Society Transactions* no.136: 175, 9,10.
9. DCRO: D/Sa/E/460.
10. Durham Recusant Estates, *Surtees Society Transactions* no.133: 173, 201.
11. DCRO: D/Sa/E/460.
12. Durham Recusant Estates, *Surtees Society Transactions* no.139: 175, 27.

13. *Newcastle Courant* 14 February 1756.
14. DCRO: D/Sa/E/401,402.
15. *Newcastle Journal* 17-24 September 1768.
16. DCRO: D/Sa/E/403-407.
17. The damp paper was usually dried on cow hair lines to avoid making marks on the paper. Using laths for drying seems unlikely, especially as 3,000 laths would be an extraordinarily high number for such a purpose in a two-vat mill. It is possible that the cow hair lines were strung from laths but, even taking that in to consideration, one would still question the number of laths ordered.
18. DCRO: D/Sa/E/636,637.
19. DCRO: D/Sa/E/698.
20. DCRO: D/Sa/E/388; *Newcastle Courant* 11 January 1772.
21. DCRO: D/Sa/E/408-418,420,421.
22. DCRO: D/Sa/E/389.
23. BL: Add.Ms.15054 Myvyrian Mss.List; Shorter (1957) 163.
24. DCRO: D/Sa/E/390.
25. *Newcastle Courant* 20 June 1795.
26. DCRO: D/Sa/E/391.
27. LG 2 August 1803.
28. DCRO: D/Sa/E/392,393.
29 DCRO: D/Sa/E/639.
30. DCRO: D/Sa/E/392.
31. EGL 8 Oct 1816.
32. EGL 21 October 1824.
33. DCRO: EP/DU/ SO 112/2/162,171,172,173 23 May 1835.
34. LG 27 June & 18 July 1826.
35. EGL 20 March 1828; 17 February 1829.
36. St Oswald, Durham City Parish Register 1818.
37. EGL 28 November 1832, 27 October 1837.
38. DCRO: EP/Mer 43/1-2.
39. DCRO: D/Fle 2/6/106.
40. NZ 150572.
41. Anderson, (1975) 167.
42. Anderson, (1975) 167.
43. Anderson, (1975) 167-168.
44. Newcastle Directory 1811.
45. Bodleian Library, Oxford: Gough Adds. Fol. A252 no.77.
46. CKS:Balston MSS: MPM: 13 Jun 1803.

References

47. DCRO: D/CG/7/1586.
48. DCRO: D/CG/7/1586.
49. EGL 30 Nov 1841, 1 Dec 1842, 1 Feb 1844.
50. Bradshaw's 1853, Kent's 1862, 1868 & 1871, Kelly's 1873 directories; PMD 1866, 1876, 1894-1899.
51. Anderson, (1975) 167-168.
52. *The Paper Record & Wood Pulp News* XI no.2 (NS) (July 1895) 55.
53. *The Paper Record & Wood Pulp News* XI no.2 (NS) (July 1895) 54.
54. HLRO: HofC 1852.
55. DCRO: D/EP/Win 3/7.
56. *The Paper Record & Wood Pulp News* XI no.2 (NS) (July 1895) 54.
57. *The Times* Engineering Supplement no.454 (5 November 1913) 23.
58. Anderson, (1975) 168.
59. NZ 117579.
60. 6 inch Ordnance Survey map 1856.
61. P/L Mr. T. Berg to Co. Durham Archivist 24 Sept 1977.
62. Bodleian Library, Oxford: Gough Adds. Fol. A252 no.77.
63. SFIP 746069, 3 Mar 1803.
64. DCRO: D/CG 6/375.
65. DCRO: EP/Win 3/7.
66. NZ 064151.
67. TNA: Recovery Roll, Trin Geo I rot,64 & 47 Geo III rot, 327: CP 43/537.
68. VCH: Yorkshire North Riding (1914) I,III.
69. Account Book of Morritt family at Rokeby Hall, Yorkshire, quoted from Bower (1994).
70. *Kentish Gazette* 27 Jun 1809; *Bath Chronicle* 29 Jun 1809.
71. *Bath Chronicle* 29 Jun 1809.
72. TNA: CUST 48/48/123.
73. NZ 122579.
74. SFIP 263906, 19 November 1768.
75. DCRO: EP/Win 3/7.
76. DCRO: D/X/530.
77. NZ 178595.
78. Unless otherwise stated, details of this mill's history are from the Strathmore Estate records under the following references:
    DCRO: D/St/C1/4/2;
    DCRO: D/St/D13/1/1:|
    DCRO: D/St/E5/3,7,8,9,10,11,12;
    DCRO: D/St/E5/5/3,6,9,10,11

DCRO: D/St/E5/18/2,3,4(3,4,12),5,6,7,8,9,10,12,13
DCRO: D/St/P6/1/3.
79. P/L Dr. M. Wills, 28 September 1999.
80. Although used here as an occupational title, 'paper miller' is not a standard term for a paper maker or paper manufacturer, nor one that is usually used colloquially.
81. P/L Dr. E. Clavering 12 January 2000.
82. P/L Dr. M. Wills 28 September 1999.
83. P/L Dr. M. Wills 28 September 1999.
84. Paper houses for growing melons are described in Gilbert White, *Garden Kalender 1751-1773* (Scolar Press) and in Thomas Mawe, *Every Man His Own Gardener* (1717).
85. *Newcastle Journal* 3 April 1742.
86. P/L Dr. M. Wills 28 September 1999.

Chapter 2 pages 49-84

1. NZ 285627.
2. EGL 8 Oct 1816.
3. *Tyne Industries* (1889) 173.
4. *Newcastle Courant* 1 Aug 1795.
5. Shorter (1971) 110.
6. Sykes Local Records II,18.
7. *The Times* 27 Dec 1803.
8. *Tyne Industries* (1889) 173.
9. LG 18-21 Jul 1807, 24 May 1808.
10. Sykes Local Records I,52.
11. *Tyne Industries* (1889):173; EGL 22 Dec 1821.
12. LG 24 Feb 1832.
13. *Tyne Industries* (1889) 173; Cornett (1908) 164.
14. *Tyne Industries* (1889) 173.
15. EGL 28 Nov 1832, 16 Mar 1833, 16 Mar 1834.
16. MacKenzie & Ross (1834) I,24.
17. *Newcastle Courant* 16 Dec 1837.
18. EGL 29 Jun 1848.
19. PMD and Ward's Trade Directory 1850-1896.
20. Reports of the Juries of the 1851 Exhibition, London (1852) Class XVII,431.
21. HLRO: HofC 1852.
22. *Tyne Industries* (1889) 173.

23. PMD 1869.
24. OSP 07/1876; Tyne Industries (1889) 173.
25. *The Gateshead Observer* 13 May 1876.
26. *The Gateshead Observer* 20 May 1876.
27. *The Gateshead Observer* 3 Jun 1876.
28. *The Gateshead Observer* 3 Jun 1876.
29. *Tyne Industries* (1889) 173.
30. PMD 1878.
31. PMD 1882, 1896.
32. *Tyne Industries* (1889) 173.
33. PMD 1897.
34. *The Paper Maker* 3 Jul 1902: XXIV,40; The Engineer 11 Jun 1909: CVII,605-606.
35. PMD 1902, 1903.
36. NZ 255573.
37. BCA: Clarke Collection MS 2092 Lamesley.
38. DUL: Durham Marriage Bonds 1753,1767,1787.
39. First Newcastle Directory 1778; Universal British Directory of Trade, Commerce & Manufacture 1791.
40. SFIP 649066, 1 Dec 1795.
41. CKS: Balston MSS: MPM 13 Jun 1803.
42. SFIP 755168, 24 Oct 1803.
43. *Durham County Advertiser* 6 Jan 1816.
44. EGL 8 Oct 1817, 6 Nov 1823.
45. EGL 17 Jun 1825.
46. LG 14 Feb & 9 Mar 1826.
47. EGL 3 May 1826, 3 May 1827.
48. EGL 29 Jan 1830.
49. NZ 055155.
50. *Newcastle Journal* 25 December 1756 & 1 January 1757.
51. LG 20-23 June 1789.
52. *Newcastle Courant* 15 April 1797.
53. *Newcastle Courant* 9 March 1799.
54. LG 6 June 1815.
55. NZ 257419.
56. P/L Mr. I. Walker 12 Oct 1991.
57. DCRO: D/Fle 2/15/4.
58. *Newcastle Courant* 3 Jan 1795.

59. EGL 8 Oct1816.
60. DUL: Dean & Chapter Registered Deed no.219,785; 24 Sep 1817; 219,778; 12 & 13 May 1819.
61. DCRO: D/Fle 2/15/1.
62. DCRO: D/Fle 2/15/4.
63. EGL 11 Jul 1822.
64. DCRO: D/Fle 2/15/4.
65. LG 27 Jun 1826.
66. DCRO: D/Fle 2/15/4.
67. *Durham County Advertiser* 12 & 15 Jul 1826.
68. DCRO: D/Fle 2/15/1.
69. EGL 3 May 1827, 20 Mar 1828; Parsons & White Trade Directory 1827; LG 26 Jun 1827; PMD 1828.
70. EGL 11 Feb 1829; DCRO: D/Fle 2/15/1.
71. DCRO: D/Fle 2/15/2.
72. EGL 9 Dec 1830, 28 Nov 1834; DCRO: EP/DU/SO/112/17/168.
73. DCRO: D/Fle 2/15/3.
74. DCRO: D/Fle 2/15/2.
75. DCRO: D/Fle 2/15/3.
76. DCRO: EP/DU/SO/1/21,2; P/L Mr. I. Walker 12 Oct 1991.
77. DCRO: D/Fle 2/15/4.
78. LG 22 July 1845.
79. DCRO: D/Fle 2/15/1,4.
80. HLRO: HofC 1852; EGL 23 Feb 1846.
81. DUL: Dean & Chapter, Deeds nos. 219777, 219778; 27 Sep 1862; P/L Mr. I. Walker 12 Oct 1991.
82. PMD 1850, 1860,1864, 1866,1875, 1876, 1885; Whellan Trade Directory 1876, 1879.
83. *A Descriptive Account of Durham & District* (nd) 26.
84. DUL: Dean & Chapter Deed no. 284,699; 1 Mar 1899.
85. DCRO: EP/BP001.
86. High Mill: NZ 085519; Low Mill: NZ 087521.
87. BL: Add. Mss. 15054 Myvyrian Mss.
88. *The Paper Makers' Circular* 10 Jun 1899: XXIX no.340,256.
89. Local News Cuttings 1899: vol.598, 316-317.
90. *The Paper Makers'* Circular 10 Jun 1899: XXIX no.340,256.
91. Local News Cuttings 1899: vol. 598, 316-317.
92. EGL 29 Jan 1830; 28 Nov 1832; 30 Nov 1861.

93. Sykes Local Records: 15 Jul 1828.
94. *Newcastle Courant* 19 Jul 1828.
95. DCRO: D/Bo/G96/232,233.
96. HLRO: Royal Commission in to the Employment of Children 1843: 28 May, no.119, paras. 23 & 57.
97. EGL 9 Jan 1830.
98. LG 31 May 1839.
99. EGL 1832.
100. HLRO: HofC 1852.
101. *The Paper Makers' Circular* 10 Jun 1899: XXIX no.340,256.
102. PMD 1862, 1872, 1882, 1890, 1894, 1898, 1900, 1904.
103. *The Paper Record & Wood Pulp News* Jul 1895: XI no.2(NS),55.
104. *The Paper Makers'* Circular 10 Jun 1899: XXIX no.340,256.
105. *The Paper Record & Wood Pulp News* Jul 1895:XI no.2(NS)54/55.
106. *The World's Pulp & Paper Industry* 15 Jul 1899:9.
107. P/L Professor A. Crocker 22 Aug 2000.
108. A Paper-Making Centenary: The Story of Shotley Grove & Lintzford in *The World's Pulp & Paper Industry* 15 Jul 1899: 9/10.
109. *The Stationer* 5 Aug 1868: 86.
110. *The Paper Record* 8 Oct 1892: VIII no.4,154.
111. A Paper-Making Centenary: The Story of Shotley Grove & Lintzford in *The World's Pulp & Paper Industry* 15 Jul 1899: 9/10.
112. *The Paper Record & Wood Pulp News* Jul 1895: XI no.2(NS)55.
113. *The Paper Record & Wood Pulp News* Jul 1895: XI no.2(NS)55.
114. *West Hartlepool Northern Daily Mail*, 23 May 1906.
115. *Durham County Advertiser* 15 Aug 1834.
116. *The Paper Record & Wood Pulp News* Jul 1895: XI no.2(NS)55.
117. *The Paper Maker & British Paper Trade Journal* 2 Jul 1906, vol.XXXII no.1,81.
118. PMD 1907-1917.
119. St Cuthbert's, Benfieldside Parish Magazine, July 1888.
120. NZ 258408.
121. DCRO: D/X487/1/77.
122. SFIP 380938, 4 Mar 1777.
123. DCRO: D/X/487/1/78,80.
124. DCRO: D/X/487/1/81,83.
125. REXFI 108151, 15 Sep 1788.
126. REXFI 174434, 3 May 1800.

127. REXFI 235238, 24 Dec 1807.
128. Whitehead's Trade Directory 1790.
129. CKS: Balston MSS: MPM 13 Jun 1803.
130. DCRO: D/X/487/1/88.
131. HLRO: HC 351 (1837) xx,35: Report of the Select Committee on Fourdrinier's Patent.
132. DCRO: D/X/487/1/90.
133. *Durham County Advertiser* 26 Apr 1828.
134. EGL 28 Nov 1832.
135. DCRO: EP/DU/SO 112/2.
136. DCRO: D/Br/P/140/112.
137. DCRO: D/X/487/1/92,93.
138. HLRO: HofC 1852.
139. 1861 Census: RG9 3736 f64v.
140. PMD 1850s,1860s,1874.
141. LG 11 May 1875.
142. LG May 1875, 1876; PMD 1875,1876.
143. Abstract of Particulars of Langley Mill and Colliery (n.d.). Transcription by Mr. T. Hay from a Durham Trade Directory 1876. As the railway opened in 1872, John Smith was declared bankrupt in 1875, and the solicitor who signed this document died early in 1876, it is thought to have been a document of c.1875.
144. Craigs's PMD 1876.
145. DCRO: D/X/487/1/95; On the back of this document is a beautiful, large coloured map with the North East railway line shown running across, parallel with and just below Langley Bridge.
146. DCRO: D/X/487/1/94,97,98.

Chapter 3 pages 85-120

1. NZ 292370.
2. *The Parliamentary Gazetteer of England & Wales 1840-1843* (1843) II, 358.
3. 6 inch Ordnance Survey Map 1857.
4. DUL: Dean & Chapter Muniments, Miscellaneous Charters 6417.
5. *Newcastle Courant* 3 Apr 1779.
6. P/L Miss S. Lister 10 Apr 2002; CKS: Balston MSS: MPM 13 Jun 1803.
7. DUL: ASC: DPRI/1/1807/C21/1-5.
8. Several members of this Cooke family were recorded on monumental inscriptions in St John the Evangelist churchyard, Kirk Merrington.

9. DCRO: D/Sa/E/847.
10. LG 26 Apr & 20 Jul 1817.
11. EGL 8 Oct 1816.
12. EGL 4 Aug 1817.
13. EGL 31 Dec 1818.
14. LG 7 Jun & 1 Jul 1825.
15. LG 14 Feb & 9 Mar 1826.
16. EGL 2 Apr 1825,1 Jan 1832,28 Nov 1832, 28 Nov 1833.
17. EGL 30 Apr 1835.
18. DCRO: EP/Mer 43/1,2.
19. LG 28 Jan & 4 Feb 1842.
20. EGL 1 Feb 1844.
21. EGL 30 Apr & 13 May 1847.
22. 1851 census: HO107 2390 f93v.
23. PMD 1850, 1853.
24. HLRO: HofC 1852.
25. NZ 253357.
26. DCRO: D/Sa/D/941; Further detailed scrutiny of this group of papers might elicit further information.
27. DCRO: D/Sa/D/940.
28. DCRO: D/Sa/D/943.
29. CKS: Balston MSS: MPM 13 Jun 1803.
30. DCRO: D/Sa/D/944.
31. DCRO: D/Sa/D951.
32. DCRO: D/Sa/D/956/1,2.
33. *Durham County Advertiser* 14 Oct 1831.
34. HLRO: House of Commons Parliamentary (or Sessional) Papers of 1831 vol.XV.
35. EGL 28 Nov 1832.
36. *Newcastle Courant* 15 Mar 1834.
37. EGL 3 Feb 1836.
38. Wallis (1981) 8.
39. DCRO: D/ Fle 2/18/35.
40. DCRO: D/Fle 2/18/44.
41. EGL 1 Feb 1844.
42. DCRO: D/Sa/E 119/23,24; D/Sa/E 121/1,6.
43. DCRO: D/Fle 2/18/46; Some words are difficult to decipher.
44. DCRO: D/Fle 2/18/48.

45. NZ 231539.
46. Ordnance Survey 6 inch map 1857, pub.1861.
47. DUL: SB 848/1.
48. CKS: Balston MSS:MPM 13 Jun 1803.
49. Beamish Museum Archives, Chester-le-Street: Urpeth Mill papers, items 7, 28.
50. PMD 1811.
51. EGL 21 Oct 1824, 2 Apr 1825.
52. LG 14 Feb & 9 Mar 1826.
53. DCRO: D/M7/21.
54. Beamish Museum Archives, Chester-le-Street: Urpeth Mill papers, item 24.
55. DCRO: D/M7/21.
56. DUL: SP 676.
57. EGL 28 Nov 1832.
58. EGL 10 Sep 1839, 30 Nov 1841.
59. HLRO: HofC 1852.
60. PMD 1850-1855.
61. PMD 1860,1868.
62. Kent's Trade Directory 1862-1867; PMD 1866.
63. Whellan's 1856, 1857; Post Office 1858; Morris, Harrison & Co. 1861.
64. PMD 1878.
65. NZ 315349.
66. VCH: Co. Durham (1928) III,205.
67. CKS: Balston MSS 13 Jun 1803.
68. DCRO: EP/BM 25/1,2.
69. DCRO: Index to Monumental Inscriptions at St Michael's, Bishop Middleham.
70. DUL: ASC: DPRI/1/1807/C21/1-5.
71. CKS: Balston MSS: MPM 13 Jun 1803.
72. DCRO: Index to Monumental Inscriptions at St Michael's, Bishop Middleham.
73. *Northern Echo* 16 Oct 1991. This may refer to Thinford Mill.
74. NZ 278375.
75. DCRO: D/Sa/D 214.7.
76. *Newcastle Courant* 20 Jun 1795.
77. DCRO: D/Sa/D/214.2.
78. DCRO: D/Sa/C/182.
79. *Durham County Advertiser* 6 Jan 1816.

80. Slater's Trade Directory 1855.
81. DCRO: D/Sa/D 214.6.
82. DCRO: D/Sa/L 127,128.
83. LG 7 Jun & 1 Jul 1825.
84. The name Teasdale is variously spelt as Teesdale.
85. LG 27 Jun & 18 Jul 1826.
86. EGL 3 May 1827, 20 Mar 1828.
87. LG 21 Feb & 15 Mar 1832.
88. EGL 28 Nov 1832; 16 Mar 1833; 3 Feb 1836; 27 Oct 1837.
89. EGL 27 Oct 1837.
90. DCRO: D/Sa/C 180.
91. Writing indistinct in places.
92. DCRO: D/Sa/C 183.
93. DCRO: D/Sa/C 184.
94. DCRO: D/Sa/C 185.
95. P/L Dr. R. L. Hills 6 Jun 1999.
96. DCRO: D/Sa/C/186.
97. EGL 30 Nov 1841; 1 Dec 1842.
98. LG 10 May & 10 Jun 1842.
99. PMD 1850, 1855; EGL 20 May 1851.
100. HLRO: HofC 1852.
101. DCRO: D/Fle 2/3/68; faint, inconsistent writing.
102. *The Times* 10,15,22 Jun 1857.
103. DCRO: D/Fle 2/3/69.
104. 1861 Census: RG9 3739 f10; PMD 1860, 1862.
105. DCRO: D/Fle/2/6/28-30.
106. NZ 151556.
107. P/L Dr. E. Clavering 12 Jan 2000.
108. Tanfield and Lanchester Parish Registers 1796 & 1797.
109. EGL 8 Oct 1816.
110. EGL 8 Oct 1817.
111. EGL 24 Jan 1824.
112. LG 16 May 1826.
113. EGL 8 Dec 1830.
114. EGL 28 Nov 1832.
115. EGL 15 Sep 1838.
116. NZ 253426.
117. EGL 8 Oct 1816.

118. LG 27 Jun 1826.
119. EGL 3 May 1827, 20 Mar 1828, 11 Jul 1832.
120. EGL 17 Sep 1831, 28 Nov 1832, 10 Sep 1839.
121. DCRO: D/EP/SO/ 2 (1)1.
122. EGL 30 Nov 1841.
123. HLRO: HofC 1852.
124. Bradshaw's Trade Directory 1853.
125. PMD 1860.
126. PMD 1860,1862,1864,1865.
127. 1861 Census: RG9 3736 f88.
128. LG 7 Jun, 23 Aug 1867; *The Stationer* 4 Jul 1867.
129. LG 15 & 22 Dec 1868.
130. PMD 1868-1880.
131. *World's Paper Trade Review* 16 Jul 1937, quoting issue 8 Jul 1887.
132. NZ 259412.
133. TNA: CUST 48/65, 48/50/347.
134. EGL 8 Oct 1816.
135. St Oswald, Durham City Parish Registers, 23 Mar & 27 Nov 1782.
136. EGL 13 May 1817, 20 Mar 1818, 21 Oct 1824.
137. DCRO: EP /DU ISo 112/2/162,171,173.
138. *Durham County Advertiser* 6 & 13 May 1826.
139. LG 27 Jun & 18 Jul 1826.
140. EGL 28 Nov 1832.
141. *Durham County Advertiser* 4 Dec 1835.
142. EGL 15 Sep 1838.
143. DCRO: EP /Du/SO/1/2/1,2.
144. NZ 28.62.
145. P/L Dr. E. Clavering 15 Feb 2000.
146. P/L Dr. E. Clavering 12 Jan 2000.
147. EGL 8 Oct 1816.
148. *Newcastle Courant* 5 Sep 1818.
149. EGL 31 Aug 1819; LG 17 Aug 1819.
150. EGL 9 Oct 1822.
151. *Newcastle Courant* 8 Aug & 30 Nov 1822.
152. EGL 28 Nov 1832.
153. Gateshead Trade Directory 1824.
154. LG 18 Aug, 2 & 26 Oct 1840.
155. EGL 30 Nov 1841.

156. Bradshaw's Trade Directory 1853.
157. P/L Dr. E. Clavering 12 Jan 2000.
158. NZ 303351.
159. CKS: Balston MSS: MPM 13 Jun 1803.
160. EGL 8 Oct 1816.
161. EGL 4 Jul 1820.
162. EGL 17 Jun 1825.
163. LG 27 Jun & 18 Jul 1826.
164. LG 27 Jul 1826.
165. EGL 13 Sep 1826.
166. EGL 17 Sep 1827.
167. EGL 29 Jan 1830, 28 Nov 1832, 1 Jul 1833, 30 Nov 1841.
168. DCRO: EP/BM25/1,2.
169. EGL 1 Dec 1842.
170. BCA: Clarke Collection MS 2092 Thinford.
171. DCRO: D/X/561 (5).

Chapter 4 pages 121 to 158

1. NZ 321567.
2. *Durham County Advertiser* 26 Nov 1814.
3. EGL 8 Oct 1816.
4. LG 31 Dec 1816, 25 Jan 1817.
5. GL 31 Dec 1818.
6. GL 4 Jul 1820.
7. GL 6 Nov 1823.
8. PMD 1828.
9. EGL 20 Mar 1828, 8 Dec 1830.
10. EGL 17 Sep 1831.
11. NZ 286222.
12. EGL 11 Jul 1822.
13. EGL 2 Apr 1825.
14. LG 26 Feb 1830.
15. EGL 8 Dec 1830.
16. NZ 27.04.
17. EGL 17 Jun 1825.
18. LG 2 & 6 Aug 1825.
19. EGL 20 Mar 1828.
20. LG 11 May 1830.

21. EGL 8 Dec 1830.
22. EGL 28 Nov 1832.
23. LG 24 Nov 1835; 12 Feb 1836; 5 Feb 1841.
24. EGL 14 Mar 1849.
25. NZ 255513.
26. BCA: Clarke Collection MS 2092.
27. EGL 19 Feb 1823, 21 Oct 1824.
28. LG 27 Jun 1826.
29. EGL 3 May 1827.
30. DCRO: Q/R/HD/814/95,96.
31. DCRO: Q/R/HD/B1/104-105, 18 Jul 1835; LG 12 Feb 1850.
32. DCRO: D/Bo/G10/XXXVIII; 6 inch Ordnance Survey map 1856; P/L Dr. C. Goldsmith 23 Oct 2001.
33. EGL 28 Nov 1832.
34. PMD 1828, 1829.
35. EGL 28 Nov 1832; PMD 1834.
36. EGL 15 Sep 1838, 10 Sep 1839.
37. EGL 16 May 1841, 16 May 1850, 20 May 1851; PMD 1864.
38. LG 20,26,29 Apr & 24 Jun 1853, 1 Feb 1856.
39. EGL 30 Nov 1841; LG 12 Feb 1850.
40. HLRO: HofC 1852.
41. PMD 1864.
42. NZ 248633.
43. EGL 1 Dec 1841,1855.
44. NCRO: NRO 4930/B1,B11.
45. *Newcastle Courant* 19 Jul 1828.
46. NCRO: NRO 4930/B2.
47. EGL 17 Feb 1829, 28 Nov 1832, 16 Mar & 16 Nov 1833.
48. NCRO: NRO 4930/B6,B20.
49. LG 4 Dec 1840; EGL 30 Nov 1841.
50. EGL 1 Dec 1842.
51. PMD 1847.
52. EGL 29 Jun 1848.
53. PMD 1850.
54. Whellan's Trade Directory 1855.
55. LG 19 Sep 1851.
56. HLRO: HofC 1852.
57. LG 12 Mar & 16 Apr 1852.

58. LG 6 Apr 1855.
59. NCRO: NRO 4930/B20.
60. PMD 1860-1871.
61. EGL 19 Mar 1865.
62. PMD 1871,1872.
63. PMD 1868.
64. PMD 1879.
65. PMD 1866,1876,1894.
66. NZ 38.57.
67. LG 26 Apr 1844; EGL 19 Mar 1845.
68. OSP AR/14.
69. *Sunderland & Durham County Herald & Shields, Hartlepool & Stockton Observer* 13 Feb 1846.
70. *Sunderland & Durham County Herald & Shields, Hartlepool & Stockton Observer* 13 Feb 1846.
71. *Sunderland & County Durham Herald & Shields, Hartlepool & Stockton Observer* 13 Feb 1846.
72. OSP AR/14.
73. LG 2 Feb 1849.
74. Reports by the Juries of 1851 Exhibition (1852) Class XVII London 429.
75. HLRO: HofC 1852.
76. Memoir from Minutes of the Proceedings of the Institute of Civil Engineers XXXIII, (Session 1871-1872) 270-271, Sper TA 114.
77. *The Sunderland Times* 1 Jun 1875.
78. PMD 1892-1902.
79. *Illustrated Guide to Sunderland & District* 1898, 69.
80. *Original Papermakers Recorder October* 1902 (Journal of trade union, OSP).
81. OSP 07/1902.
82. OSP 07/1919.
83. BLPES: Webb Trade Union Collection E, Section B, vol.73, item 18.
84. NZ 419132. Egglescliffe Mill has been included in this work as Yarm was in Co. Durham at some periods; at others it was part of Yorkshire as a result of changes to county boundaries.
85. VCH: Yorkshire North Riding (1923) II,320-321.
86. VCH: Co. Durham (1928) III,222.
87. Easingwold, Yorkshire Parish Register 1808.
88. Directories are sometimes a year or so out of date, leaving the possibility that the same man moved on to papermaking, but as a business man rather

than a paper maker.
89. *The Times* 17 Oct 1846.
90. HLRO: HofC 1852.
91. 1851 Census: HO107 2383 f103a.
92. 1861 Census: RG9 4898 f41; 1871 RG10 4866 f72. DCRO: Index to Monumental Inscriptions and Burial Register of 1881 for Yarm.
93. *The Paper Record* 8 Oct 1892, VIII,IV,103,185.
94. *Paper Makers' Monthly Journal* 5 Jun 1896, XXXIV no.6,188.
95. 1881 Census: RG11 4893 f9,10; RG11 4023 f59.
96. Amalgamated Society of Papermakers: Membership list 1896.
97. NZ 35. 57.; BCA: Clarke Collection MS 2092 Ford.
98. TWAS: *North East Archives Bulletin* 1987: no.2,9.
99. *Sunderland Herald* 6 Apr 1849.
100. DCRO: EP/Biw 220/1,2.
101. HLRO: HofC 1852.
102. EGL 20 May 1851.
103. *The Paper Makers' Circular*, 9 Sep 1861:2.
104. Will of J. B. Falconer, Probate 17 Sep 1864.
105. Patent 31 Jul 1856.
106. PMD 1864-1865.
107. A detailed description of the processes also appeared in *The Sunderland Times* 1 Jun 1875, as well as in Chester (1976).
108. TWAS: 202/1960.
109. *The Sunderland Times* 1 Jun 1875.
110. *The Sunderland Times* 20 Jun 1871.
111. Routledge's Improvement Extension Cost Book gives more details of changes between 1866 and 1886. See Chester (1976) 6-13.
112. *The Paper Record* 7 Nov 1891, Contemporary Pictures no.XXXI,162.
113. *The Sunderland Times* 1 Jun 1875.
114. *The Times* 5 Apr 1887.
115. TWAS:MF 71; 1881 Census: RG11 4992 f32.
116. *The Paper Record* 8 Sep 1892:VIII,no.3,128.
117. *The Times* 5 Nov 1913, Engineering Supplement no.454,23a. For a more detailed account of events and changes in equipment, processes and personnel from the time of the First World War see Chester (1976) 16-19 and Walker (1984) 67-69.
118. *The Times* 5 Nov 1913, Engineering Supplement no.454.
119. *Sunderland Daily Echo & Shipping Gazette* 19 Jun 1913.
120. *Sunderland Daily Echo* 12 Jul 1913.

121. Register of Defunct & Other Companies Removed from the Stock Exchange: Official Year Book edn. 1978/1979.
122. *World's Paper Trade Review* 13 Nov 1947.
123. Wiggins Teape house magazine *Gateway* 1954.
124. *The Paper Maker*, Apr 1971:161,no.4,28.
125. Detailed extracts from Thomas Routledge's Improvement & Extension Cost Book describes changes in processes and equipment. See Chester 1976:6-13.

Chapter 5 pages 159 to 188

1. NZ 330641.
2. O.S. 6 inch map 1856.
3. DCRO:Q/R/HD/327 (7 Mar 1927 & 17 Apr 1928).
4. LG 17 & 29 Feb 1848.
5. HLRO: HofC 1852.
6. LG 22 Mar,19 Apr,14 May,19 & 23 Jul 1852; 4 Jan, 1 Feb, 19 Jul, 11 Nov 1853.
7. *The Times* 10 & 12 Apr 1852.
8. *The Times* 25 Apr 1857.
9. *Jarrow Express* 29 Aug 1874.
10. PMD 1862, 1864.
11. *Jarrow Express* 29 Aug 1874.
12. *Jarrow Express* 29 Aug 1874.
13. *The Times* 25 Aug 1874; *Jarrow Express* 29 Aug 1874.
14. *The* [Jarrow] *Guardian* 29 Aug 1874.
15. PMD 1876, 1885.
16. *Review of Newcastle & District* 1896, 82-83.
17. Obituary in *The Paper Record & Wood Pulp News* Jul 1985, 83.
18. PMD 1905.
19. P/L Miss A. Cook 26 Jun 1995.
20. *The Times* 5 Nov 1913, Engineering Supplement no.454,23.
21. DCRO:D/TVP/1.
22. *The Paper Maker & British Paper Trade Journal* 2 July 1906 XXXII,65; Monumental Inscription, Lasswade Parish Churchyard.
23. PMD 1906, 1911, 1922.
24. PMD 1921,1922.
25. P/L Miss A. Cook 26 Jun 1995.
26. PMD 1961.
27. NZ 238618.

28. P/L Dr. E. Clavering 28 Aug 2000.
29. *Gateshead Guardian* 28 Apr 1900.
30. DCRO: D/CG/15/1.
31. P/L Dr. E. Clavering 28 Aug 2000.
32. DCRO: D/CG/15/11,14,59.
33. Gateshead Public Library: BP 1/83.
34. PMD 1868, 1869, 1871-1875.
35. PMD 1876-1892; *The Paper Record* 8 Oct 1892, VIII no.IV,152.
36. PMD 1892,1894.
37. DCRO: D/TVP 24.
38. *Gateshead Guardian* 28 Apr 1900.
39. *Gateshead Guardian* 28 Apr 1900.
40. *World's Paper Trade Review* 15 Mar 1951, vol.135 no.11,782.
41. The Letter Book was a daily log with copies of all letters sent; it included an analysis of manufacturing costs by item type and contained an index.
42. DCRO: D/TVP/1/8.
43. *Gateshead Guardian* 28 Apr 1900.
44. DCRO: D/TVP/1/8.
45. DCRO: D/TVP/1/16.
46. DCRO: D/TVP/1/58-59.
47. PMD 1902-1915; DCRO: D/TVP/24; *World's Paper Trade Review* 15 Mar 1951, vol.135 no.11,782.
48. DCRO: D/TVP/24.
49. *World's Paper Trade Review* 15 Mar 1951, vol.135 no.11,782.
50. PMD 1902, 1908-1911.
51. *World's Paper Trade Review* 15 Mar 1951, vol.135 no.11, 782.
52. DCRO: D/TVP/1/298; D/TVP/24.
53. PMD 1906, 1908; *World's Paper Trade Review* 15 Mar 1951, vol.135 no.11,782.
54. PMD 1909-1912.
55. *The Times* 5 Nov 1913, Engineering Supplement no.454,23.
56. *World's Paper Trade Review* 15 Mar 1951, vol.135 no.11, 782.
57. *World's Paper Trade Review* 15 Mar 1951, vol.135 no.11, 782.
58. PMD 1922-1934.
59. *World's Paper Trade Review* 15 March 1951, vol.135 no.11, 782.
60. NZ 408558.
61. *The Sunderland Times* 1 Jun 1875.
62. *The Sunderland Times* 1 Jun 1875.

63. *The Sunderland Times* 24 Oct 1873.
64. *The Sunderland Times* 26 Nov, 7 Dec 1875.
65. *Sunderland Daily Echo* 8 Jul, 26 Jul 1876.
66. *Sunderland Daily Echo* 16 Jun 1876.
67. *The Sunderland Times* 7 Jul 1876.
68. PMD 1882.
69. PMD 1895,1896,1898.
70. *World's Pulp & Paper Industry* 6 Sep 1899, 301.
71. *Sunderland Daily Echo & Shipping Gazette* 24 Aug 1899.
72. *World's Pulp & Paper Industry* 6 Sep 1899:301.
73. *The Times* 5 Nov 1913, Engineering Supplement no.454, 23.
74. Beamish Hall Archives, photograph no.40499/3.3211.
75. *World's Paper Trade Review* 13 Mar 1931.
76. PMD 1851,1961.
77. NZ 203623.
78. P/L Dr. E. Clavering 28 Aug 2000.
79. TWAS: 2644.
80. P/L Dr. E. Clavering 28 Aug 2000.
81. PMD 1887-1908.
82. PMD 1894.
83. PMD 1902,1906 1909.
84. NZ 411632.
    Unless otherwise stated, details of Marsden Mills' history is from Duncan/ Maidwell notes (1952,15-17) and TWAS: 1847/2 documents. See bibliography and abbreviations.
85. *The Paper Record* 8 Jul 1892, VIII no.1,28; 8 Sep 1892, VIII no.3,128.
86. DCRO: D/CB/1/23/0.780.
87. DCRO: D/CB 1/23.
88. Duncan/Maidwell (1952) 16.
89. *The Times* 5 Nov 1913, Engineering Supplement no.454,23.
90. NZ 50.32.
91. *Stock Exchange Register* ed.1891.
92. PMD 1892.
93. *World's Pulp & Paper Industry Journal* 21 Jun 1899,329; 12 Jul 1899, 40-41.
94. *The Times* 5 Nov 1913, Engineering Supplement no.454,23a.
95. *The Paper Record & Wood Pulp News* Jun 1895,XI no.1, 29-31.

96. *The Paper Record & Wood Pulp News* Jun 1895, XI no.1,29-31.
97. *Northern Daily Mail & South Durham Herald* 18 Jun 1906.
98. *The Times* 5 Nov 1913, Engineering Supplement no.454,23.
99. *Paper Maker's Monthly Journal* 15 Sep 1921, LIX 349; *Stock Exchange Register*: List of Defunct & Other Companies Removed from the *Stock Exchange Official Year Book* edn. 1978/1979.
100. *Stock Exchange Register* edn.1920.
101. *Stock Exchange Register*: List of Defunct & Other Companies Removed from the *Stock Exchange Official Year Book* edn.1978/1979.
102. *Stock Exchange Register*: List of Defunct & Other Companies Removed from the *Stock Exchange Official Year Book*, edn.1978/1979.
103. *The Paper Maker* Sep 1965, 150 no.3,52.

Chapter 6 pages 189 to 196

1. *The World's Pulp & Paper Industry,* 2 Nov 1898,186; The Paper Record, 8 Mar 1892, 342.

Index

Abbott, John 53
Abbott, Patrick 53
accidents 52, 53, 148
    boiler explosions 145, 192
    see also fires; flooding
Addison, John William 59, 112
Aitkin, Wm. R. 177
Aldin Grange Estate 111
Allen, Mr (*c. 1762*) 58
Amalgamated Society of Papermakers (ASPM) 186, 199
Anderson, F. 130
Anderson, Isabella 91-2
Anderson, James 119
Anderson, John, snr 91, 92, 119
Anderson, John, jnr 91, 92
Anderson, Thomas, snr 91, 119
Anderson, Thomas, jnr 92
Andrew, Walter 185
Angerstein, Reinhold 25, 32-3, 39, 41
Annandale, Alexander 65, 66, 70, 74, 130
Annandale, Andrew 70
Annandale, James 27, 28, 29, 66, 67, 70, 75
Annandale, James, JP 74, 75
Annandale, John, snr 27, 65, 66-7, 69, 75
Annandale, John, jnr 66, 68-9, 70
Annandale, Peter 27, 28, 29, 66, 70, 75
Annandale, William 66-7, 70
Annandale, William M. 74, 75
Annandale & Son(s), John 65-7, 68-9, 70, 71, 72-6
Annandale family 27-30, 65-75
apprenticeship 8, 133
Armstrong, R. W. 178
Armstrong, Robert 113
Aycliffe Mill 123
Ayre, Amoras 86
Ayre, Joseph (*c. 1798*) 86
Ayre's Quay 136, 137, 138

B

Babcock & Wilcox 169
Backhouse, James 112
Backhouse, Jonathan 112
Bage, Thomas (of Armonside farm) 24
Bage, Thomas (m. *1781*) 55
Bainbridge, Charles T. 138, 139-40, 141
Bainbridge, Emerson Muschamp 131
Bainbridge, Richard 139
Bainbridge, William 131, 140
bankruptcy and insolvency 56, 57, 62, 82, 88, 103-4, 115, 117, 118, 123, 125, 130, 131, 156, 161
    District Court of Bankruptcy, Newcastle 160
Barker, T. B. 151, 152
Barlow, F. B. 151, 152
Barnard Castle 34, 35, 57, 58
Barras, James 43, 44
Bartram & Sons, Jas. 169
Beckett, Thomas 95
Bedson, Henry 43
Bell, Errington 160, 161
Bell, Henry 173
Bell, James 25, 33, 38
Bell, Richard Hansell 160, 161
Bell, Robert 18
Bell, Thomas 160
Bellerby, Michael 122
Bennet, Thomas 26
Bensham Colliery 165
Benson, John 18
Bentley & Jackson 148
Bertram, G. & W. 150, 174
Best, Robert 62
Bewick, Margaret 97
Bewick, Thomas 11, 71
Binns, Ellen 113
Binns, John 113
Black & Gainsford 61
Blackbird, Francis 145
Blackbird & Co, F. 161
Blackhall Mills 31-2, 33, 36-9
Blackhill: Highgate Baptist Church 75

Blackwall Mill 118, 124-5
Blackwell, George 145
Blackwell, John 133, 135, 144, 145, 146
Blackwell & Co, J. 145
bleaching agents 11
Blenkinsop, Richard 51, 116
Bond, George (Frederick) 113
Bonsor, William 32
Boulfield, William 40
Bourn, Thomas William 116, 117
Bowes, George 39, 40, 43-4, 46
Bowes, Mary 46
Bowes, Robinson Stoney 47
Bowmaker, Edward 56
Bowman, Christopher 32
Brough, W. 127
Browney, River 58, 60, 76
Burdon, Augustus Edward 170
Burdon, Thomas 95
Burdon, William W. 166
Burn, Mary 131
Burns, Edward 53
Butterby Mill 21, 23, 102-8, 192
       inventory of implements 107

C

Cail's wharf 168-9
Calvert, John 56
Cargey's cement works 118
Carolin, Thomas 148
Charlton, Matthew 78
Chater, George 151, 152
Chater, G., jnr 152
Chater, Lionel G. 152
chemicals 148, 181, 185, 186, 193
Chester, C. A. 2
Chester-le-Street 125, 126, 127
child employment 69
Chilton, Nicholas 77
China 3
Chopwell Estate 26, 29, 33, 34, 39
Chopwell Mill 31-4, 38, 39, 97, 194
Chopwell Wood 33, 38
Clark, James 120
Clark, Richard 33
Clark(e) (Clerk), Edward 18, 19
Clarke, John 90
Clarke, Richard 19, 32
Clavering, Sir James 179

Clavering, Sir Thomas John 28
Clerk, William 19
Cleveland Bridge & Engineering Co Ltd 182
coal 7, 13, 15, 84, 108, 168, 181, 189, 193
coal mill 165
Cockburn, Thomas 81
Cockram, Joseph 45
Coltman, Thomas 41
Cong Burn 109, 125, 128
Cooke, Catherine 35
Cooke, Elizabeth 35
Cooke, Henry 34, 35, 36, 133
Cooke, James (d. *1807*) 86-7, 88, 100
Cooke, James (of Henry Cooke & Co) 34-5
Cooke, James (son of James d. *1807*; of Tudhoe Mill) 92-3, 94, 106-7
Cooke, John (son of James d. *1807*; of Lendings Mill) 57, 87
Cooke, Lane 108
Cooke, Matthew 108, 113
Cooke, Robert (son of James; d. *1819*) 87, 88, 89
Cooke, Robert, snr (d. *1855*) 88, 89
Cooke, Robert, jnr 108
Cooke & Co, James 112
Cookson, Daniel 126, 127
Cookson, Isaac 33
Cookson, John (of Blackhall Mill) 39
Cookson, John (of White Hill) 126
Cornett, James P. 149-50, 151
Cornforth Beck 99, 101, 119
Cornforth (Cornfourth) Mills 2, 7, 99-102
       plan *101*
Court of Common Relief for Insolvent Debtors 118
Coward, Thomas 62
Cowper, Earl 33
Cox, Hannah 124, 125
Cox, John, snr 124, 125
Cox, John, jnr 124, 125
Craig's Trade Directory 29
Crampton, Robert 34, 57
Crankshaw, A. E. 172
Crankshaw, C. T. 172
Crankshaw, Turner 170, 172
crepe papermaking 156
Crowley, Ambrose 179
Croxdale Beck 17, 18, 108
Croxdale Mill 17-24, 102, 193, 194

Crozier, Ralph 112
Crozier, William 112
Crudden, William 26
Cuming (Cummins), Thomas 20

D

Dartford, Kent 4
Davidson, Ian 178
Davidson, John 113
Davidson, Percy 178
Dean and Chapter of Durham Cathedral 62, 63, 112
Deerness, River 76
Deptford Mill 34, 132
Derwent, River 2, 10, 24, 28, 29, 32, 36, 37, 41, 42, 47, 64, 67, 72-3, 179
    Damhead dam 179
Dickinson, John 146, 147, 192
Dickson, Mr (of Springwell Mills) 164
Dixon, John 131
Dixon, William 47
Dobson, William 78
Dock, Wharf, Riverside & General Workers' Union 186
Donkinson, Archibald 38
double paper mill 25
Douglas, Joseph 59, 111, 114
drying process 36
Dufay Paints 31
Dunn, Matthew (Matthias) 122
Durham City 10, 19, 62, 81, 112
    Elvet 62
    map, *1767* 40
    St Cuthbert's parish 64, 65
    St Margaret's parish 58, 111, 114
    St Oswald's parish 18, 19, 21, 23, 58, 78, 81, 126
Durham Gaol 89, 92, 118
Durham Paper Mills Ltd 187
Durham University 5
Dyson, W. 186

E

Ebchester parish 32, 33, 37, 38
effluent 175, 190
Egglescliffe (Eaglescliffe) Mill *see* Tees Mill
Eggleston, James 77, 79
Eggleston, John 100

Eggleston(e), Thomas 99-100
Egglestone Abbey (Athelstone, Eccleston) Mill 5, 34-6, 57
electricity 181
Elerington, Ralph 96
Elliot, Richard 42
Elliott, William 98
Ellison, Cuthbert 128
esparto grass 6, 72, 73-4, 146-8, 149, 150, 153, 161, 164, 177, 190
    imports 14
Evans, Sir John 146, 151, 152
Evans, Lewis 151, 152
Ewhurst Mill 37, 109-11
Excise
    Duty 9, 11, 13-14, 59, 70-1, 114, 147, 191
    Label *13*
    licences issued 192
explosions, boiler 145, 192
Eynsham Mill, Oxfordshire 146
Eyre (Ayres, Eyres), Joseph (*c. 1738*) 19, 20
Eyre, Thomas 86

F

Falconer, Charles 146
Falconer, John Brunton 133, 135, 144, 145, 146
Farrow, John 90
Fellingshore Mill 49-54, 168, 199
Feltine 170
Fielding, Eliz Eleanor 81
finance 8-9. 191-2
fires 29, 35, 50, 51, 54, 73-4, 79-80, 111-12, 117, 139, 150-1, 154, 192
    incendiary 133-5, 191
    Marsden Mills 183
    Monkton Mills 162-3, 164
    smoke 174-5
    Team Valley Mills 167-8
flax 177
Fleming, Mr (of Monkton Mills) 162
Fleming, Mr (of Tudhoe Mill) 107
Fleming, Temple 60
Fleming, W. 58
Fletcher, John 160
Fletcher, Joseph 145
Fletcher, Thomas 133, 135, 144, 145

flooding 42-3, 56, 67, 129, 170, 192
Ford (Hylton) Mill, near Sunderland 2, 7,
    14, 34, 115, 132, 143-57, 190,
    192, 199
    Opening Commemoration Sheet
    142
    plan *153*
Forster, John 61
Forster, P. 61
Forster, William Charlton 52
Fourdrinier Committee 79
Friendless Poor Society 75
Fryer, William 124, 125
Fryer, William Brown 125

G

Gallon, Mary 127
Gallon, Mr and Mrs
    (visitors to Jarrow Mill) 160
Gallon, Simon 126, 127
Gallon, Thomas 52, 54, 127
Galpin, Percy (Herbert) 170
Galpin, Stanley (Ingram) 170
Garling, Simon 26
Garton, Mrs 47
Gasworkers & General Labourers Union
    177
Gates, Mr (of Thinford Mill) 119
Gateshead 12, 51, 55, 117, 122,
    128-9, 131
Gateway 156
Gibside Mill 39-47
Gibson, Thomas Cummings 124
Gilder, Isaac 25
Girling, Simon 95
Gladston (Gledstone), Thomas 33, 97
Gleddle, Danl 60
Gledston (Glidstone), John 97
Gloucester Paper Mills 31
Golden Leather Brown 132
Goodall, Thomas 174, 177
Gordon & Co, James 30
Gowland, Ralph 115
Grace, John 50, 51
Grace, Nathaniel 27
Grace & Co, William 179
Graham, John 59, 111, 114
Graham, Matthew 97
Graham, Thomas 56

Granger (Grainger), William 60, 61, 62
Gray, James Wilson 110
Gray, John, 96
Gray, Joseph 96, 110
Gray, Ralf 114, 115
Gray, Robert 26
Gray, Thomas (of Lintzford Mill) 26
Gray, Thomas (of Urpeth Mill) 96
Great Exhibition, *1851* 52
Green & Son(s), E. 30, 169
Grey, George 114
Grey, Mary 114
Grey, Ralph 114
Grey, William 114

H

Hagan, John Short 84
Hall, Thomas 43
Hamilton, John 185-6
Hampson, Ralph 115
Hand, John 60
Hand & Simmons 60
Harden, Thomas 133
Hargrave, J. 160
Hargrave, W. H. 160
Hargrave(s), Joseph 160, 161
Harker, Joseph 33, 97
Harrison (baker) 51
Harrison, Catharine 129
Harrison, John Jefferson 33, 38, 39, 128-
    9, 130
Harrison, Robert 58
Hartlepool Mill 184-7, 199
Hartley, William 97
Harvey, George 125
Harvey, Joseph 124
Harvey, William (of Aycliffe Paper Mill) 123
Harvey, William (of Gateshead) 125
Harvey, Wm (of Tyne Mill) 130, 131-2
Hassan, Isaak 165
Hastings, R. 160
Haughton Mill, Northumberland 27, 65,
    71
Hauxwell, G. 23
Hawks, Sir Robert 50, 52
Hawks, Robert Shafto 50, 51
Haworth, Hargreaves, Henry and James 84
Hayle Mill, Kent 14
Head, George 103
Heel, Thomas 26

Hendon Lonnin windmill 56
Hendon Mill, Sunderland 15, 149, 172-9, 194, 199
Her Majesty's Stationery Office 70
Hett Mill 85-9, 199
Heworthshore *see* Fellingshore Mill
High Team (Law) Mill 166
Holdin, Thomas 95
Hollander beater 11
Hollingworth, James 82
Hood, Tom 167
Hopper, John 41
Hopper, Thomas 102
House of Commons Papers, *1852* 107
Hudson, Henry 98
Hudson, James 98
Hudson of Newcastle 95-6, 98
Hull Pulp Co 185
Hunt, William 133, 144
Hunter, Christopher 24
Hunter, George 40
Hunter, Thomas 27
Hurst, Nicholas 32
Hutchinson, Ralph 122
Hutton, Michael 136, 137, 144
Hutton, Robert 34, 133, 135, 143, 144
Hutton, William 133, 135
Hutton & Co, M. 136-7
Hylton Mill *see* Ford Mill

I

India 76
Inland Revenue 147
Inveresk Group 187

J

Jackson, John 32
Jackson, Vincent 30
Jarrow (Paper) Mill 159-60, 165
Jarrow Hall Estate 161
Jefferson, Henry 131
Jefferson, John 57
Jefferson, Matthew (of Hett Mill) 88
Jefferson, Matthew (of Lendings Mill) 57-8
Jefferson & Co, Henry 33
Johnson, Alderman 137
Johnson, Hannah 65
Johnson, John 65, 122, 128
Johnson, Richard 65

Johnson, Thomas 65
Jones, Samuel 164
Jopling, Mark 61
jute 14

K

Kalmeter, Henrik 37
Kellner & Partington Paper Pulp Co 185
Kent 8
   see also place names
King, James 126, 127
King, John 162
Kirk Merrington Parish Registers 86
Kirkup (injured boy) 52
Kraft paper 54, 171, 187

L

labour relations *see* strikes; trade unions
Lacey, Henry 59, 111, 114
Laing & Co, shipbuilders 137
Lamb, George 124
Lambert, Ralph 79
Lamesley Mills 20, 54-7
Lancashire & Yorkshire Paper Makers Association 72
Langley Mills 7, 23, 76-84, 194, 199
Langley Paper Co Ltd 84
Langley Park 77
Lawes, Robert 26
Leadbitter, John 69
Lendings Mill 57-8
Lewer, H. W. (Henry William) 169, 170
Lightfoot, George 28
Lightfoot, John 28
Lightfoot, Thomas 101, 117-18, 124
Lintz Old Paper Mill 37, 109
Lintzford House 27
Lintzford Mill 7, 24-31, 194, 195, 199
London, Joseph Augustus 149
Longman, A. H. 151, 152
Lonsdale, John, snr 21-2, 102
Lonsdale, John, jnr 21-2
Low Team (Teams) Mill 166, 199
Lowe, Peter 84
Lowther, John 77
Lumley, William 21, 102, 103-4
Lynas, H. 177

M

machinery 8-9, 189
   accidents 52
   Butterby Mill, inventory 107
   early papermaking machines 5, 9, 11, 12, *87*, 132
   Fellingshore 54
   fire caused by 111
   Ford Mill 150, 152, 154, 156, 157
   Hartlepool Mill 184, 187
   Hendon Mill 174, 175-6, 178
   Hollander beater 11
   Kraft machine 54
   Langley Mills 79, 80, 82, 83, 84
   Lintzford 29, 31
   Marsden Mills 180, 182, 183
   seizure 9
   Shotley Grove 66, 68, 72
   Springwell Mills 160
   Robert Stephenson & Co 67-8, 80, 124
   Team Valley Mills 166, 171, 172
   see also steam power; waterwheels
MacKey, Alexander 25, 38
MacKinlay, Archibald (of Ewhurst and Blackwall Mills) 110, 124, 125
MacKinlay, Edward 96, 110, 127
Mackinlay, Edward, jnr 127
MacKinlay, Roger Patterson 127
Makin, J. 185, 186
market 5, 189
Markham, J. 155
Marsden & Co Ltd, Charles 31
Marsden Chemical Company 181
Marsden Mills 14-15, 180-4, 192, 193
'Marsden Rattler' steam engine 181, 183
Martin, Ebenezer 106
Martin, Robert, snr and jnr 104-6
Martin, William 106
Marwood, Thomas 143
Masson, Scott & Co, 30
Master Paper Makers 191
   meetings 26, 55, 78, 86, 91, 96, 99-100, 118
materials for paper 4, 190
   see also esparto grass; pulp; rags
Maugham, John 40-1, 42, 44

McKinlay, Archibald (d. *1807*) 25, 26, 65, 95, 96, 127
McLeod, David 26, 51, 116
Miller, Frederick Norton 149, 173, 174
Miller, Ingelby 90
Miller, Mr (of Moorsley Banks Mill) 112
Miller & Co, John 96
Millwood, John 113
Mitchell, J. (of Shotley Grove Mill) 74
Modern Society 138
Monkton: Paper Mill Path 159
Monkton Mills 160-2
Moon, John 119, 120
Moon, Robert 118
Moon, Thomas 118
Moor Paper Mill *see* Lamesley Mills
Moore, George 126, 127
Moore, James 95
Moore, William 86
Moorsley (Morsley) Bank(s) Mill 58, 81, 107, 111-14, 199
Moorsley Banks Paper Co 113
Morritt family (c 1773) 34
Mowbray (valuer) 102
Murray, John 86
Muschamp, J. B. 132
Muschamp, John (Jno. 130), 132
Muschamp, John Dover 131
Muschamp, William 130, 131, 132
Musgrave & Sons, J. 30

N

Napoleonic Wars 11, 191
National Coal Board 184
National Union of Paper Mill Workers (NUPMW) 138, 154-5, 186, 199
Nelson, George 108
New Stourbridge Mill 128, 129-30, 131
Newcastle Browns papers 5
Newcastle upon Tyne 25, 38, 78, 98
newsprint and newspapers 10, 11, 180-1, 182, 183
Nichol, John 124
North Brancepeth Coal Co Ltd 84
North Eastern Paper Mills Company 14-15, 180, 181
Northumberland Paper Mills 179
Nottingham 118

O

Oates, Anthony 86
Oates, George 119
Oates, John 119
Olde Mill, The, restaurant, Ferryhill 102
Olive & Partington Ltd 187
Ord, Ann 56, 110
Ord, Benjamin (*1694-1771*) 21, 40, 43-4, 45
Ord, Benjamin (remarried *1753*) 55
Ord, Benjamin (m. *1790*) 55
Ord, Benjamin (*c. 1816*) 111, 112
Ord, Benjamin (bankrupt *1826*) 56, 59, 60
Ord, Christopher (m. *1767*) 55
Ord, Christopher (*c. 1778*) 55
Ord, Christopher (m. *1787*) 55
Ord, Christopher (*c. 1792*) 20-1, 55
Ord, Christopher (*c. 1823*) 125
Ord, David 45-6
Ord, John (*c. 1760*) 46
Ord, John (d. *1819*) 59
Ord, John (*c. 1862*) 62
Ord, Jonathan (of Lamesley Mill) 20-1, 32, 37, 40
Ord, Jonathan, snr (of Tudhoe; d. *1805*) 90, 91
Ord, Jonathan, jnr 91
Ord, Robert 40, 43-4, 45
Ord, Thomas (of Ewhurst Mill) 110
Ord, Thomas (of Gibside Mill) 46
Ord [Benjamin] & Addison 59, 112
Ord family 20-1, 40, 43-6, 55-7, 59
  watermark *90*
Original Society of Papermakers, The (OSP) 8, 133, 134-5, 190-1, 199

P

Palliser, Cuthbert 41
Palliser, Joseph 40, 42, 43, 44
Palliser, William 29
Palmer, John 17
Paper Makers Association 150
Papermakers Association of Northern Manufacturers 71-2
Paper-Makers Club 150
Paper Makers' Combination Act 12

paper sorts 70-1
  see also names of sorts
Papyrus Fibre Company 166
paraffin 185-6
parchment 3
Parish, John 148
Parker, John 167
Partington, Edward 185
partnership laws 9
Patent Fuel Company 172
patent infringement 185-6
Pattinson, John 177
Pearson, Francis 26
Pearson, George 26-7, 28
Pearson, John (Jno), snr 100-1
Pearson, John, jnr 101
Pearson, Richard (of Chopwell Mill) 33
Pearson, Richard (of Ewhurst Mill) 110
Pearson, Thomas 26-7
Pearson & Co, Geo. 51
Pembertons of Gateshead 194
Phillip, William 99
Phillips, Nicholas 123
Phillips, William 123
Pinkney, William 53
Pirie & Sons Ltd, Alex 156
pollution
  smoke 174-5
  see also under water
Pont, River 32, 37
Poor Law Settlement Examinations 22, 81, 115
price-fixing 71-2
printing presses 10
Public Health Act 174
pulp 4-5, 7, 11
  sulphite 181
  wood 6, 14, 180
  imported 181, 183, 190

R

rags
  cutting 69
  prices 9
  shortage 190
  trade 6
Read, James 115
Reed, Eleanor 50-1
Reed, Will(iam) (of Blackwall Mill) 124, 125

Reed, William (of Fellingshore) 50
Reid, Ralph 26
Relly (Releigh) Mill 7, 58-63, 81, 111, 112
Richardson, Albert 161
Richardson, E. (Edmund) 164, 168-9
Richardson, E. R. (Edmund Rich) 170, 172
Richardson, Edward 136, 145, 166
Richardson, Henry Yarker 136
Richardson, O. B. 172
Richardson, Peter 91
Richardson, W. H. (William Henry) 135, 136, 144, 161, 164, 165
Richardson, Wm H. & A. 164
Richardson & Son(s), E. 54, 170
Richardson('s) Printing Ink Co Ltd 31, 167
Ridley, William 117
River Wear Commissioners 148
Robertson, A. 30
Robinson, Bartholomew 115
Robinson, John 141
Robinson, Robert 141
Robinson, Thomas 141
Robinson, Thomas May 141
Robson, Daniel 130
Robson, Joseph 117, 130
rope 8, 19, 127
rope browns 52, 63, 136, 137
Ropemakers, Guild of 114
Routledge, Thomas 6, 145, 146-8, 149, 150-1, 153, 173, 190
Royal Commission into the Employment of Children 69
Russell, William 81
Ruthverd, John 105
Ruthverd Patent Press & Steam Engine Manufactory 104-5
Rymer, John 130-1
Ryton parish 32, 36, 37

S

Sage, Thomas 32
Salter, William 51, 52
Salvin, Anthony 18
Salvin, Bryan (of Croxdale Mill) 19
Salvin, Bryan John 91
Salvin, Gerard 18

Salvin, Gerrard 17
Salvin, James 17-18
Salvin, Jerrard 18
Salvin, Marmaduke Charles 84, 108
Salvin, W. T. (*c. 1816*) 22, 103
Salvin, William (*c. 1752*) 19, 20-1
Salvin, William Thomas (*c. 1838*) 105-6
Salvin Estate 17, 91, 102
Salvin family 17, 18-19, 102
Salvin's paper mill, Croxdale Glen 18
Sandford, John 24
Sandilands, R. A. 178
Savage, Alfred 141
Savage, Edward 122
Savage, Henry 141
Scaife, John, snr and jnr 27 (*c. 1840*)
Scaife, Mr 25, 26 (*c. 1811*)
Scales, Shillington 137
Scales, William 127
Scotswood Mill, Northumberland 135, 144, 179
Scott, Robert 124
Seel, C. 140
Sele Mill, Hertfordshire 3-4
Sharp, Thos. 65
Sheffield 31
Shevill, Ralph 25
shipyards 6
Shotley Bridge
    Baptist Chapel 75
    Ealands 64, 65
    Presbyterian Church 75
Shotley Bridge Co-operative Society 75
Shotley Grove Mills (Grove Mill; High Mill; Low Mill), 2, 15, 27, 28, 29, *63*, 63-76, 199
    Excise label *13*
Sill, Thomas 116, 117
Simonds, John 60
Simpson, Anthony, snr 96, 110
Simpson, Anthony, jnr 96, 110
Simpson, Henry 110
Simpson, Thomas 110
Skelton, George 77, 79
Skerne, River 123
Smales, Francis 59
Smales, Henry 59
Smart, Robert 53
Smith, Alfred 53

Index

Smith, Anwick 23, 62, 78, 79, 80, 81, 84, 112
Smith, Cuthbert 64
Smith, Edward 52, 54
Smith, Elizabeth 78, 79
Smith, Howard 178
Smith, J.E. 54
Smith, John (of Relly Mill) 58, 62
Smith, John (father of Anwick, at Langley Mills) 77, 78
Smith, John (son of Anwick? at Langley Mills) 80, 82, 84
Smith, John (of Moorsley Banks) 112
Smith, Robert 59, 111, 114
Smith Bros 62-3
smoke 174-5
Snipe's Dene 41
Snowden Hole Mill 49, 116-18
Sodfine reservoir 65, 76
South Shields Fibre Company 166
Southeron Closes Mill 103
Sowerby, George 128-9
Sowerby, John 130
Spilman, John 4
Springwell Mills 159-65, 199
    plan *163*
St Cuthbert's Works, London 74
St Edmund Bearpark 63
steam power 7, 10-11, 70, 94, 108, 137, 181
    Marsden Rattler' 181, 183
    rotary steam engine 105-6
Stephenson, Jonathan 25
Stephenson & Co, Robert 67-8, 80, 124, 136
Stevens, C. L. 169
Stock Exchange Register 31, 155, 156, 187
Stoker, William 59
Stone Bridge Mill 58, 61, 114-16, 144
Stoyel, Alan 128
Strathmore Estate 39
strikes 133-5, 154-5, 176-7, 191
Summerson, Sarah 110
Sunderland 12, 14, 19, 23, 89, 90, 94, 132, 154, 172-3
Sunderland Water Company 154
Surtees, Robert 37, 64, 81, 116, 119
Sutton, Robert 133
Swalwell Mill 15, 179-80

T

Tanfield parish 25
Tate, John 3-4
Taylor, F. B. 60, 61, 62
Taylor, John 59
Taylor (valuer) 102
Team, River 54, 94, 168
Team Valley Mills 54, 165-72, 192, 199
Teasdale, James 23
Teasdale, Jane 23
Teasdale, Joseph 104
Teasdale, Mary 23
Teasdale (Teesdale), Robert, snr 22-3, 104, 115, 125-6
Teasdale (Teesdale), Robert, jnr 22-3, 104, 115, 125
Tees (Egglescliffe; Eaglescliffe; Yarm) Mill 138-42
Tees, River 34, 57
Teesdale, James 23, 80, 104
Teesdale, Joseph 104
Teesdale, Robert *see* Teasdale
Teesdale, William 104
Telford, Robert 97-8
Telford, William 97, 122
Telford & Sons, William 98
Thinford Mill 91, 118-20
Thompson, Edward 179
Thompson, James 27
Thwaites, Thomas 88
Timber, John Snowball 61
Times, The 107, 182
Tithe Apportionment (Schedule) 3, 39, 62, 81, 92, 94, 100, 112, 115, 119-20, 144
Tithe Map 81, 92, 100, 120, 144
Tovil Mill, Maidstone 169
Town, W. R. 74
trade unions 186, 191, 199
    see also National Union of Paper Mill Workers; Original Society of Papermakers, The
Tudhoe Mill 7, 89-94
Turn Paper Mill *see* Lamesley Mills
Turnbull, Jack & Grant 162
Turner, Joseph Mallord William 34, 36
Tursdale Beck 85
Tweddell, John 130
Tyne, River 10, 49, 67, 128, 129
Tyne Casings (Scotch papers) 5
Tyne Dock 180

Tyne Industries 50
Tyne (Muschamp's) Mill 15, 128-32, 199
Tyne Paper Mill Co 131-2
Tyne Steam Engine Paper Mill 50

U

Union Works, Rochdale 185
United Brotherhood of Paper Makers 138, 199
United Society of Master Paper Makers of Great Britain 12
Urpeth Mill 25, 26, 94-9, 199

V

Venables, Messrs 135-6
Victoria County History: Durham 2
Vint, Hutton & Co 132, 133, 143
Vint, James 130-1, 133, 143, 144
Vint, Robert, snr 132, 143
Vint, Robert, jnr 133
Vintin, John 32

W

wages 155, 177, 191
Walmsley & Co, (C.) 30, 182
Ward, George 124
Ward, Robert 103
Wardell, John 97
Warrell, W. C. 141-2
Washington Mills 121-3
waste disposal 68-9, 146
water rates 151
water supplies 7, 41, 69, 72-3, 85, 102, 118, 161, 172, 179, 190
  Ford Mill 148-9, 151, 154, 190
  pollution 7, 25, 32, 37, 64, 72, 108, 109, 140, 168, 190
  shared 40, 86-7
  wells sunk 7, 154
watermarks 25, *90*, 95
waterwheels 7, 10-11, 73, 93-4, 102, 106, 118-19
Wear, River 7, 10, 17, 41, 85, 89, 146
  Commissioners 148
Wearmouth (Deptford) Mill 132-8, 144, 191, 194, 199
Wearmouth Paper Company 135-6
Weatherley, Thomas 24
wells, sunk 7, 154

Wells, William 92
Wennington, Thomas 58-9, 111, 114
Westoe Soda Works 166
Whatman, James 10
wheat straw 156
Whitburn Colliery 181
Whitcliffe Mill 36
White, William 22, 115
White Hill Mill 125-8, 199
Whitfield, Joseph 33
Whitfield, William 33
Whittaker, John 137-8
Wiggins Teape Group 156, 157
Wilkinson, Benjamin 84
Wilkinson, Hannah (later Cooke) 36
Willan & Smith 63
winds, gale force 103, 192
wood *see* pulp
Wood, Sir Arthur 180, 181
Wood, Sir Lindsay 181
Woodifield, Matthew 78, 79
Wouldhave, William 41
wove paper 10
Wrigley, Thomas 72